Pericyclic Reactions

Chapman and Hall Chemistry Textbook Series

Pericyclic Reactions

G. B. Gill
M. R. Willis

Department of Chemistry, University of Nottingham

LONDON
CHAPMAN AND HALL

First published in 1974
by Chapman and Hall Ltd.
11 New Fetter Lane, London EC4P 4EE

© 1974 G. B. Gill and M. R. Willis

Printed in Great Britain by
William Clowes & Sons Limited
London, Colchester and Beccles

ISBN 0 412 12490 4

Distributed in the U.S.A.
by Halsted Press, a Division
of John Wiley and Sons, Inc., New York

Contents

Preface

Molecular orbital theory has had some notable successes in the analysis of individual organic reactions and in correlations between reaction series. Generally the theory has been invoked to explain known chemical phenomena, and rather infrequently for broadly-based predictions. In 1965 Woodward and Hoffmann published a series of papers on the molecular orbital interpretation of various types of concerted cyclo-addition reactions, which hitherto had been rather poorly understood. Because these processes (now known as pericyclic reactions) had great synthetic importance, and because the Woodward–Hoffmann theory was stated so explicitly as to allow for useful and far-reaching predictions to be made, the general acceptance of the so-called Woodward–Hoffmann Rules was very rapid. Judging from the vast number of publications that have appeared, a great deal of experimental effort has been channelled into this general area since that time, the results of which provide a vindication of the rules. The theoretical basis of Woodward and Hoffmann's method has, however, been the subject of criticism and controversy, and a number of alternative theoretical methods have also appeared.

Many university departments (including our own) have for some time covered pericyclic reactions in their undergraduate and graduate courses. Because aims, teaching methods, and personal preferences differ widely, each of the various theoretical methods have achieved some currency. We have sought to place these methods in some sort of perspective. The book is intended to be introductory, being aimed primarily at final year undergraduates and first year postgraduates.

Readers with a limited knowledge of molecular orbital theory and its applications to aromaticity will find concise coverage of the various points pertinent to the later discussions in Chapters 1 and 2. Some may prefer to start in at Chapter 3, whilst others with some knowledge of concerted reactions, seeking clarification on specific problems, will wish to read individual

Sections in Chapters 4 to 6. We hope that the organization of the book will prove suitable for the rather heterogeneous requirements of the readership for which it was intended. A few problem exercises have been written into Chapters 1 to 5, and the answers appear in Appendix IV. The Appendices I to III were created in order to avoid digression or clutter in Chapters 1 and 2.

Because of the introductory nature of this book, prominence has been given among the references to review articles; original papers are cited only occasionally. The literature in this field continues to accrue rapidly, and hence in the discussion of experimental results (Chapter 6) limitations on space have precluded any sort of exhaustive coverage.

Finally, we thank numerous colleagues who have helped either directly or indirectly in formulating the content and lay-out of this manuscript. We are grateful to our families and to the publishers for their forebearance.

Nottingham   G. B. Gill
September 1973   M. R. Willis

Atomic and molecular orbitals　1

1.1　Introduction

Many reactions in organic chemistry involving olefinic compounds take place by concerted mechanisms, i.e. the changes in σ and π bonding and in the position of nuclei occur in a continuous or synchronous manner rather than in a series of steps. The reactions may be brought about thermally and/or photo-chemically (e.g. Fig. 1.1). Furthermore the reactions are highly stereospecific. Clearly, where such reactions are used in organic synthesis it is highly desirable to be able to predict the stereochemistry of the product.

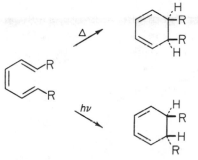

FIGURE 1.1
Example of concerted reactions

Recently, Woodward and Hoffmann (1965, 1968, 1969), Longuet-Higgins and Abrahamson (1965), and Fukui (1971) have suggested that the stereochemical courses of these reactions are controlled by the symmetry properties of the orbitals of the reactants and products. Two approaches are employed, the frontier orbital method, and the correlation diagram method. The first approach requires a knowledge of the molecular orbitals of unsaturated hydrocarbons and consideration of the way in which they can interact.

The second method requires a knowledge of the symmetry of the molecular orbitals of both reactants and products. To predict the more favourable steric pathway it may be necessary to construct a correlation diagram to relate the symmetry of the reactant to that of the product.

In this chapter the necessary theory to understand these two approaches is outlined. Orbital symmetry is introduced by consideration of atomic orbitals and their interaction to form molecular orbitals. The construction of correlation diagrams is illustrated for the formation of molecular orbitals of diatomic molecules.

An alternative approach, due to Dewar, considers the aromatic properties of the transition state of the concerted reaction. The background theory for this method is covered in Chapter 2.

1.2   The representation of atomic orbitals

In polar co-ordinates (Fig. 1.2) the position of a point P in space is specified with respect to the origin O in terms of the distance r and angles that OP makes with the x axis (ϕ) and the z axis (θ).

If the nucleus of a hydrogen atom is placed at the origin, then the potential energy of the electron at distance r from the nucleus is $-e^2/r$, where e is the electronic charge. The Schrödinger equation for the system is:

$$\nabla^2 \psi + \frac{8\pi^2 m}{h^2}\left(E + \frac{e^2}{r}\right)\psi = 0$$

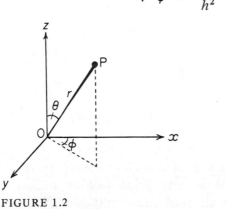

FIGURE 1.2
Polar co-ordinates for a point P

2

Converting to polar co-ordinates and using the appropriate boundary conditions we obtain solutions of the general form:

$$\psi = R(r)\Theta(\theta)\Phi(\phi)$$

i.e. the wave function ψ may be divided into the radial part ($R(r)$) which depends only on the distance from the nucleus, and the angular part $\Theta(\theta)\Phi(\phi)$ which depends on the angles θ and ϕ. The wave function ψ is most easily thought of as a quantity which varies in a wave-like manner. As with other waves it can have both positive and negative values as well as zero values (nodes), e.g. the sine wave (Fig. 1.3).

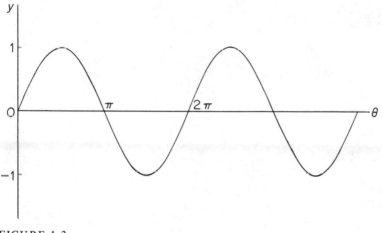

FIGURE 1.3
Plot of $y = \sin \theta$

To represent these solutions (orbitals) on paper is difficult and it is common practice to represent only the angular part. This gives the basic shape of the orbitals and their relative direction in space. The angular parts of some of the wave functions for the hydrogen atom are shown in Fig. 1.4.

Although the orbitals whose angular parts are shown are for hydrogen, approximate calculations show that the shapes of the orbitals for other atoms are similar, although their sizes and energies differ. Furthermore, whereas the orbitals with the same principal quantum number all have the same energy in the case of hydrogen, in other atoms this is not the case, the p-orbitals being above the s-orbital on the energy scale.

Now it is the square of the wave function which has physical significance in that $\psi^2 \, d\tau$ is the probability that the electron is to be found in a volume element $d\tau$ (when ψ is a complex quantity, then ψ^2 is replaced by $\psi\psi^*$, where ψ^* is the complex conjugate of ψ). One convenient and widely used representation

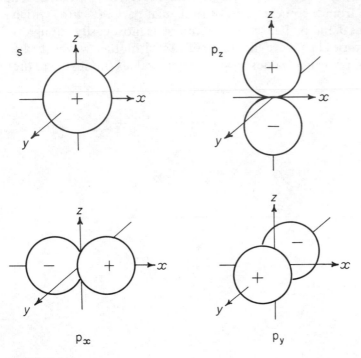

FIGURE 1.4
Angular part of the wave functions for the H atom

is the boundary surface which is the contour within which the electron spends say 90 per cent of its time. An alternative but less satisfactory interpretation is to consider the electron as a diffuse charge cloud and that the boundary surface outlines the area containing say 90 per cent of the charge. The shapes of the boundary surfaces are rather similar to the angular parts of the wave function shown in Fig. 1.4, but of course since they are derived from ψ^2 the signs of the lobes are all positive. There is no physical significance in the signs of the orbital lobes in that ψ^2 does not depend on them. However when we

4

come to consider the overlap of atomic orbitals, the *relative* signs of the overlapping lobes do become important. For this reason we shall frequently use the convention adopted by Coulson (1951) and represent orbitals by their boundary surfaces, whilst indicating the signs of the wave functions themselves. In more complicated diagrams the orbitals are often drawn with elongated lobes, for the sake of clarity.

The hybrid orbitals, constructed by the combination of atomic orbitals, can be represented in a similar way (Fig. 1.5). Only the two *sp*-hybrid orbitals are shown but the trigonal sp^2- and tetrahedral sp^3 hybrid orbitals have similar shapes. In each case the large bonding lobes have the same sign, taken as positive.

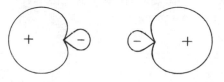

FIGURE 1.5
sp-hybrid orbitals

1.3 Molecular orbitals of diatomic molecules

The method most frequently used to construct molecular orbitals is to take linear combinations of the appropriate atomic orbitals (LCAO method). Thus, we can construct a molecular orbital (ψ) from say two atomic orbitals (ϕ_a, ϕ_b) associated with two atoms bonded together:

$$\psi = c_a \phi_a + c_b \phi_b$$

The pairs of atomic orbitals which may be combined in this way are determined by the following rules.

(a) The energies of the orbitals ϕ_a and ϕ_b must be comparable. In homonuclear diatomic molecules orbitals of identical energy are normally combined, but this is not the case for heteronuclear diatomics.

(b) The orbitals must overlap significantly.

(c) The orbitals must have the same symmetry with respect to the internuclear axis (taken as the z axis). An *s*-orbital, which is symmetric

5

with respect to rotation (e.g. rotation of the orbital about the z axis by any angle produces an orbital indistinguishable from the original) can thus combine with a p_z-orbital which has the same symmetry with respect to the z axis. In contrast, p_x- and p_y-orbitals are said to be antisymmetric with respect to a $180°$ rotation about the z axis, since the rotation produces an orbital indistinguishable from the original except that the signs of the lobes are reversed. Thus two p_x-orbitals or two p_y-orbitals can combine, but rule (b) eliminates the combination of p_x with p_y.

Table 1.1 summarizes the allowed and forbidden combinations of s and p-orbitals, provided that the energies are comparable. The first column gives, for example, possible atomic orbitals for ϕ_a. The second and third columns gives orbitals (ϕ_b) with which they may and may not combine.

TABLE 1.1
Allowed and forbidden combinations of atomic orbitals

	Allowed	Forbidden
s	s, p_z	p_x, p_y
p_x	p_x	s, p_y, p_z
p_y	p_y	s, p_x, p_z
p_z	s, p_z	p_x, p_y

1.4 Homonuclear diatomics

The combination of each pair of atomic orbitals leads to two molecular orbitals.

(a) A lower energy orbital of the general form

$$\psi_1 = c_a\phi_a + c_b\phi_b$$

Since ψ_a and ψ_b are normally identical atomic orbitals, symmetry requires that c_a and c_b be of equal magnitude. Thus the molecular orbital may be written

$$\psi_1 = N_1(\phi_a + \phi_b)$$

Where N_1 is the appropriate normalization factor which ensures that an electron in this orbital has unit probability of being found somewhere in space, i.e. $\int \psi \psi^* \, d\tau = 1$. An electron in the orbital contributes to the bonding between the nuclei and hence the orbital is termed a bonding orbital.

(b) A higher energy orbital of the general form,

$$\psi_2 = N_2(\phi_a - \phi_b)$$

An electron in this orbital reduces the net bonding between the nuclei and hence the orbital is termed anti-bonding.

For any two wave functions to be proper wave functions of the same system it is necessary for them to be orthogonal i.e. the product of their wave functions integrated over all space must be zero. That this condition is satisfied for this pair of bonding and antibonding orbitals is readily demonstrated.

$$N_1 N_2 \int (\phi_a + \phi_b)(\phi_a - \phi_b) \, d\tau = N_1 N_2 \int (\phi_a^2 - \phi_b^2) \, d\tau$$

Since the atomic orbitals are themselves normalized

$$\int \phi_a^2 \, d\tau = \int \phi_b^2 \, d\tau = 1$$

Thus $N_1 N_2 \int (\phi_a^2 - \phi_b^2) \, d\tau = 0$.

Fig. 1.6 gives the approximate shapes of the molecular orbitals of a homonuclear diatomic molecule, labelled according to their symmetry properties. Molecules which have cylindrical symmetry about the z axis (i.e. symmetric with respect to rotation about any angle) are designated σ orbitals. The π-orbitals are antisymmetric with respect to reflection in a plane containing the two nuclei, e.g. the π-orbital formed by overlap of two p_y orbitals is antisymmetric with respect to reflection in the xz plane. Orbitals which are symmetric with respect to inversion (i.e. reflection through the centre of symmetry) are indicated by a subscript g (for *gerade* meaning *even*), and those which are antisymmetric are indicated by a subscript u (for *ungerade* meaning *odd*). In addition, antibonding orbitals, which have a node on the bond axis, are indicated by an asterisk. Finally, the atomic orbitals from which the molecular orbital is constructed are also given. Thus an orbital designated $\pi_g^* 2p_y$ is an antibonding orbital of π-symmetry, which is symmetric with respect to inversion in the centre of symmetry, and is formed by the overlap of two $2p_y$ orbitals.

Atomic orbitals

Molecular orbitals

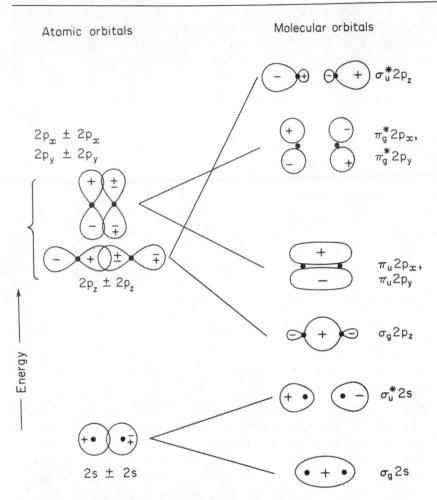

FIGURE 1.6
Molecular orbitals of diatomic molecules

The sequence of energies of the molecular orbitals in homonuclear diatomics is normally determined by experiment, and for most diatomic molecules of first row elements is as shown in Fig. 1.7.

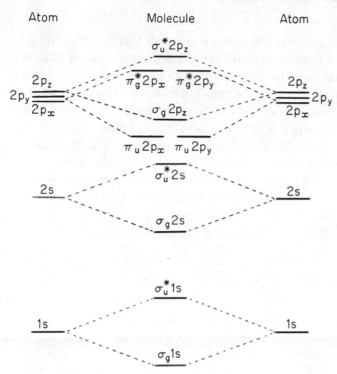

FIGURE 1.7
Orbital energies of homonuclear diatomic molecules

1.5   Molecular orbitals of heteronuclear diatomic molecules

In contrast to homonuclear diatomics, the molecular orbitals of heteronuclear diatomics cannot be constructed from a linear combination of two identical atomic orbitals. The atomic orbitals may differ in energy and type and hence do not contribute equally to the molecular orbitals. In the general case,

$$\psi = c_a\phi_b + c_b\phi_b$$

c_a and c_b will normally differ in magnitude. The molecular orbitals are frequently written as

$$\psi = N(\phi_a + \lambda\phi_b)$$

where λ reflects the polarity of the orbital. One consequence is that the u and g classification is lost since the orbitals no longer possess an inversion centre.

9

1.6   Correlation diagrams

In discussing the sequence of orbital energies it is helpful to consider the way these energies change with internuclear distance. Taking the process to its logical conclusion we must consider how the energies vary as we go from two separate atoms to the situation where the two atoms have coalesced (ignoring nuclear repulsions). This is known as the united atom approximation. Clearly the process is a gradual one which will not cause abrupt changes in the symmetry of the orbitals. Thus the atomic orbitals of the separate atoms may be correlated with the molecular orbitals of the diatomic molecule, which in turn correlate with those of the united atom. The construction of a correlation diagram of this type may be illustrated by considering the simplest possible case, that of the H_2^+ ion, for which the orbital correlation diagram is shown in Fig. 1.8. For clarity only the lower orbitals are included.

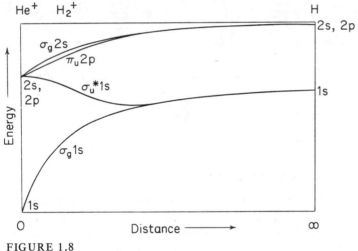

FIGURE 1.8
Correlation diagram for H_2^+

The H_2^+ ion, which has only one electron, is formed by the overlap of hydrogen atomic orbitals. Thus the orbitals of the separate atoms (shown on the right-hand side of Fig. 1.8) are those of H atoms. As the internuclear distance is reduced the orbitals change gradually to those of the H_2^+ ion and eventually the two atoms merge to form the He^+ ion (the united atom). As with the H atom, the $2s$- and $2p$-levels of the He^+ ion have the same energy.

10

The lowest molecular orbital of H_2^+ (the σ_g 1s orbital) is formed by the overlap of two 1s-orbitals of hydrogen, and as the nuclei are brought closer together then it becomes the lowest orbital of He^+, the 1s-orbital. Thus the 1s-orbital of the separate atoms, the σ_g 1s of H_2^+, and the 1s-orbital of He^+ may be correlated. Note that symmetry with respect to the bond axis, and the centre of symmetry, are maintained. Similarly the antibonding orbital formed by the overlap of the two 1s-orbitals (σ_u^* 1s) must merge into an He^+ atomic orbital with the same symmetry (i.e. cylindrical symmetry about the bond axis and antisymmetric with respect to inversion). The lowest He^+ orbital to meet these requirements is one of the 2p-orbitals (the $2p_z$). The process is shown diagrammatically in Fig. 1.9. Similarly, the σ_g 2s and σ_u^* 2s correlate with the 2s and the $3p_z$-orbitals of He^+, and the π_u 2p-orbitals correlate with the remaining 2p-orbitals. The curvature of the correlation lines is determined by calculation.

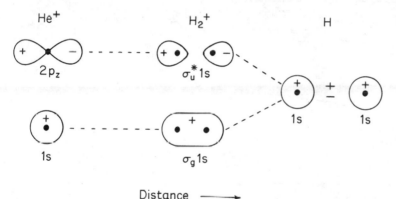

Distance ⟶

FIGURE 1.9
Orbital changes associated with the formation of the united atom He^+

1.7   The non-crossing rule

In constructing correlation diagrams in more complicated cases it is important to bear in mind the *non-crossing rule*, which is an important general principle in quantum mechanics. This states that electronic potential energy-curves corresponding to orbitals or states (see Section 1.8) with the same symmetry do not cross.

11

Consider the correlation diagram for homonuclear diatomic molecules (Fig. 1.10), constructed in the same way as that for H_2^+. The significance of the non-crossing rule becomes apparent when we consider the details of this diagram. In terms of symmetry the σ_g 2s molecular orbital could correlate with either the 2s- or the 3s-orbital of the united atom. Similarly the σ_g 2p molecular orbital could correlate with either the 2s or the 3s united atom orbital. As a consequence of the non-crossing rule, the correlation of the σ_g 2s is with 2s and the σ_g 2p with the 3s.

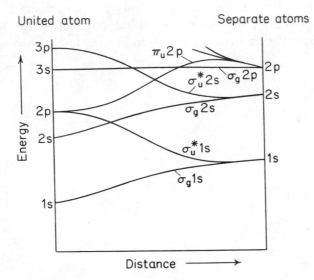

FIGURE 1.10
Part of the correlation diagram for a homonuclear diatomic molecule

Apparent exceptions to the non-crossing rule usually result from the use of too approximate wave functions. In other cases they may be due to the breakdown of the Born-Oppenheimer approximation (which allows the electronic energy to be treated separately from vibrational and rotational energy). The situation is more complex for polyatomic molecules, but the rule is generally applicable although exceptions are known.

12

1.8 Electronic states of diatomic molecules

Having considered the symmetry of individual molecular orbitals it is now necessary to consider the symmetry of electronic states resulting from the distribution of electrons amongst the various molecular orbitals to form the ground state or one of the many excited states. Consider first the hydrogen molecule in its ground state. The two electrons are paired in the bonding σ_g 1s-orbital, and the wave function for the state is the product of the wave functions for each electron,

$$\Psi_1 = \psi_1(1)\psi_1(2)$$

where $\psi_1(1)$ represents electron 1 in orbital ψ_1 (the σ_g 1s-orbital) and $\psi_1(2)$ represents electron 2 in the same orbital. In fact this is only the space part of the wave function, which has to be multiplied by an appropriate spin function. The configuration is frequently written as $(\sigma_g\ 1s)^2$, reflecting the product nature of the function.

Consider now an excited state of hydrogen with one electron in the σ_g 1s-orbital (ψ_1) and the other in the σ_u^* 1s-orbital (ψ_2). The wave function for the state might be written,

$$\Psi = \psi_1(1)\psi_2(2)$$

However, it might equally well be written with electrons exchanged,

$$\Psi = \psi_2(1)\psi_1(2)$$

An acceptable wave function must take into account both these terms, thus we may write,

$$\Psi = N(\psi_1(1)\psi_2(2) \pm \psi_2(1)\psi_1(2))$$

When the spin functions are included it can be shown that the wave function

$$\Psi_2 = N(\psi_1(1)\psi_2(2) - \psi_2(1)\psi_1(2))$$

is associated with the triplet state (Fig. 1.11b) and the function,

$$\Psi_3 = N(\psi_1(1)\psi_2(2) + \psi_2(1)\psi_1(2))$$

is associated with the singlet state (Fig. 1.11a)

Finally consider the hypothetical excited state with both electrons in the antibonding orbital, i.e. $(\sigma_u^*\ 1s)^2$. Here we may write

$$\Psi_4 = \psi_2(1)\psi_2(2)$$

In order to describe fully the symmetry of the various electronic states it is necessary to see how the wave function transforms under the various symmetry

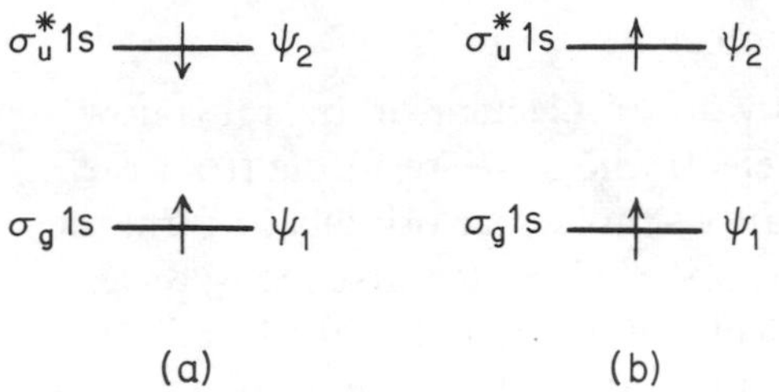

$\sigma_u^* 1s$ ___↓___ ψ_2 $\sigma_u^* 1s$ ___↑___ ψ_2

$\sigma_g 1s$ ___↑___ ψ_1 $\sigma_g 1s$ ___↑___ ψ_1

(a)   (b)

FIGURE 1.11
Two excited states of H_2 (a) singlet state (b) triplet state.

operations. We can illustrate the method by considering just one symmetry operation with respect to which the orbitals are either symmetric (S) or anti-symmetric (A), for example, inversion through the centre of symmetry.

(a) In the ground state of the molecule both electrons are in an orbital which is symmetric with respect to inversion and thus the state is symmetric with respect to inversion, i.e. the wave function Ψ_1 is symmetric because it is the product of two symmetric functions.

(b) In the excited singlet state one electron is in an orbital which is symmetric with respect to inversion and the other is in an orbital which is antisymmetric with respect to inversion. The wave function Ψ_2 contains two terms each of which is the product of an antisymmetric and a symmetric function, making the state antisymmetric (i.e. $(S) \times (A) = (A)$)

(c) The triplet state has the same symmetry with respect to inversion as the singlet state since it also contains terms which are the product of symmetric and antisymmetric functions.

(d) The hypothetical state $(\sigma_u^* 1s)^2$ has both electrons in an orbital which is antisymmetrical with respect to inversion. The symmetry operation produces a reversal of sign for each orbital leaving the product (Ψ_4) unchanged. The state is therefore overall symmetric (i.e. $(A) \times (A) = (S)$).

The symmetries of the four states considered are summarized in Table 1.2.

We can generalize these results into a set of simple rules for determining the symmetry of electronic states. Note that these rules may not be applicable where degenerate orbitals occur, in which case it is necessary to use group theory.

(1) Define the symmetry operation(s) of interest.

14

TABLE 1.2
Symmetry of electronic states with respect to inversion

Configuration	Symmetry
$(\sigma_g\ 1s)^2$	$(S) \times (S) = (S)$
Singlet $(\sigma_g\ 1s)(\sigma_u^*\ 1s)$	$(S) \times (A) = (A)$
Triplet $(\sigma_g\ 1s)(\sigma_u^*\ 1s)$	$(S) \times (A) = (A)$
$(\sigma_u^*\ 1s)^2$	$(A) \times (A) = (S)$

(2) The overall symmetry with respect to a symmetry operation is the product of the symmetries for each electron.

(3) For a given symmetry operation

$(S) \times (S) = (S)$

$(S) \times (A) = (A)$

$(A) \times (A) = (A)$

(4) We need only consider singly occupied orbitals in determining the overall symmetry, since doubly occupied orbitals are overall symmetrical.

1.9   Localized and delocalized orbitals of polyatomic molecules

The σ- and π-orbitals of diatomic molecules extend over the whole structure. In a similar way, orbitals could be constructed which extend over the whole of polyatomic molecules. In the case of conjugated systems it is normal to describe π-electrons in terms of orbitals of this type. This is clearly in accord with chemical experience for it is found that the behaviour of one double bond is strongly influenced by other double bonds in conjugation, and that electronic effects are readily transmitted along the conjugation pathway.

In the case of σ-bonds the effects of neighbouring groups are less apparent. Indeed, many bond properties show remarkably little variation from molecule to molecule. Thus it is normal to regard the σ-framework as a series of localized bonds, although it can be shown that the two approaches are virtually equivalent.

The C—C bonding in conjugated hydrocarbons may be conveniently separated into a σ-framework formed by the overlap of sp^2-hybrid orbitals of carbon, and π-orbitals formed by the sideways overlap of p-orbitals. The π-orbitals may be constructed by the linear combination of the atomic p-

15

orbitals involved (referred to as the basis set). In general there are as many π-orbitals as there are atomic p-orbitals in the basis set. Furthermore, these orbitals have differing numbers of nodes as well as differing energies. For the purpose of discussing orbital symmetry conservation we normally need to know:

(a) the number and position of the nodes in a given molecular orbital which determine the symmetry properties of interest.

(b) The relative energies of the molecular orbitals.

In the case of ethylene the σ framework is formed by the carbon sp^2-orbitals and the π-bond is formed by the sideways overlap of the remaining two p-orbitals. The two π-orbitals have the same symmetry as the $\pi_u 2p$ and $\pi_g^* 2p$-orbitals of a homonuclear diatomic molecule (Fig. 1.6), and the sequence of energy levels of these two orbitals is the same (Fig. 1.7). We need to know how such information may be deduced for ethylene and larger conjugated hydrocarbons. In most cases the information required does not provide a searching test of a molecular orbital approximation. Indeed for π-orbitals the information can usually be provided by the simple Hückel (1931) molecular orbital method (HMO) which uses the linear combination of atomic orbitals (LCAO), or even by the free electron model (FEM). These methods and the results they give are outlined in the remainder of this chapter.

1.10 The LCAO method for π-orbitals in conjugated systems

Using the LCAO method, π-molecular orbitals (ψ) may be expressed as a linear combination of the atomic p-orbitals (ϕ) involved. Thus the molecular orbitals of a molecule containing carbon atoms in conjugation may be represented by,

$$\psi = c_1\phi_1 + c_2\phi_2 + c_3\phi_3 \ldots c_n\phi_n \qquad (1.1)$$

where the coefficients $c_1, c_2, c_3, \ldots, c_n$ reflect the different contribution of the atomic orbitals to the molecular orbitals.

Any wave function constructed in this way is inevitably an approximate one. The coefficients have to be chosen to give the best wave functions possible within the limits of the approximation. The *variation principle* tells us that the energy corresponding to an approximate wave function is always

16

greater than that of the true wave function, and that the lower the energy the better the approximation. Now the energy can be calculated by substitution into the Schrödinger equation appropriate to the system. Because of the complexity of the potential energy function it is convenient to use the Hamiltonian form of the wave equation without specifying the operator in detail. Thus

$$H\psi = E\psi \tag{1.2}$$

To calculate the energy associated with a wave function both sides of Equation (1.1) are multiplied by ψ (or ψ^* if ψ is complex) and integrated over space.

$$E = \frac{\int \psi H \psi \, d\tau}{\int \psi^2 \, d\tau} \tag{1.3}$$

For the general case, substituting Equation (1.1) into Equation (1.3) gives

$$E = \frac{\int (c_1\phi_1 + c_2\phi_2 + \ldots c_n\phi_n)H(c_1\phi_1 + c_2\phi_2 \ldots c_n\phi_n) \, d\tau}{\int (c_1\phi_1 + c_2\phi_2 \ldots c_n\phi_n)^2 \, d\tau} \tag{1.4}$$

The coefficients are now chosen to give minimum energy. This is achieved by differentiating Equation (1.4) with respect to each coefficient in turn and equating to zero. Whilst the differentiation could be performed for the general case it is sufficient for our purpose to consider a simple example and generalize the result. Consider then the case where

$$\psi = c_1\phi_1 + c_2\phi_2$$

$$E = \frac{\int (c_1\phi_1 + c_2\phi_2)H(c_1\phi_1 + c_2\phi_2) \, d\tau}{\int (c_1\phi_1 + c_2\phi_2)^2 \, d\tau}$$

Expanding this expression, remembering that H is an operator, we get

$$E = \frac{\int (c_1^2\phi_1 H\phi_1 \, d\tau + \int c_2^2\phi_2 H\phi_2 \, d\tau + \int c_1\phi_1 Hc_2\phi_2 \, d\tau + \int c_2\phi_2 Hc_1\phi_1 \, d\tau}{\int c_1^2\phi_1^2 \, d\tau + \int c_2^2\phi_2^2 \, d\tau + 2\int c_1c_2\phi_1\phi_2 \, d\tau}$$

$$\tag{1.5}$$

For simplicity we introduce the abbreviations,

$$\int \phi_1 H\phi_1 \, d\tau = H_{11} \qquad \int \phi_1^2 \, d\tau = S_{11}$$

$$\int \phi_2 H\phi_2 \, d\tau = H_{22} \qquad \int \phi_2^2 \, d\tau = S_{22}$$

$$\int \phi_1 H\phi_2 \, d\tau = H_{12} \qquad \int \phi_1\phi_2 \, d\tau = S_{12}$$

$$\int \phi_2 H\phi_1 \, d\tau = H_{21}$$

17

It can be shown that $H_{12} = H_{21}$.

Thus substitution into Equation (1.5) gives

$$E = \frac{c_1^2 H_{11} + c_2^2 H_{22} + 2c_1 c_2 H_{12}}{c_1^2 S_{11} + c_2^2 S_{22} + 2c_1 c_2 S_{12}} \tag{1.6}$$

Putting

$$\left(\frac{\partial E}{\partial c_1}\right)_{c_2} = 0$$

gives

$$c_1(H_{11} - ES_{11}) + c_2(H_{12} - ES_{12}) = 0 \tag{1.7}$$

Putting

$$\left(\frac{\partial E}{\partial c_2}\right)_{c_1} = 0$$

gives

$$c_1(H_{12} - ES_{12}) + c_2(H_{22} - ES_{22}) = 0 \tag{1.8}$$

Equations (1.7) and (1.8) are called the *secular equations*. Solutions of a set of equations of this type may be expressed as a determinant (see Appendix I), in this case referred to as the *secular determinant*.

$$\begin{vmatrix} H_{11} - ES_{11} & H_{12} - ES_{12} \\ H_{21} - ES_{21} & H_{22} - ES_{22} \end{vmatrix} = 0 \tag{1.9}$$

For the general case of a linear combination of n atomic orbitals the secular equations are,

$$c_1(H_{11} - ES_{11}) + c_2(H_{12} - ES_{12}) + \dots c_n(H_{1n} - ES_{1n}) = 0$$
$$c_1(H_{21} - ES_{21}) + c_2(H_{22} - ES_{22}) + \dots c_n(H_{2n} - ES_{2n}) = 0$$
$$\vdots \qquad\qquad \vdots \qquad\qquad \vdots \tag{1.10}$$
$$c_1(H_{n1} - ES_{n1}) + c_2(H_{n2} - ES_{n2}) \dots c_n(H_{nn} - ES_{nn}) = 0$$

The secular determinant for the general case is,

$$
\begin{vmatrix}
H_{11} - ES_{11} & H_{12} - ES_{12} \ldots H_{1n} - ES_{1n} \\
H_{21} - ES_{21} & H_{22} - ES_{22} \ldots H_{2n} - ES_{2n} \\
\vdots & \vdots \\
H_{n1} - ES_{n1} & H_{n2} - ES_{n2} \ldots H_{nn} - ES_{nn}
\end{vmatrix} = 0 \qquad (1.11)
$$

This determinant is widely used in molecular orbital theory and should be memorized. Notice that the terms on the leading diagonal are of the form $H_{11} - ES_{11}, H_{22} - ES_{22}$ etc., and that the determinant is symmetrical about the leading diagonal (since $H_{12} = H_{21}$ etc., and $S_{12} = S_{21}$ etc.).

1.11 The Hückel molecular orbital (HMO) method

The secular determinant requires some simplification to enable simple calculations to be made. Consider the various integrals,

(a) Integrals of the type S_{11}, S_{22} etc.

Assuming that the atomic orbitals are themselves normalized, then

$$
S_{11} = \int \phi_1 \phi_1 \, d\tau = 1, \quad S_{22} = \int \phi_2 \phi_2 \, d\tau = 1 \text{ etc.}
$$

(b) Integrals of the type S_{12}, S_{23}, S_{13} etc. (i.e. S_{ij}, where $i \neq j$).

These integrals are called *overlap integrals* and reflect the extent to which two atomic orbitals overlap. Clearly where the two atomic orbitals are on non-adjacent carbon atoms the overlap is very small and may be neglected. In the Hückel approximation even overlap of orbitals on adjacent atoms is neglected (i.e. $S_{12} = S_{23} = S_{13}$ etc. $= 0$). At first sight this may appear to be such a gross approximation as to invalidate the results, for in qualitative descriptions bonding is said to result from the overlap of atomic orbitals. In practice, however, the interaction between adjacent atoms (say 1 and 2) is reflected in the value of both H_{12} and S_{12}, and the former is much more significant. Although this approximation greatly simplifies the mathematics, overlap can be included in the calculation but little improvement results.

(c) Integrals of the type H_{11}, H_{22}, H_{33} etc.

19

At this level of approximation these terms may be associated with the energy of an electron in the field of atom 1, 2, 3 etc. and are called *Coulomb integrals*. The integrals are assumed to be equal for all carbon atoms and are given the symbol α.

(d) Integrals of the type H_{12}, H_{23}, H_{13} etc. (i.e. H_{ij}, when $i \neq j$).

H_{ij} may be associated with the energy of an electron in the combined fields of atoms i and j, and is referred to as the *resonance integral*, it is normally regarded as a constant for adjacent carbon atoms and is given the symbol β, but for non-adjacent atoms the integral is neglected.

These various assumptions greatly simplify the calculation of relative energy levels and wave functions. We can now consider a number of examples, relevant to later chapters, which illustrate the use of the method.

1.12   HMO treatment of ethylene

The secular determinant simplifies thus:

$$\begin{vmatrix} H_{11} - ES_{11} & H_{12} - ES_{12} \\ H_{21} - ES_{21} & H_{22} - ES_{22} \end{vmatrix} = \begin{vmatrix} \alpha - E & \beta \\ \beta & \alpha - E \end{vmatrix} = 0$$

As a general rule it is helpful to divide each term in the determinant by β and put

$$\frac{\alpha - E}{\beta} = x$$

Thus,

$$\begin{vmatrix} x & 1 \\ 1 & x \end{vmatrix} = 0$$

Multiplying out the determinant (Appendix I) gives

$$x^2 - 1 = 0$$

$$\therefore x = \pm 1 \qquad \text{i.e.} \qquad \frac{\alpha - E}{\beta} = \pm 1$$

$$\therefore E_1 = \alpha + \beta, \qquad E_2 = \alpha - \beta$$

Now it can be shown that β is a negative quantity and hence $\alpha + \beta$ is the energy of the lower occupied orbital (ψ_1) and $\alpha - \beta$ is the energy of the upper orbital (ψ_2) (Fig. 1.12).

Energy   Occupancy   Wave function

$\alpha - \beta$ ————— ψ_2

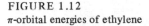

$\alpha + \beta$ 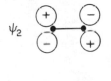 ψ_1

FIGURE 1.12
π-orbital energies of ethylene

To obtain the wave functions corresponding to these energies it is necessary to solve the secular equations using the appropriate values of E. A general method is given in Appendix II.

In this case the wave functions are,

$$\psi_1 = \frac{1}{\sqrt{2}} (\phi_1 + \phi_2)$$

$$\psi_2 = \frac{1}{\sqrt{2}} (\phi_1 - \phi_2)$$

Molecular orbitals   Atomic orbitals

ψ_2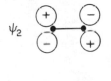

ψ_1

FIGURE 1.13
π-molecular orbitals of ethylene

21

The shapes of the orbitals are shown in Fig. 1.13. The two frequently used representations are employed. The orbitals may be represented either by their boundary surfaces or by the atomic orbitals from which they are built up (their sizes and the signs of the lobes reflecting the sizes and signs of the coefficients). For ψ_1 the two coefficients are of the same sign and magnitude and thus the orbital is a bonding orbital with the two atomic p-orbitals contributing equally, as in the π-orbital of a homonuclear diatomic molecule. For the ψ_2 orbital, although the two p-orbitals again contribute equally, there is a change of sign indicating a node between the atoms showing that the orbital is antibonding. The fact that its energy $(\alpha - \beta)$ is higher than an electron not involved in bonding (α) also reflects its antibonding character.

1.13   HMO treatment of allyl

When an allyl compound $CH_2=CH-CH_2-X$ loses the group X as a positive ion, radical or negative ion, the remaining hydrocarbon fragment has delocalized π-bonding resulting from the overlap of p-orbitals for each carbon atom. Numbering the atoms in the following way,

$$CH_2\text{---}CH\text{---}CH_2$$
$$1 \qquad 2 \qquad 3$$

the secular determinant becomes,

$$\begin{vmatrix} \alpha - E & \beta & 0 \\ \beta & \alpha - E & \beta \\ 0 & \beta & \alpha - E \end{vmatrix} = 0$$

Dividing each term by β and putting $\alpha - E/\beta = x$, we get

$$\begin{vmatrix} x & 1 & 0 \\ 1 & x & 1 \\ 0 & 1 & x \end{vmatrix} = 0$$

Multiplying out (Appendix I) gives

$$x^3 - 2x = 0$$
$$\text{or} \quad x(x^2 - 2) = 0$$
$$\therefore \quad x = 0, \pm\sqrt{2}$$

Thus the three energy levels are,
$$E_1 = \alpha + \sqrt{2}\beta, \qquad E_2 = \alpha, \qquad E_3 = \alpha - \sqrt{2}\beta$$
The energy levels, and their occupancy are shown in Fig. 1.14

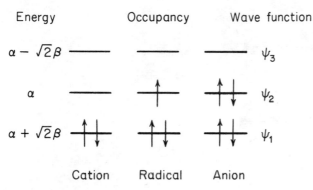

FIGURE 1.14
Energy levels and their occupancy in the allyl system.

Solution of the secular equations (Appendices II and III) gives the wave functions ψ_1, ψ_2, ψ_3 corresponding to energies E_1, E_2 and E_3:

$$\psi_1 = \tfrac{1}{2}(\phi_1 + \sqrt{2}\phi_2 + \phi_3)$$

$$\psi_2 = \frac{1}{\sqrt{2}}(\phi_1 - \phi_3)$$

$$\psi_3 = \tfrac{1}{2}(\phi_1 - \sqrt{2}\phi_2 + \phi_3)$$

The shapes of the orbitals are shown in Fig. 1.15.

The lowest orbital ψ_1 is clearly a bonding orbital since it has no nodes on the bond axis and its energy is less than α. Likewise the highest orbital is antibonding since it has a node between each atom and an energy greater than α. The ψ_2 orbital, however, has a node at atom 2 and an energy equal to α, the energy of an electron not involved in bonding. An electron in ψ_2 does not contribute to the bonding in the molecule and, hence ψ_2 is called a *non-bonding molecular orbital* (NBMO).

23

Molecular orbitals   Atomic orbitals

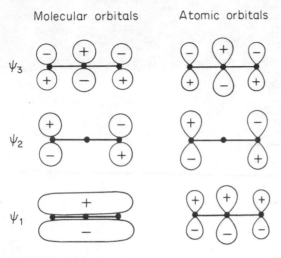

FIGURE 1.15
π-Molecular orbitals of allyl

Thus in the allyl radical the odd electron in the NBMO is distributed equally between the two terminal carbon atoms, and the bonding corresponds directly to that predicted by the familiar valence bond description

$$CH_2{=}CH{-}\dot{C}H_2 \leftrightarrow \dot{C}H_2{-}CH{=}CH_2$$

1.14   Non-bonding orbitals

The presence of a non-bonding orbital in a conjugated hydrocarbon can be readily deduced from a consideration of the carbon skeleton. Conjugated hydrocarbons may be classified as *alternant hydrocarbons* (AH) or *nonalternant hydrocarbons* according to whether or not it is possible to divide the atoms into two groups, starred and unstarred, in such a way that no two starred and no two unstarred atoms are directly linked. It is customary to denote the more numerous set by stars. Thus, it may be seen from Fig. 1.16 that naphthalene (a) is alternant and fulvene (b) is nonalternant. All conjugated systems are alternant, except those which contain rings of odd numbers of carbon atoms. Conjugated hydrocarbons are also classified as *odd* or *even* according to whether the number of conjugated atoms is odd or even.

For even alternant hydrocarbons the Hückel energy levels occur in pairs.

24

Thus for every bonding level of energy $\alpha + n\beta$ there is a corresponding anti-bonding level of $\alpha - n\beta$. There may also be pairs of non-bonding orbitals of energy α (i.e. $n = 0$). For odd alternant hydrocarbons there are, of course, an odd number of energy levels. The pairing property is also present but in addition there is a non-bonding level of energy α. Ethylene is an example of an even alternant and allyl an odd alternant hydrocarbon.

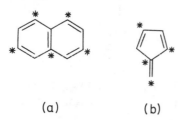

(a)   (b)

FIGURE 1.16
Example of alternant and nonalternant hydrocarbons

Using a method devised by Longuet-Higgins (1950) the coefficients of the non-bonding orbital in odd alternant hydrocarbons may be easily obtained without solving the secular equations. He showed that the coefficients of the unstarred atoms are zero and also that the sum of the coefficients of the atoms (i) directly bonded to a particular unstarred atom is also zero.

i.e. $\Sigma c_i = 0$

Consider the non-bonding orbital of allyl. The starred atoms are 1 and 3. (Fig. 1.17).

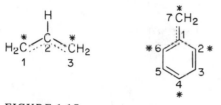

FIGURE 1.17
Odd alternant hydrocarbons

It follows that $c_1 + c_3 = 0$. Let $c_1 = a$. Then, $c_2 = 0$ and $c_3 = -a$. Normaliz-ation requires that $c_1^2 + c_3^2 = 1$ (see footnote p. 215). Hence $a = 1/\sqrt{2}$. The

25

non-bonding orbital is therefore

$$\psi = \frac{1}{\sqrt{2}}(\phi_1 - \phi_3)$$

Consider a less trivial example, the benzyl radical (Fig. 1.17). The unstarred atoms have zero coefficients and, hence $c_1 = c_3 = c_5 = 0$. Also $\Sigma c_i = 0$, hence

$$c_2 + c_6 + c_7 = 0$$
$$c_4 + c_6 = 0$$
$$c_4 + c_2 = 0$$

Solution of these equations by putting $c_4 = a$ gives $c_2 = -a$ and $c_6 = -a$. Hence $c_7 = 2a$. Normalization requires that $c_2^2 + c_4^2 + c_6^2 + c_7^2 = 1$ and hence $a = 1/\sqrt{7}$. Thus, the non-bonding orbital for the benzyl radical is

$$\psi = \frac{1}{\sqrt{7}}(-\phi_2 + \phi_4 - \phi_6 + 2\phi_7)$$

The same result can usually be obtained even more rapidly in the following way. Consider an unstarred carbon atom in the unbranched part of the ring, for example, the C3 carbon of benzyl. If one neighbour (say C4) has the coefficient a, then the other (C2) has coefficient $-a$. Similarly, C6 has coefficient $-a$. Finally, summation of the coefficients adjacent to C1 gives the coefficient at C7 as $2a$. Normalization gives $a = 1/\sqrt{7}$.

1.15   HMO treatment of the cyclopropenyl system

$$\text{1 CH}\!\!-\!\!\text{CH 2}$$
$$\text{CH}$$
$$3$$

The calculation of the energy levels and wave functions of this system are carried out in detail in Appendix III as an illustration of the method of working. The energy levels are shown in Fig. 1.18. Note that the two upper energy levels are of the same energy, i.e. degenerate.

26

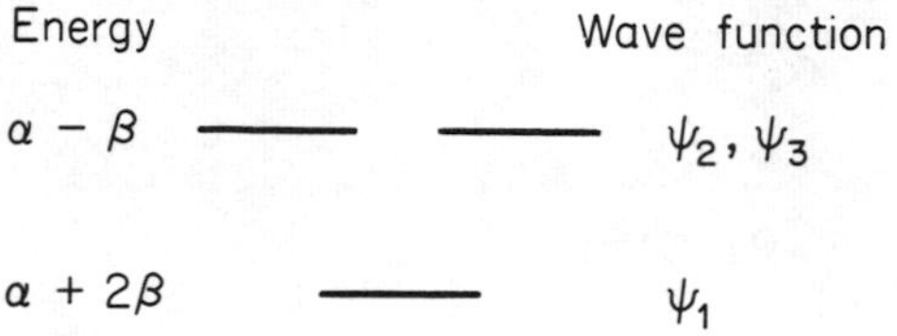

Energy   Wave function

$\alpha - \beta$ ——   —— ψ_2, ψ_3

$\alpha + 2\beta$ —— ψ_1

FIGURE 1.18
Energy levels of cyclopropenyl

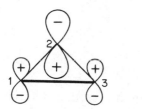 ψ_3

ψ_2

ψ_1

FIGURE 1.19
Molecular orbitals of cyclopropenyl

There are no unique solutions for the wave functions of degenerate levels (see Appendix III). A set of solutions which satisfy the necessary conditions are:

$$\psi_1 = \frac{1}{\sqrt{3}}(\phi_1 + \phi_2 + \phi_3)$$

27

$$\psi_2 = \frac{1}{\sqrt{2}}(\phi_1 - \phi_3)$$

$$\psi_3 = \frac{1}{\sqrt{6}}(\phi_1 - 2\phi_2 + \phi_3)$$

The orbitals are sketched in Fig. 1.19. For clarity only the atomic orbitals contributing to the molecular orbitals are shown.

1.16   HMO treatment of butadiene

$$CH_2=CH—CH=CH_2$$
$$1 \quad\ \ 2 \quad\ \ 3 \quad\ \ 4$$

Since there are four p-orbitals involved in the π-bonding the secular determinant is fourth order. The four roots are shown in Fig. 1.20.

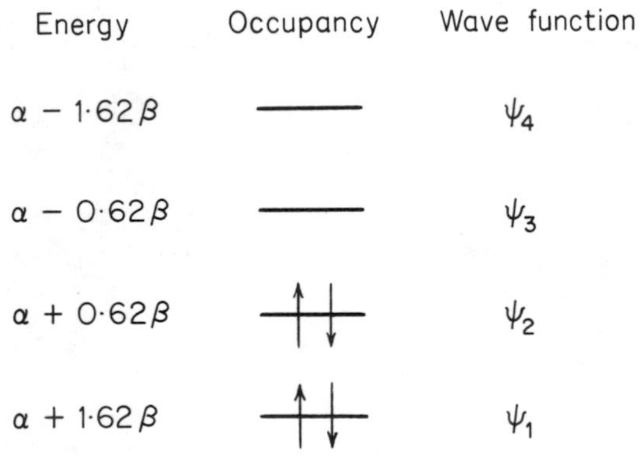

Energy	Occupancy	Wave function
$\alpha - 1\cdot62\beta$	——	ψ_4
$\alpha - 0\cdot62\beta$	——	ψ_3
$\alpha + 0\cdot62\beta$	⥮	ψ_2
$\alpha + 1\cdot62\beta$	⥮	ψ_1

FIGURE 1.20
Energy levels of butadiene

The corresponding wave functions are:

$$\psi_1 = 0\cdot3717\phi_1 + 0\cdot6015\phi_2 + 0\cdot6015\phi_3 + 0\cdot3717\phi_4$$
$$\psi_2 = 0\cdot6015\phi_1 + 0\cdot3717\phi_2 - 0\cdot3717\phi_3 - 0\cdot6015\phi_4$$
$$\psi_3 = 0\cdot6015\phi_1 - 0\cdot3717\phi_2 - 0\cdot3717\phi_3 + 0\cdot6015\phi_4$$
$$\psi_4 = 0\cdot3717\phi_1 - 0\cdot6015\phi_2 + 0\cdot6015\phi_3 - 0\cdot3717\phi_4$$

The shapes of the orbitals are shown in Fig. 1.21. Note that the number of nodes increases as the energy increases, a general property of molecular orbitals.

Molecular orbitals   Atomic orbitals

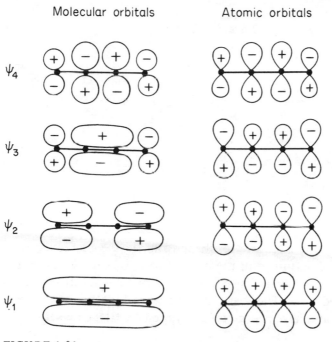

ψ_4

ψ_3

ψ_2

ψ_1

FIGURE 1.21
The molecular orbitals of butadiene

1.17   HMO treatment of cyclobutadiene

$$
\begin{array}{cc}
1 & 2 \\
CH{=}CH \\
| \quad \quad | \\
CH{=}CH \\
4 & 3
\end{array}
$$

The four solutions of the secular determinant are shown in Fig. 1.22. The energy levels E_2 and E_3 associated with the wave functions ψ_2 and ψ_3 are identical and are thus described as degenerate. Degeneracy is common to all monocyclic polymethines (i.e. cyclic compounds of general formula

29

—(CH)$_N$—). In this case the degenerate levels are non-bonding levels having an energy α. This treatment suggests that the ground state has two unpaired electrons.

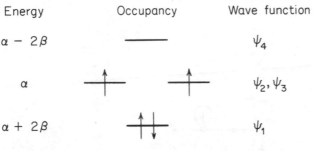

Energy	Occupancy	Wave function
$\alpha - 2\beta$		ψ_4
α		ψ_2, ψ_3
$\alpha + 2\beta$		ψ_1

FIGURE 1.22
The energy levels of cyclobutadiene

The wave functions display a feature resulting from the degeneracy. Whilst ψ_1 and ψ_4 can be determined in the normal way, ψ_2 and ψ_3 do not have unique solutions. There is an infinite number of pairs of solutions which satisfy the necessary conditions. These are that the wave functions must be normalized, orthogonal, and have energy α (see Appendix III). One set of wave functions is:

$$\psi_1 = \frac{1}{2}(\phi_1 + \phi_2 + \phi_3 + \phi_4)$$

$$\psi_2 = \frac{1}{\sqrt{2}}(\phi_1 - \phi_3)$$

$$\psi_3 = \frac{1}{\sqrt{2}}(\phi_2 - \phi_4)$$

$$\psi_4 = \frac{1}{2}(\phi_1 - \phi_2 + \phi_3 - \phi_4)$$

These orbitals are sketched in Fig. 1.23.

30

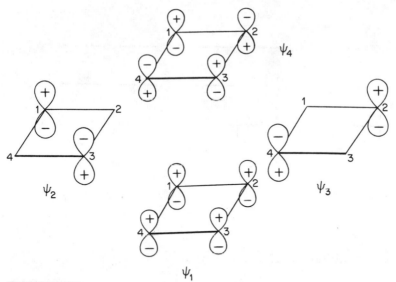

FIGURE 1.23
The molecular orbitals of cyclobutadiene (atomic orbital representation).

1.18   HMO treatment of cyclopentadienyl

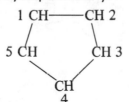

Cyclopentadienyl is an odd non-alternant hydrocarbon. Being cyclic, it has degenerate energy levels, but they do not show the pairing property nor is there a non-bonding orbital. The energy levels are shown in Fig. 1.24.

One set of wave functions for cyclopentadienyl is as follows:

$$\psi_1 = \frac{1}{\sqrt{5}}(\phi_1 + \phi_2 + \phi_3 + \phi_4 + \phi_5)$$

$$\psi_2 = 0.602\phi_1 + 0.372\phi_2 - 0.372\phi_3 - 0.602\phi_4$$
$$\psi_3 = 0.196\phi_1 - 0.512\phi_2 - 0.512\phi_2 + 0.196\phi_4 + 0.633\phi_5$$
$$\psi_4 = 0.372\phi_1 - 0.602\phi_2 + 0.602\phi_3 - 0.372\phi_4$$
$$\psi_5 = 0.512\phi_1 - 0.196\phi_2 - 0.196\phi_3 + 0.512\phi_4 - 0.633\phi_5$$

31

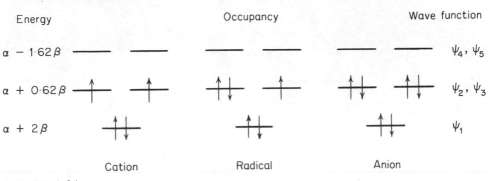

FIGURE 1.24
Energy levels for cyclopentadienyl

The five molecular orbitals are shown in Fig. 1.25

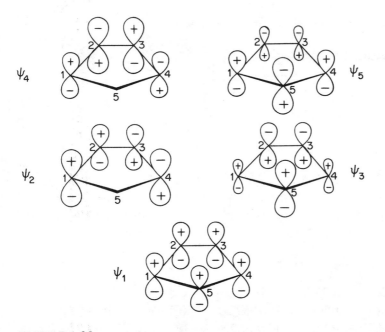

FIGURE 1.25
The molecular orbitals of cyclopentadienyl (atomic orbital representation)

1.19   HMO treatment of benzene

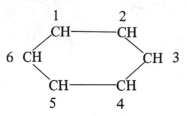

Being an even, alternant, cyclic hydrocarbon benzene has orbitals which exhibit the pairing property as well as degeneracy. The energy levels are shown in Fig. 1.26.

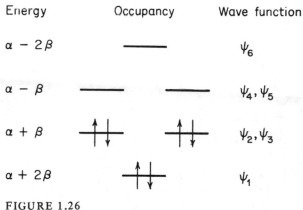

FIGURE 1.26
The energy levels of benzene

One set of wave functions for the π-orbitals of benzene is as follows:

$$\psi_1 = \frac{1}{\sqrt{6}}(\phi_1 + \phi_2 + \phi_3 + \phi_4 + \phi_5 + \phi_6)$$

$$\psi_2 = \frac{1}{2}(\phi_1 + \phi_2 - \phi_4 - \phi_5)$$

$$\psi_3 = \frac{1}{\sqrt{12}}(\phi_1 - \phi_2 - 2\phi_3 - \phi_4 + \phi_5 + 2\phi_6)$$

$$\psi_4 = \frac{1}{2}(\phi_1 - \phi_2 + \phi_4 - \phi_5)$$

$$\psi_5 = \frac{1}{\sqrt{12}}(\phi_1 + \phi_2 - 2\phi_3 + \phi_4 + \phi_5 - 2\phi_6)$$

$$\psi_6 = \frac{1}{\sqrt{6}}(\phi_1 - \phi_2 + \phi_3 - \phi_4 + \phi_5 - \phi_6)$$

The shapes of the orbitals are as shown in Fig. 1.27.

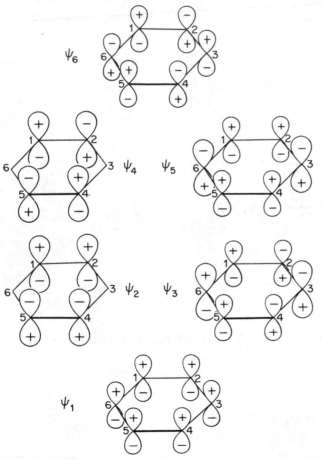

FIGURE 1.27
Molecular orbitals of benzene (atomic orbital representation)

Benzene itself has a sixfold axis of symmetry through the molecular centre, normal to the plane of the ring, i.e. rotation of the molecule by one sixth of a revolution leaves the molecule indistinguishable from the original. The molecular symmetry is reflected in the symmetry of the non-degenerate molecular orbitals. Thus ψ_1 is symmetric and ψ_6 antisymmetric with respect to a 60° rotation. The individual degenerate orbitals do not necessarily reflect the molecular symmetry. A pair of degenerate orbitals must however reflect the molecular symmetry since the π-bonding electrons (occupying ψ_1, ψ_2 and ψ_3) are distributed symmetrically around the ring. Similar symmetry behaviour is shown by the molecular orbitals of other polymethines.

1.20   Hetero-atoms

It is possible to extend the HMO method to cases where a hetero-atom is included in the π-system. Because of the difference in electronegativity the value of the Coulomb integral for the hetero-atom (α_x) will be different from that of carbon (α). Similarly the resonance integral for the interaction between the hetero-atom and the adjacent carbon (β_{cx}) will differ from that between two adjacent carbon atoms (β). It is normal to express these differences thus:

$$\alpha_x = \alpha + h_x \beta$$

$$\beta_{cx} = k_{cx} \beta$$

h_x and k_{cx} are adjustable parameters, normally chosen to give the best fit with experiment. In practice it is found that the values vary somewhat according to the property measured. Streitweiser (1961) has summarized attempts to evaluate these parameters and has recommended a set of values for general use. The following simplified set of values (Roberts, 1962) is sufficiently accurate for the present discussion (Table 1.3).

TABLE 1.3

Atom	h_x	k_{cx}
C	0	1
N	1	1
0	2	$\sqrt{2}$

The effect of introducing a hetero-atom can be illustrated by considering one of the simplest possible cases, that of the carbonyl group in an otherwise saturated compound.

The secular determinant is,

$$\begin{vmatrix} x & \sqrt{2} \\ \sqrt{2} & x + 2 \end{vmatrix} = 0$$

The roots are $x = 0.7$ and $x = -2.7$, corresponding to energies of $E_1 = \alpha + 2.7\beta$ and $E_2 = \alpha - 0.7\beta$. The corresponding wave functions are

$$\psi_1 = 0.44\phi_1 + 0.90\phi_2$$
$$\psi_2 = 0.89\phi_1 - 0.46\phi_2$$

Fig. 1.28 shows the approximate shapes of the orbitals. Notice that the oxygen atomic orbital contributes more to the bonding orbital than does the carbon atomic orbital, but the reverse is true for the antibonding orbital.

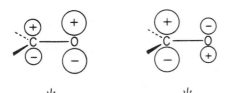

ψ_1 ψ_2

FIGURE 1.28
Molecular orbitals of the carbonyl group

1.21   The Free Electron Model (FEM)

An even simpler treatment of the π-electrons in a conjugated polyene is the free electron model. The basis of the model is the particle-in-a-box which is used in elementary quantum mechanics as an example of the solution of the

Schrödinger equation. In the one dimensional case an electron is confined to a region between $x = 0$ and $x = a$ by potential barriers of infinite height (Fig. 1.29).

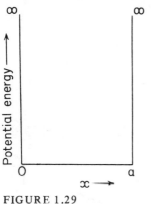

FIGURE 1.29
Square well potential

Solution of the Schrödinger equation for this solution yields wave functions with the form,

$$\psi = N\sin\left(\frac{n\pi x}{a}\right),$$

where n is an integer having values 1, 2, 3 etc. The allowed energies corresponding to these wave functions are given by,

$$E = \frac{h^2 n^2}{8ma^2}$$

where h is Planck's constant and m the electron mass. The form of the four lowest wave functions is shown in Fig. 1.30.

If we assume that the π-electrons of a polyene are free to move within the molecule but are not free to leave the molecule, then the situation is directly analogous to the electron-in-a-box. The dimension of the box is related to the length of the conjugation path. In practice it is frequently assumed that the π-electrons are free to travel one half a bond length beyond either end of the conjugated system. Thus for butadiene the length of the box is taken as four average bond lengths. The appropriate number of π-electrons are then fed into

37

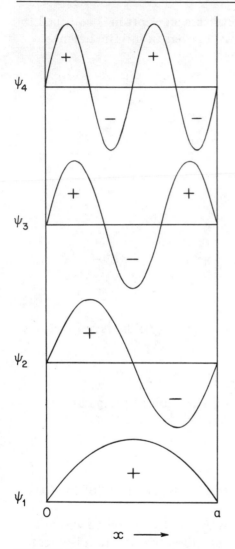

FIGURE 1.30
Wave functions for an electron-in-a-box

the energy levels, two at a time, and electron repulsion is neglected. The FEM has been extended to cyclic conjugated hydrocarbons (Platt, 1949).

The purpose of introducing the FEM into the present discussion is twofold.

38

Firstly it provides a rather convenient mental picture of delocalized π-electrons and the nodal properties of their wave functions. Secondly, it is a convenient way of remembering the number and position of the nodes in the π-orbitals of linear polyenes. The wave functions obtained by the HMO and FEM methods are shown in Fig. 1.31.

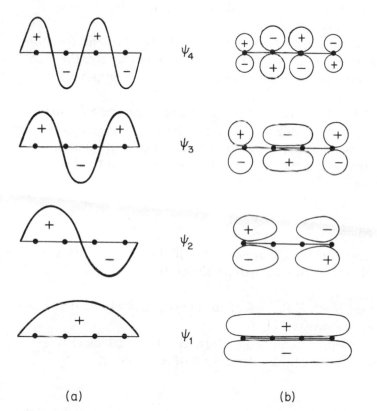

(a)   (b)

FIGURE 1.31
The butadiene wave functions (a) using the free electron model and (b) using the Hückel method

1.22   The validity of simple molecular orbital theory

The Hückel approach makes a number of simplifying assumptions of doubtful validity. Amongst these is the neglect of overlap, the absence of any specific electron-electron interaction terms and the assumption of constant exchange integrals, irrespective of bond length. Despite these and other approximations, the energies (in terms of α and β) correlate remarkably well with a wide range of experimental data, particularly for structurally related polycyclic hydrocarbons. Similarly, the unpaired electron density of their radical ions correlates well with electron spin resonance data. The correlation between the results of HMO calculations and experimental measurements has been discussed in detail by Streitweiser (1961).

The method is less successful for non-alternant hydrocarbons and for molecules containing hetero-atoms. As will be seen in the next chapter, the method is of limited value for the prediction of the aromatic properties of cyclic compounds.

The prediction of the configuration of the products of concerted reactions using the Woodward–Hoffmann rules does not require very accurate molecular orbitals. It merely requires that the symmetry of the orbitals and the signs of the coefficients are correct. In almost every case, the Hückel method is satisfactory for this purpose.

1.23 Further Reading

A more detailed discussion of Hückel molecular orbital theory and its applications is given by Roberts (1962) and Streitweiser (1961).

Problem 1.1 Using the methods described in the Appendices calculate the π-energy levels and wave functions of allyl.

Problem 1.2 Use the method described in Section 1.14 to calculate the coefficients of the non-bonding molecular orbital of pentadienyl.

Aromaticity   **2**

2.1   Introduction

It is well known that the benzene ring exhibits unusual chemical stability. This is exemplified by its tendency to undergo substitution reactions which leave the π-system intact, rather than the addition reactions commonly associated with olefines. The term aromatic is used to describe this characteristic stability of benzene and a number of other cyclic conjugated systems.

A variety of criteria for aromaticity have been proposed. One is based on the existence of a diamagnetic ring current. Another is based on the existence of a large resonance energy, which is defined as the difference in energy between the molecule and some reference structure, usually a hypothetical molecule with localized bonds (e.g. for benzene this might be a Kekulé structure). Values of resonance energy can be deduced from heats of hydrogenation or combustion.

The treatment of concerted reactions advocated by Dewar (1966) involves a consideration of the aromatic properties of the transition state. In this approach the reference structure is chosen as the corresponding open chain compound. The transition state is classified as aromatic if it is lower in energy than the reference structure, non-aromatic if of the same energy, and anti-aromatic if of higher energy. Transition states are too short-lived to permit experimental criteria of aromaticity to be used. However the information can be readily deduced from molecular orbital theory.

In this chapter the molecular orbital theory covered in Chapter 1 is applied to the problem of aromaticity. The HMO approach is shown to be somewhat limited in its usefulness. However the PMO (perturbational molecular orbital) method, which uses Hückel orbitals, does lead to satisfactory criteria of

41

aromaticity. A summary of the PMO approach is given in the latter part of this chapter. Although this is a very useful and powerful approach, some readers may prefer to take the results (given in Table 2.1, p. 57) on trust.

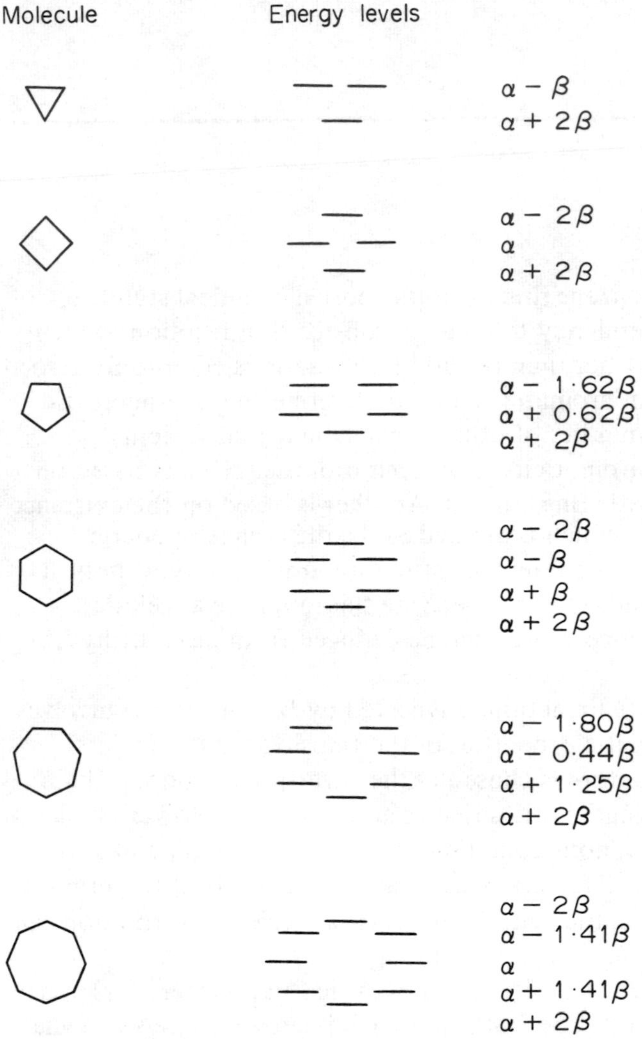

Molecule	Energy levels

$$\alpha - \beta$$
$$\alpha + 2\beta$$

$$\alpha - 2\beta$$
$$\alpha$$
$$\alpha + 2\beta$$

$$\alpha - 1 \cdot 62\beta$$
$$\alpha + 0 \cdot 62\beta$$
$$\alpha + 2\beta$$

$$\alpha - 2\beta$$
$$\alpha - \beta$$
$$\alpha + \beta$$
$$\alpha + 2\beta$$

$$\alpha - 1 \cdot 80\beta$$
$$\alpha - 0 \cdot 44\beta$$
$$\alpha + 1 \cdot 25\beta$$
$$\alpha + 2\beta$$

$$\alpha - 2\beta$$
$$\alpha - 1 \cdot 41\beta$$
$$\alpha$$
$$\alpha + 1 \cdot 41\beta$$
$$\alpha + 2\beta$$

FIGURE 2.1
Hückel energy levels of the cyclic polymethines from $N = 3$ to $N = 8$

42

2.2 π-Energy levels of cyclic polymethines $(-CH-)_N$

The energy levels of several cyclic polymethines have already been discussed in Chapter 1. The general result is that the HMO energies of planar monocylic polymethines are given by

$$E = \alpha + 2\beta \cos \frac{2\pi r}{N}$$

where N is the number of carbon atoms and

$$r = 0, 1, 2 \ldots (N - 1)$$

The π-energy levels of the lower members of the series are shown in Fig. 2.1.

The same results may be obtained using a simple geometrical method (Frost and Musulin, 1953). The molecule is represented by a regular polygon inscribed in a circle of diameter 2β, such that there is an atom at the bottom of the vertical (C_2) axis. The vertical axis is regarded as an energy scale whose fixed points are $\alpha + 2\beta$ at the bottom of the circle, α at the centre of the circle and $\alpha - 2\beta$ at the top of the circle. The N energy levels are given by the positions of the N atoms on this energy scale. To illustrate the method, consider the cyclopropenyl system (Fig. 2.2).

Energy scale   Energy levels

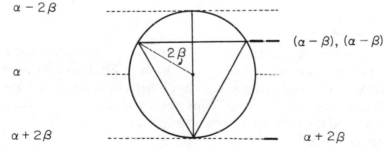

$\alpha - 2\beta$

$\quad\quad 2\beta \quad\quad\quad\quad (\alpha - \beta), (\alpha - \beta)$

α

$\alpha + 2\beta \quad\quad\quad\quad\quad \alpha + 2\beta$

FIGURE 2.2
Geometrical method for Hückel energy levels

The lowest π-energy level in this (and other) cyclic polymethines is $\alpha + 2\beta$. The other two energy levels are both $\alpha - 2\beta \cos \theta$ where θ is 60°. Thus, the energy levels are $\alpha + 2\beta, \alpha - \beta, \alpha - \beta$.

43

2.3 The Hückel $(4n + 2)$ rule

Hückel pointed out that, on the basis of molecular orbital theory, monocyclic conjugated polymethines have filled shells of π-electrons when the number of π-electrons is $4n + 2$, where n is an integer. These systems may be expected to be stable. The rule may be illustrated by reference to Fig. 2.1. If $n = 0$, then a system with 2π-electrons should be stable. Such a situation is found in the cyclopropenyl positive ion, which has been isolated as the hexachloroantimonate. For $n = 1$, the prediction is that the cyclopentadienyl anion, benzene and the cycloheptatrienyl (tropylium) cation are stable. This is certainly in accord with experience. The stability of benzene is well known, the cyclopentadienyl anion is readily formed by the action of potassium metal on cyclopentadiene, and the cycloheptatrienyl cation is one of the most stable carbonium ions known. Hückel's rule also predicts that some of the larger cyclic conjugated systems are stable, e.g. those with 10, 14 and 18 π-electrons. However, the situation is complicated by steric problems (see for example Garratt, 1971) and need not be considered further here.

In contrast systems wth $(4n)$ π-electrons are expected to be less stable. Cyclobutadiene, with 4π-electrons, is only a transient compound. Cyclooctatetraene, with 8π-electrons, has chemical properties similar to those expected for an olefine. These and other observations lead to the conclusion that in general cyclic polymethines with $(4n + 2)$ π-electrons are aromatic.

2.4 Resonance energy

It might be expected that the relative stabilities of $(4n + 2)$ and $4n$ systems suggested by the Hückel rule would be reflected in the π-electron energies of the compounds. As a reference compound, a hypothetical structure is chosen in which the double bonds are localized. Thus, the resonance energy (RE) is assumed to be equal to the total π-electron energy (E_π) minus the total π-electron energy of the reference structure (E_π^{ref})

$$\mathrm{RE} = E_\pi - E_\pi^{\mathrm{ref}}$$

E_π is obtained by summing the energies of all the π-electrons in the molecule. The energy of a π-electron is the energy of the orbital it occupies. Thus, for benzene (Fig. 1.26), E_π is $2(\alpha + 2\beta) + 4(\alpha + \beta) = 6\alpha + 8\beta$.

The reference structure contains three localized double bonds (a Kekulé

44

structure), each having the same π-orbitals as ethylene (Fig. 1.12). Thus, the π-electron energy for ethylene is $2 \times (\alpha + \beta) = 2\alpha + 2\beta$, and that for the reference structure is $3 \times (2\alpha + 2\beta) = 6\alpha + 6\beta$.

$$\therefore \quad RE = (6\alpha + 8\beta) - (6\alpha + 6\beta) = 2\beta.$$

The resonance energy of conjugated cyclic polyenes as a function of the number of atoms in the ring (N) is shown in Fig. 2.3.

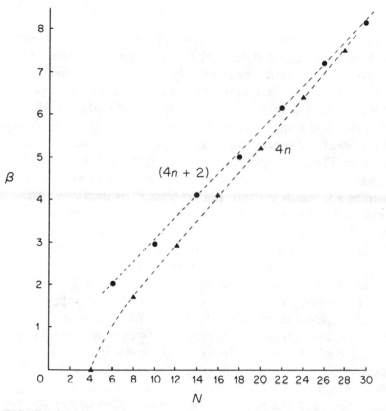

FIGURE 2.3
Hückel resonance energies (in units of β) of cyclic conjugated polyenes

Thus, the method suggests that there is significant stabilization for all the compounds, but that the stabilization for compounds with $(4n + 2)$ π-electrons is greater than for those with $(4n)$ π-electrons. However, this difference

45

decreases with increasing ring size. More sophisticated methods suggest that, whilst the Hückel method is qualitatively correct in its predictions of the differences between $(4n)$ and $(4n + 2)$ compounds, the resonance energy of $(4n + 2)$ polyenes decreases with ring size, and that of $(4n)$ polyenes is negligible or even negative (Dewar and Gleicher, 1965). Nevertheless, these more accurate calculations support the $(4n + 2)$ rule as a criterion of aromaticity.

2.5　The PMO method

The classification of aromaticity depends on the comparison of the energies of related chemical structures. In general, it is very much more accurate to calculate these relatively small differences directly than to obtain them by subtraction of the total energies. In quantum mechanics, such differences are calculated by perturbation theory. This approach has been applied to HMO calculations by Coulson and Longuet-Higgins (1947, 1948), Longuet-Higgins (1950) and Dewar (1952) and is referred to as the perturbational molecular orbital (PMO) method. The applications of this very powerful and elegant method to problems in organic chemistry has been discussed by Dewar (1969).

The method can be applied directly to the problem of aromaticity. An aromatic compound is defined as a cyclic polymethine which is lower in energy (i.e. more stable) than its open chain analogue. An anti-aromatic compound has higher energy and a non-aromatic compound the same energy as the open chain reference structure. Thus the problem is immediately reduced to a calculation of the energy change on ring formation. In the case of cyclopentadienyl the energy change on union (signified by the symbol $\leftarrow u \rightarrow$) at the terminal carbon atoms of pentadienyl is required (Fig. 2.4a). For an even alternate hydrocarbon such as benzene the cyclization of hexatriene could be considered. However, it turns out to be much simpler to compare the energy of formation of the linear and cyclic structure from the union of two odd alternate hydrocarbons (Fig. 2.4b and c). For this purpose the methyl radical is regarded as a simple odd alternant hydrocarbon.

Union involves the breaking and formation of σ-bonds as well as changes in π-bonding. However, only changes in π electron energy need be considered and Hückel orbitals form a satisfactory basis for the calculation. Before proceeding to the two rules necessary to apply the PMO theory to aromaticity it is first necessary to define bond order.

46

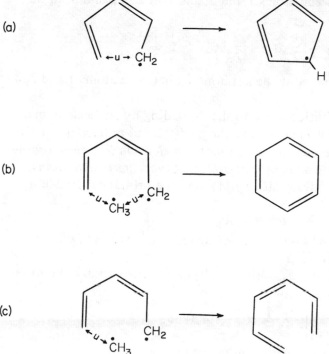

(a)

(b)

(c)

FIGURE 2.4
The concept of union as employed by the PMO method

2.6 Bond order

The contribution to the total π-bonding between two adjacent atoms due to electrons in a given orbital clearly depends on the size and signs of the orbital coefficients. For instance in the lowest orbital of allyl,

$$\psi_1 = \frac{1}{2}\phi_1 + \frac{1}{\sqrt{2}}\phi_2 + \frac{1}{2}\phi_3$$

there is strong π-bonding between atoms 1 and 2, and between atoms 2 and 3. On the other hand, in the non-bonding orbital

$$\psi_2 = \frac{1}{\sqrt{2}}\phi_1 - \frac{1}{\sqrt{2}}\phi_3$$

there is zero bonding between atoms 1 and 2, and between 2 and 3. In the uppermost orbital,

$$\psi_3 = \frac{1}{2} \phi_1 - \frac{1}{\sqrt{2}} \phi_2 + \frac{1}{2} \phi_3$$

if occupied, the interaction would be antibonding between atoms 1 and 2, and between 2 and 3.

To quantify the contribution made to the π-bonding by an electron in a given orbital Coulson (1939) has defined the partial bond order. The *partial bond order between two adjacent atoms due to an electron in a given orbital is the product of the coefficients of that orbital at those particular atoms.* Thus, if the two atoms are designated i and j, and the orbital designated μ, then

$$p_{ij}^{\mu} = c_{\mu i} c_{\mu j} \tag{2.1}$$

where p_{ij}^{μ} is the partial bond order between adjacent atoms i and j due to an electron in a particular orbital μ.

Consider an electron in the ψ_1 orbital of allyl, then the partial bond order between atoms 1 and 2 is given by

$$p_{12}^{1} = \frac{1}{2} \times \frac{1}{\sqrt{2}} = 0 \cdot 353$$

The positive value indicates a bonding interaction.

For an electron in ψ_2 the partial bond order between atoms 1 and 2

$$p_{12}^{2} = \frac{1}{\sqrt{2}} \times 0 = 0$$

Thus an electron in ψ_2 does not contribute to the π-bonding.

For an electron in ψ_3,

$$p_{12}^{3} = -\frac{1}{2} \times \frac{1}{\sqrt{2}} = -0 \cdot 353$$

The negative sign reflects the antibonding nature of the interaction.

The total π-bonding is the sum of the bonding interactions of each of the electrons. *Thus the total π-bond order (commonly called bond order) is the sum of the partial bond orders for the bond.* Thus

$$p_{ij} = \sum_{\text{all electrons}} p_{ij}^{\mu} \tag{2.2}$$

For example, consider the total π-bond order of the bond between atoms 1 and 2 in the allyl radical

$$p_{12} = 2 \times p_{12}^1 + 1 \times p_{12}^2$$

$$= 2 \times (0 \cdot 353) + 0 = 0 \cdot 707$$

When cyclization is being considered it is necessary to calculate the bond order between the two atoms at the point of union. Thus for the conversion of allyl into cyclopropenyl the bond order between atoms 1 and 3 is required

$$p_{13} = 2 \times \frac{1}{2} \times \frac{1}{2} + 1 \times \frac{1}{\sqrt{2}} \times \left(-\frac{1}{\sqrt{2}}\right)$$

$$= \frac{1}{2} - \frac{1}{2} = 0$$

This last result is an example of an important general result. In a neutral alternate hydrocarbon (AH) the bond order between two atoms which are either both starred or both unstarred (referred to as being of like parity) is zero.

Thus for a neutral AH

$$p_{ij} = 0 \text{ if } i \text{ and } j \text{ are of like parity} \tag{2.3}$$

The odd AH ions differ from the odd AH by one electron. The bond orders between atoms i and j therefore differ only by the partial bond orders of this electron, which is either added to or removed from the NBMO. Thus the anion, which has one more electron than the radical, has an additional contribution to the bond order of $c_{0i}c_{0j}$, where c_{0i} and c_{0j} are the coefficients of the NBMO at atoms i and j.

Thus for an odd AH anion

$$p_{ij} = c_{0i}c_{0j}, \text{ where } c_{0i} \text{ and } c_{0j} \text{ are} \tag{2.4}$$

the NBMO coefficients at atoms i and j of like parity..

The cation on the other hand has one electron less in the NBMO than the radical and the total bond order is therefore reduced by $c_{0i}c_{0j}$.

Thus for an odd AH cation

$$p_{ij} = -c_{0i}c_{0j} \text{ when } i \text{ and } j \text{ have like parity} \tag{2.5}$$

49

2.7   The PMO method and aromaticity

The application of the PMO method to the problems of aromaticity Dewar (1966, 1967) requires only two rules, which will be stated here without rigorous proof.

Intramolecular union (Rule I)

The change in π-energy on intramolecular union between two positions i and j in an alternant hydrocarbon (AH) (e.g. Fig. 2.4(a)) might be expected to depend on the coefficients of the occupied orbitals at the point of union. These coefficients are reflected in the calculated π-bond order between atoms i and j in the original structure. The energy change is given by rule I.

Rule I. The energy change (δE) on union between two positions i and j in the same AH is given by

$$\delta E = 2p_{ij}\beta \qquad (2.6)$$

where p_{ij} is the π-bond order between positions i and j and β is the C—C resonance integral.

Intermolecular union (Rule II)

It can be shown that in the union of two odd AH radicals (Fig. 2.4(c)) the bonding molecular orbitals survive effectively unchanged. The change in π-energy results from the interaction of the two NBMOs to form two new MOs (Fig. 2.5).

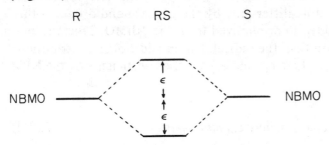

FIGURE 2.5
Interaction of NBMOs on union between two odd AHs R and S to form even AH, RS.

The magnitude of the splitting (ϵ) reflects the interaction between the two NBMO and depends on the NBMO coefficients at the point of union. Thus,

$$\epsilon = c_{0r}c_{0s}\beta$$

Since there are two electrons in the new orbital, the total π-energy change,

$$\delta E = 2c_{0r}c_{0s}\beta$$

Where the union occurs at more than one pair of sites (e.g. Fig. 2.4(b))

$$\delta E = 2 \overset{\text{bonds}}{\underset{rs}{\Sigma}} c_{0r}c_{0s}\beta$$

where the summation is over all pairs of atoms at which union occurs. Thus,
Rule II:

The change in energy (δE) when two odd AH radicals, R and S, combine to form an even AH, RS is given by

$$\delta E = 2 \overset{\text{bonds}}{\underset{rs}{\Sigma}} c_{0r}c_{0s}\beta \tag{2.7}$$

The two Rules given above form a basis for calculating the difference in energy between cyclic polymethines and their open chain analogues and, hence, classifying them as aromatic, non-aromatic or anti-aromatic. Furthermore, the results may be generalized as a simple set of rules for the prediction of aromatic properties.

2.8 Aromaticity in even AHs

Rule II (Equation 2.7) can be readily applied to the problem of aromaticity in conjugated cyclic polyenes, which are even AHs. Such a compound with, say N carbon atoms, may be regarded as being formed by the union of an odd AH radical with (N − 1) atoms and a methyl radical (Fig. 2.6a).

Likewise, the reference structure (the open chain compound) may also be formed by the union of these two radicals (Fig. 2.6(b)). For this purpose, the methyl radical may be regarded as a simple case of an odd AH radical, the electron being in a normalized atomic orbital of energy α and with a coefficient of unity.

The lowest cyclic even AH is cyclobutadiene, which may be regarded as being formed by the union of an allyl with a methyl radical, as also is the reference compound, butadiene (Fig. 2.7). The NBMO coefficients at the

51

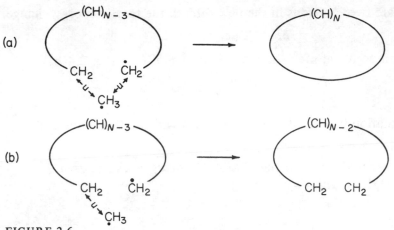

(a)

(b)

FIGURE 2.6
Formation of an AH by union of an odd AH radical with a methyl radical. (a) cyclic compound;
(b) open chain compound

terminal atoms of allyl are readily seen to be $1/\sqrt{2}$ and $-1/\sqrt{2}$ (Section 1.14).
Thus, for the formation of cyclobutadiene

$$\delta E = 2\beta\left(\frac{1}{\sqrt{2}} - \frac{1}{\sqrt{2}}\right) = 0$$

and for butadiene, taking the positive coefficient of allyl.

$$\delta E = 2\left(\frac{1}{\sqrt{2}}\right)\beta$$

Since β is a negative quantity, the cyclic compound is *less* stable than the open
chain compound. Cyclobutadiene is, therefore, anti-aromatic since it has a
negative resonance energy.

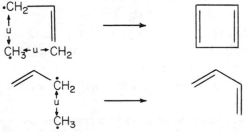

FIGURE 2.7
Formation of cyclobutadiene and butadiene

The next highest cyclic, even AH is benzene, which is regarded as formed by union of pentadienyl with methyl (Fig. 2.8). The coefficients at the terminal carbon atoms of pentadienyl are both $1/\sqrt{3}$. The energy change on formation of benzene is, therefore,

$$\delta E = \frac{4}{\sqrt{3}} \beta$$

The energy change for the formation of the reference structure hexatriene is

$$\delta E = \frac{2}{\sqrt{3}} \beta$$

Benzene is thus aromatic, having a positive resonance energy of $2/\sqrt{3}\beta$.

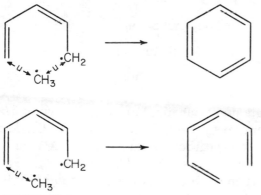

FIGURE 2.8
Formation of benzene and hexatriene

Thus, it can be seen that odd AHs will have coefficients at the terminal carbon atom of opposite sign if the number of carbon atoms is 3, 7, 11, etc. This gives a negative resonance energy for the cyclic compound with 4, 8, 12, etc. carbon atoms (i.e. $4n$ carbon atoms). On the other hand, odd AHs with 5, 9, 13, etc. carbon atoms will have coefficients at the terminal carbons which have the same sign. This gives a positive resonance energy for cyclic compounds with 6, 10, 14, etc. carbon atoms, i.e. those with $(4n + 2)$.† Thus, the PMO theory forms the basis for a derivation of Hückel's rule.

† Note that in the PMO method, polymethines are classified according to the number of carbon atoms. Hückel's $(4n + 2)$ rule refers to the number of π-electrons which only equals the number of carbon atoms in neutral hydrocarbons.

2.9 Aromaticity in odd non-alternant hydrocarbons

The systems can exist as positive ions, negative ions or radicals. Hence, the number of carbon atoms and the number of π-electrons are no longer equal. The reference structures are again chosen as the open chain compounds, although these have delocalized bonds.

The cyclic odd non-AH may be regarded as being formed by intramolecular union of the corresponding open chain odd AH (as the cation, anion or radical). Rule I gives the energy as

$$\delta E = 2p_{ij}\beta$$

From Equations (2.4–2.6), it follows that since the atoms at which union occurs have the same parity

$$\delta E = 2c_{0r}c_{0s}\beta \qquad \text{for odd AH anion}$$

$$\delta E = 0 \qquad \text{for odd AH radical}$$

$$\delta E = -2c_{0r}c_{0s}\beta \qquad \text{for odd AH cation}$$

Thus, cyclic radicals of this type are non-aromatic. For ions, the sign of δE depends on the signs of the coefficients at the point of union. As mentioned in Section 2.8 the coefficients at the terminal carbon atoms of an odd AH are of opposite sign when the number of carbon atoms is 3, 7, 11, etc. (i.e. $4n + 3$). The coefficients have the same sign when the number of carbon atoms is 5, 9, 13, etc. (i.e. $4n + 1$). Thus, anions with ($4n + 1$) carbon atoms and cations with ($4n + 3$) carbon atoms are aromatic. Cations with ($4n + 1$) and anions with ($4n + 3$) carbon atoms are anti-aromatic.

2.10 Anti-Hückel systems

The π-orbitals are written as a linear combination of atomic p-orbitals of the conjugated carbon atoms. The basis set is normally chosen so that the p-orbitals overlap in phase, as for example, Fig. 2.9(a). However, there are certain situations where this condition cannot be achieved. One such example was proposed by Heilbronner (1964), who considered the case of a conjugated chain which is twisted through 180° (or in general $n\pi$) before union at the terminal carbon atoms to form a cyclic conjugated hydrocarbon (Fig. 2.9(b)). The effect is to introduce a phase dislocation into the system. The resulting orbital has the topology of a Möbius strip.† A somewhat similar configuration can also arise during the course of a concerted reactions.

(a)   (b)

FIGURE 2.9
(a) Hückel system; (b) Anti-Hückel system

The orbital energies for these Möbius or anti-Hückel systems are given by

$$E = \alpha + 2\beta \cos \frac{\pi(2r + 1)}{N}$$

where $r = 0, 1, 2, \ldots N - 1$.

The π-energy levels of the lower members of the series are shown in Fig. 2.10.

As with Hückel systems, the same result can be obtained by the geometrical method (Section 2.2). In this case, however, the polygon is drawn with a bond at the bottom of the vertical (C_2) axis.

Applying the PMO method to these systems in the same way as to Hückel systems, it can be readily shown that neutral polymethines with $4n$ carbon atoms are aromatic and those with $(4n + 2)$ atoms anti-aromatic. This is the opposite result to Hückel systems.

The results for ions are also reversed. Cations are aromatic with $4n + 1$

---

† A Möbius strip is a strip with only one side. To construct such a system, take a narrow strip of paper, twist one end through 180° and join the two ends together. The resulting shape has only one side, as an attempt to colour one side red and the other side blue will show!

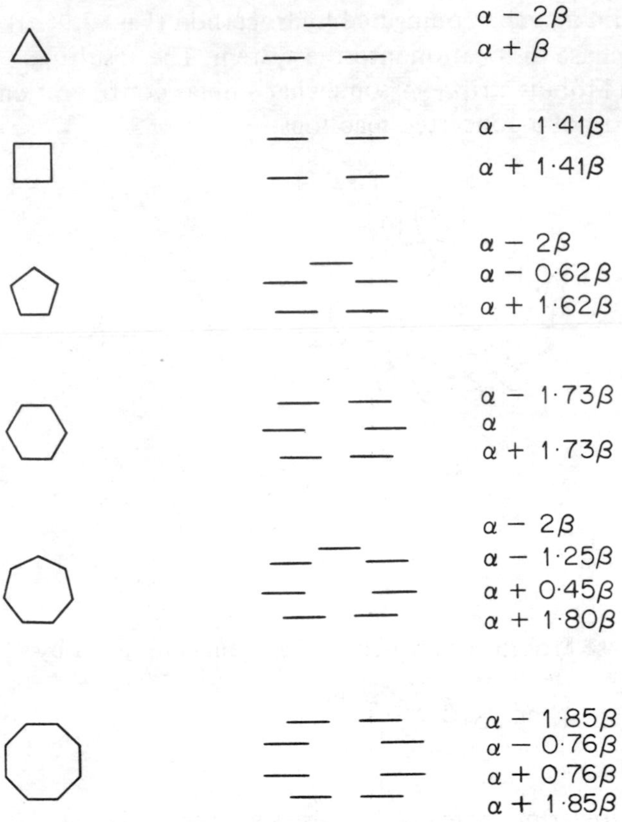

$$\alpha - 2\beta$$
$$\alpha + \beta$$

$$\alpha - 1\cdot41\beta$$
$$\alpha + 1\cdot41\beta$$

$$\alpha - 2\beta$$
$$\alpha - 0\cdot62\beta$$
$$\alpha + 1\cdot62\beta$$

$$\alpha - 1\cdot73\beta$$
$$\alpha$$
$$\alpha + 1\cdot73\beta$$

$$\alpha - 2\beta$$
$$\alpha - 1\cdot25\beta$$
$$\alpha + 0\cdot45\beta$$
$$\alpha + 1\cdot80\beta$$

$$\alpha - 1\cdot85\beta$$
$$\alpha - 0\cdot76\beta$$
$$\alpha + 0\cdot76\beta$$
$$\alpha + 1\cdot85\beta$$

FIGURE 2.10
π-energy levels of Anti-Hückel systems from $N = 3$ to $N = 8$

atoms and anti-aromatic with $4n + 3$. Anions are aromatic with $4n + 3$ atoms and anti-aromatic with $4n + 1$ atoms. The results are summarized in Table 2.1.

2.11   Aromaticity in heterocyclic systems and polycyclic systems

The PMO method can be applied to heterocyclic systems by merely replacing the heteroatom by a carbon atom whilst maintaining the number of π-electrons constant. Thus, the rules for aromaticity in pyridine are the same as

TABLE 2.1
Aromaticity of polymethines $-(CH)_N-$

Ring size (N)	Neutral molecule	Cation	Anion
4n	−H, +A-H	...	...
4n + 1	0	−H, +A-H	+H, −A-H
4n + 2	+H, −A-H	...	...
4n + 3	0	+H, −A-H	−H, +A-H

H = Hückel
A-H = Anti-Hückel
+ = Aromatic
− = Anti-aromatic
0 = Non-aromatic

for benzene, but pyrrole should be compared with the cyclopentadienyl anion.

When considering polycyclic systems, it is necessary to delete all essential single or essential double bonds. These bonds can be readily identified since they are the same in all classical resonance structures of the molecule. Consider azulene; the classical resonance structures are shown in Fig. 2.11. Notice that the central bond is always single and is, therefore, omitted, leaving a monocyclic system with ten carbon atoms, i.e. an aromatic system.

FIGURE 2.11
Classical resonance structures of azulene

2.12 Aromaticity in excited states

In photochemical reactions, it is desirable to classify the transition state according to its aromatic properties. In hydrocarbons, the excited states most likely to be involved are those in which an electron is transferred from a π-bonding orbital to a π^*-antibonding orbital ($\pi \to \pi^*$), or in which an electron is transferred from a nonbonding orbital to a π^*-antibonding orbital ($n \to \pi^*$). In principle, the excited states could be singlet or triplet states, but simple molecular orbital theory does not distinguish between the two.

57

The criterion for aromaticity is again the comparison of the energy of the cyclic and linear structures, but in this case, both structures are in an equivalent excited state, normally the lowest excited state.

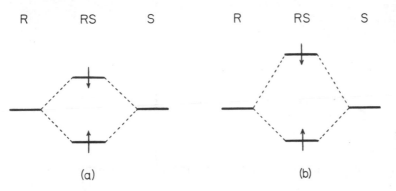

FIGURE 2.12
Interaction of NBMOs of two odd AHs to form an even AH. (a) simple MO result; (b) more accurate result

Consider first an even AH which, as before, may be regarded as being formed by the union of an odd AH (R) and a methyl (S). We now have to compare the energy of the cyclic compound with the open chain compound, both in their lowest excited ($\pi \to \pi^*$) states. The interaction only involves the NBMOs of R and S. If, as previously assumed (Section 2.7), the splitting is symmetrical (Fig. 2.12(a)), the energy gain by one electron exactly balances the energy loss by the other. Thus, on this basis, the energy change on union to form either the excited cyclic or the excited linear structure is zero, and the excited cyclic structure is non-aromatic. However, in this instance, the simple MO method is misleading in that it underestimates the energy of the antibonding orbital (Fig. 2.12(b)). Thus, the greater the interaction, the greater the energy of the excited state. This is the exact opposite to the situation in the ground state and leads to a reversal of the rules for aromaticity. Hence, the first ($\pi \to \pi^*$) excited state of an aromatic AH is anti-aromatic and that of an anti-aromatic AH is aromatic.

Simple MO theory does form a satisfactory basis for the prediction of aromaticity in odd non-AH ions and radicals. Consider union at the terminal carbon atoms of a linear odd AH radical or ion in its excited state to form a cyclic AH also in its excited state.

Rule I states that the energy of union in the ground state given by $2p_{ij}\beta$ and Equation 2.3 states that p_{ij} is zero for a radical in the ground state. Consider now how the situation in the excited state differs from that in the ground state. The relevant energy levels of an odd AH and their occupancy in the first excited state of the cation radical and anion are shown in Fig. 2.13. There are two alternative configurations of equal energy for the radical.

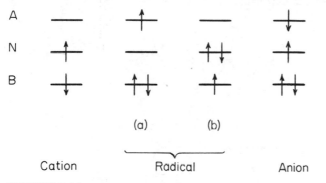

(a)　　　(b)

Cation　　　Radical　　　Anion

FIGURE 2.13
The uppermost bonding MO (B), the NBMO (N) and the lowest antibonding orbital (A) of an odd AH

The bond order at the site of union in the excited cation differs from the ground state radical by the partial bond order of an electron in the bonding orbital. Thus, for the cation

$$\Delta E = -2\beta p_{ij}^{B}$$

where p_{ij}^{B} is the partial bond order between the terminal atoms i and j from the bonding orbital. Similarly, for the excited radical, the bond order differs from that of the ground state by the bond orders associated with the excited electron and with the vacancy created in the lower orbital. Thus, for the radical

$$\Delta E = 2\beta(p_{ij}^{A} - p_{ij}^{N}) \quad \text{or} \quad 2\beta(p_{ij}^{N} - p_{ij}^{B})$$

where p_A and p_N are the partial bond orders between the terminal atoms from the antibonding and non-bonding orbitals. Similarly, for the anion

$$\Delta E = 2\beta p_{ij}^{A}$$

The signs of the partial bond orders depend on the relative signs of the appropriate orbital coefficients at the terminal carbons. This is a reflection of the

59

symmetry of the orbitals. Consideration of the orbital symmetries of odd AH, of which allyl and pentadienyl (Fig. 2.14) are typical, shows that if the NBMO is symmetric with respect to reflection in the plane perpendicular to the molecular axis and passing through the central carbon atom (as in pentadienyl), then the highest bonding and lowest antibonding MOs are antisymmetric. If, however, the NBMO is antisymmetric (as in allyl), then the highest bonding and lowest antibonding MOs are symmetric.

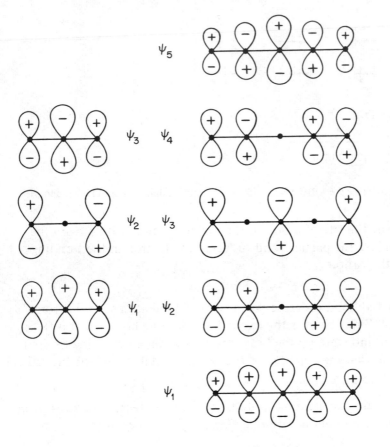

Allyl   Pentadienyl

FIGURE 2.14
Orbitals of allyl and pentadienyl

60

If the NBMO is symmetric, then p_{ij}^N is positive and p_{ij}^A and p_{ij}^B are negative. Thus, the cation and radical (b) (Fig. 2.13) are aromatic and the anion anti-aromatic. On the other hand, if the NBMO is antisymmetric, then the anion and radical (a) are aromatic and the cation anti-aromatic.

The results for the radicals depend on the excited state involved. For the two ions, since antisymmetric NBMOs occur for $(4n + 3)$ carbon atoms and symmetric NBMOs for $(4n + 1)$ carbon atoms (Sections 2.8 and 2.9) the rules for the excited state are again the reverse of those for the ground state.

2.13   Aromaticity of transition states

In the discussion of reaction paths of concerted reactions, it is helpful to classify transition states according to their aromatic properties. As an example, consider the Diels-Alder reaction between butadiene and ethylene. The transition state is shown in Fig. 2.15. Note that the orbitals of the basis sets are

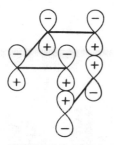

FIGURE 2.15
An aromatic transition state

elongated for clarity and that the overlap is such as to give a bonding inter-action. Clearly, the structure has a six-membered ring with delocalized bonding. Despite the non planar configuration and the combination of σ-π bonding involved, the same arguments concerning aromaticity as for a cyclic poly-methine can be applied. This transition state is therefore aromatic for a thermal reaction (i.e., not involving excited electronic states).

Problem 2.1   Assuming a reference structure consisting of two ethylene double bonds, calculate the resonance energy of cyclobutadiene.

61

Problem 2.2   Assuming the wave functions given in Section 1.16, calculate the total π-bond orders between atoms 1 and 2, 2 and 3, 3 and 4 in butadiene.

Problem 2.3   Use the PMO method (Equation 2.6) to decide whether fulvene is aromatic, anti-aromatic, or non-aromatic.

Problem 2.4   Use the PMO method (Equation 2.7) to determine the reson-ance energy of cyclo-octatetraene (consider the union of heptatrienyl and methyl).

The stereochemical requirements **3** of concentrated pericyclic reactions

3.1 Concerted reactions

A concerted reaction is one in which the conversion of reactants (R) into the products (P) occurs directly by way of a *single* transition state (T.S.). An exothermic concerted reaction is represented by the potential energy profile of Fig. 3.1(a). When the conversion of reactants into products proceeds by way of more than one transition state, such that one or more intermediates (I) are formed, the processes are accordingly non-concerted. A two-step process involving one (metastable) intermediate is represented by Fig. 3.1(b). However, since each elementary step of any chemical reaction must be concerted, by definition, then case (b) may be divided into the two concerted sequences: $R \rightarrow I$ and $I \rightarrow P$.

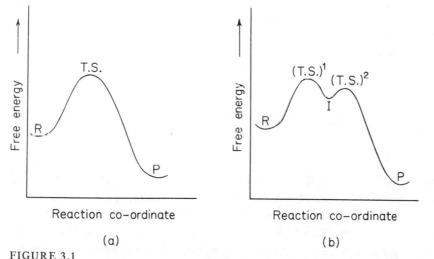

FIGURE 3.1

Reaction profiles for (a) a concerted reaction, and (b) a two-step reaction

63

Concerted reactions are usually stereospecific, and this becomes evident when a suitably substituted molecule is employed in the reaction as the starting material. The classical S_N2 reaction is a good example of a thoroughly concerted stereospecific chemical process, reaction (3.1). Non-concerted reactions are not usually stereospecific simply because the stereochemical integrity may be lost in the formation of the reactive intermediate. A suitable example is given by the S_N1 hydrolysis of an optically active halide, reaction (3.2). Ideally, of course, reactions of type (3.1) should be 100 per cent stereospecific,

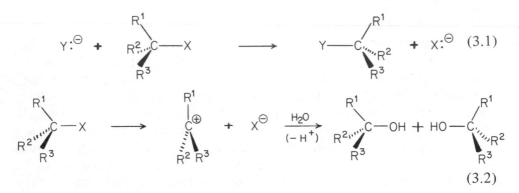

whereas type (3.2) reactions should completely lack specificity. Organic reactions are often not as well-behaved as this, however, since other factors may influence the stereochemical course of a given reaction. In Equation (3.2) for example, the formation of ion-pairs or the unsymmetrical solvation of the carbonium ion may lead to a slight preference for nucleophilic attack along one co-ordinate axis, and therefore to a slight over-production of one optical antipode.

3.2 Pericyclic reactions

The electronic structure of the transition state complex of a given reaction is, of course, unique for that reaction. Within a given reaction series, however, there will be various stereo-electronic features common to each of the transition states which themselves characterize individual processes in the reaction series. Thus, for example, all S_N2 reactions of alkyl halides have similarities in the geometrical disposition of nucleophile, the electron deficient centre, and the leaving group, and in the dispersal of charge among these groups, in the activated complex. The various points in common largely disappear when the comparison is made between two reactions from different reaction series and only the gross features such as charge separation or charge dispersal may then link the two processes. In this context the transition states of organic reactions may be placed into one of three broadly-defined categories (Kosower, 1968):

(i)   polar (involves separation or dispersal of charge);
(ii) free radical (involves creation or transfer of unpaired electrons);
(iii) isopolar (neither polar nor radical in nature).

A number of important concerted organic reactions proceed through iso-polar transition states: examples are the Diels-Alder reaction, and the Cope and Claisen rearrangements. These processes are in fact specific cases of a whole family of reactions which have been termed *pericyclic* processes (Woodard and Hoffmann, 1969). Concerted pericyclic reactions proceeding via polar transition states are also well-known.

Pericyclic reactions commonly have three additional features:

(i)   among the reactants and products usually at least one molecule is unsaturated;
(ii) the reactions involve the formation or scission of σ-bonds and the consumption or generation of π-bonds;
(iii) the electronic reorganization occurs in some sort of cyclic array of the participating atomic centres.

Because of condition (iii) all pericyclic reactions may formally be regarded as cyclo-addition processes or their retrogressions, but it is generally more useful to divide pericyclic reactions into a number of more distinct reaction series. These are: electrocyclic reactions (e.g. Equations 3.3 and 3.4), cyclo-addition reactions (e.g. Equations 3.5 and 3.6), sigmatropic reactions (e.g. Equations 3.7 and 3.8), cheletropic reactions (e.g. Equations 3.9 and 3.10), group transfers (e.g. Equation 3.11), and eliminations (e.g. Equations 3.12 and 3.13). Examples in other categories are less numerous, and will not be considered in this volume.

65

1 σ-bond ⇄ 1 π-bond

$$\square \;\rightleftharpoons\; \diagup\!\!\diagdown \tag{3.3}$$

$$\diagup\!\!\diagdown \;\rightleftharpoons\; \hexagon \tag{3.4}$$

m σ-bonds ⇄ m π-bonds

$$\diagup\!\!\diagdown + \| \;\rightleftharpoons\; \hexagon \tag{3.5}$$

$$\| \diagdown \;\rightleftharpoons\; \hexagon \tag{3.6}$$

1 σ-bond + m π-bonds ⇄ 1 σ-bond + m π-bonds

$$\tag{3.7}$$

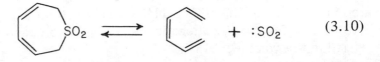

$$\tag{3.8}$$

2 σ-bonds + m π-bonds ⇄ (m + 1) π-bonds + 1 'lone pair'

$$\| \;+\; :CX_2 \;\rightleftharpoons\; \triangle\!\!\!<^{X}_{X} \tag{3.9}$$

$$\langle\!SO_2 \;\rightleftharpoons\; \diagup\!\!\diagdown \;+\; :SO_2 \tag{3.10}$$

n σ-bonds + m π-bonds ⇄ n σ-bonds + m π-bonds

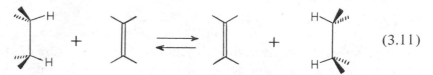

$$(3.11)$$

n σ-bonds + m π-bonds ⇄ (n − 1) σ-bonds + (m + 1) π-bonds

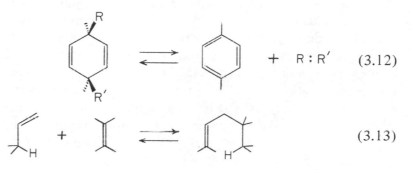

$$+ \quad R : R' \qquad (3.12)$$

$$(3.13)$$

Pericyclic reactions, which are typified in the above examples, are highly stereospecific. They may be initiated by thermal energy (Δ) or by photochemical excitation ($h\nu$), and in some cases either thermal or photochemical activation can be employed. In this last case the stereochemical consequences of the thermal and photochemical reactions are different.

3.3   Stereochemistry

Before we proceed further and examine the theoretical interpretations for the stereospecificity of concerted pericyclic reactions, it is advantageous at this stage to discuss the general stereochemical requirements of these processes.

3.3.1   Cyclo-addition reactions

Reactions (3.5) and (3.6) respectively delineate a simple two-component and a three-component cyclo-addition. The two-component system is by far the most common; a few three-component cases have been discovered, but the four-component system is almost unknown.

There are good physico-chemical reasons for these observations. Consider, for example, the dependence of reaction rate constant (k) on the activation

67

parameters as deduced from transition state theory:

$$k = \kappa \frac{(kT)}{h} e^{-\Delta H^{\neq}/RT} e^{\Delta S^{\neq}/R}$$

The rate constant increases with the value of the temperature ($T°K$) and with increases in the value of the activation entropy ($\Delta S^{\neq}$) if positive. Large activation enthalpies ($\Delta H^{\neq}$, which is always positive) and negative activation entropies serve to decrease the numerical values of the exponential terms, and hence the value of k. Since cyclo-addition reactions proceed by way of cyclic transition states, the formation of which inevitably involves the loss of degrees of freedom, they are characterized by negative $\Delta S^{\neq}$ values, which in turn serves to limit the magnitude of k.† The $\Delta S^{\neq}$ term deteriorates to an even more negative value as the number of atomic centres participating in the cyclo-addition increases. The limiting factor in a two-component cyclo-addition is therefore the ring size, and the formation of a cyclic array of more than seven or eight members is likely to be very improbable except in a few special cases. The $\Delta S^{\neq}$ term even more severely limits three-component cyclo-addition processes. The cyclic trimerization of three ethylene molecules, reaction (3.6), is so improbable that the reaction rate is negligible.

The adverse entropy factor ($\Delta S^{\neq}$ highly negative) can be circumvented by embedding two of the olefinic components within one molecule so that they are held rigidly in the correct configuration for interaction with the third component to be statistically likely. Reaction (3.14) is a good example of the practical use of these principles. An alternative answer to the entropy problem

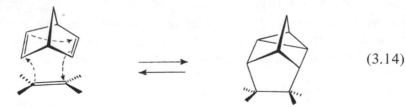

$$(3.14)$$

might be to use a suitable metal atom or ion as a species around which the olefin molecules could be arranged as ligands. In certain circumstances it

† For the Diels-Alder reaction typical values for the activation parameters are $\Delta H^{\neq} \sim 16$ kcal mole^{-1}, $\Delta S^{\neq} \sim -8$ cal deg^{-1} mole^{-1}. The sigmatropic rearrangement shown in Equation (3.8), which also proceeds by way of a six-membered cyclic transition state, has $\Delta H^{\neq} = 31 \cdot 1$ kcal mole^{-1} and $\Delta S^{\neq} = -12$ cal deg^{-1} mole^{-1} (at 185°C).

might then be possible to arrange for a concerted cyclic trimerization or tetramerization to occur.

It can also be anticipated that an activation enthalpy which is tenable (under a given set of experimental conditions) for a particular reaction, will be increased in related cases where more bond-elongations and bond-contractions must occur. The magnitude of the $\Delta H^{\ddagger}$ term will also, therefore, impose limitations on the ring size and on the number of components.

The two-component cyclo-addition reactions are conveniently classified as $[m+p]$ reactions, where m and p represent the *maximum* number of participating π-electrons on each of the two components. Likewise the general three component cyclo-addition becomes an $[m+p+q]$ process. On this basis, reactions (3.5) and (3.6) are respectively classified as $[4+2]$ and $[2+2+2]$ cyclo-addition reactions.

The simplest cyclo-addition is the two component $[2+2]$ process; the prototype reaction is the cyclic dimerization of two ethylene molecules, reaction (3.15). In this, and indeed in all cyclo-addition processes, the pro-

$$(3.15)$$

gress of the reaction depends upon the substantial overlap between the π-orbitals of the two components. Even with this limitation there are a large number of possible geometrical arrangements for the simple $[2+2]$ reaction defined by Equation (3.15). However, there are but four important stereo-chemical consequences for all two-component cyclo-addition reactions, and these depend upon whether the new σ-bonds are made on the same face of each reacting molecule (*suprafacial*), or on opposite faces (antarafacial). The terminology is that suggested by Woodward and Hoffmann (1969). For our two component cases, therefore, the four possible combinations are *supra-supra, supra-antara, antara-supra*, and *antara-antara*. These interactions for the general $[m+p]$ cyclo-addition are shown in Fig. 3.2, where the shading and the broken lines indicate the orbitals that overlap. For simplicity in presen-tation the polyenes are drawn as if they were linear, and the cyclic products as rectangular rings. In actual reactions, of course, the geometries will depart greatly from those indicated in Fig. 3.2. In addition, the polyenes are labelled

69

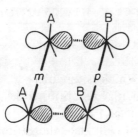
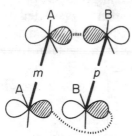

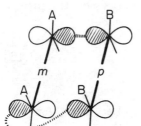
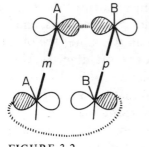
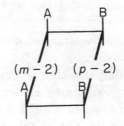
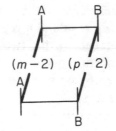
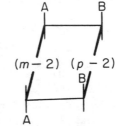
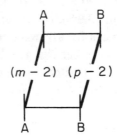

$\xrightarrow[\text{supra}]{\text{supra} -}$ $(m-2)$ $(p-2)$

$\xrightarrow[\text{antara}]{\text{supra} -}$ $(m-2)$ $(p-2)$

$\xrightarrow[\text{supra}]{\text{antara} -}$ $(m-2)$ $(p-2)$

$\xrightarrow[\text{antara}]{\text{antara} -}$ $(m-2)$ $(p-2)$

FIGURE 3.2

Possible stereochemical modes of combination of two olefins participating in an $[m+p]$ cyclo-addition reaction with the substituents A,A and B,B in order to show more clearly the stereo-chemical consequences of each mode of cyclo-addition, and only the terminal *p*-atomic orbital components of the π-system are illustrated. Only one reaction product is shown for each case; alternative possibilities arise if one of the acyclic components is first rotated through 180°.

A good example of a cyclo-addition is the Diels-Alder reaction, a [4 + 2] process. The formation of (1) from dimethyl *trans,trans*-2,5-hexadienoate and maleic anhydride illustrates very well the high stereospecificity of these processes. The relative stereochemistry of the two methoxycarbonyl groups in

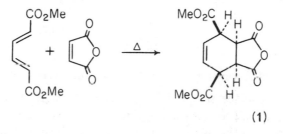

(1)

the reactant is retained in the product molecule so that the diene component must have been involved in a *supra* interaction. Likewise, the two hydrogen atoms of the maleic anhydride are *cis*-related in the product molecule, so that the dienophile has also reacted in a suprafacial manner. The topology of the reaction is therefore *supra-supra* which, other things being equal, is usually the most favourable of the four possible modes shown in Fig. 3.2.

Three important points can be deduced from Fig. 3.2.

(i) Antarafacial interactions necessarily lead to the inversion of groups at the termini in question.

(ii) The *supra-antara* and *antara-supra* modes are indistinguishable when the two reactant olefines are identical; specifically A = B, *m* = *p*.

(iii) There are two possible *supra-supra* combinations when *m* or *p* > 2; these correspond to *exo*-addition and *endo*-addition (Fig. 3.3).

Problem 3.1

(a) Classify the following cyclo-additions as [*m* + *p* + . . .] processes.

(b) What interactions (i.e. *supra-supra*, etc.) are involved?

(c) Is *exo* or *endo* addition involved in reaction (i)?

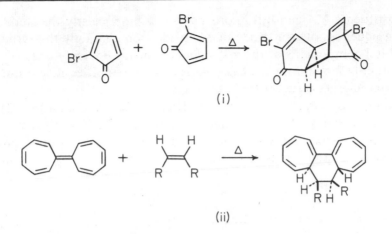

(i)

(ii)

(d) Is *exo* or *endo* addition involved in the reaction giving product (1)?

Let us now return to the simple [2 + 2] reaction, Equation (3.15), which should be defined more precisely as a $[_\pi 2 + _\pi 2]$ addition so as to distinguish it from reactions in which σ-bonds are participants. With the results of Fig. 3.2 in mind, it is readily seen that there are only three modes of combination, namely $[_\pi 2_s + _\pi 2_s]$, $[_\pi 2_s + _\pi 2_a]$, and $[_\pi 2_a + _\pi 2_a]$. The separate identity of the $[_\pi 2_a + _\pi 2_s]$ combination is eliminated by the rule (ii), above. The subscripts s and a refer to the suprafacial and antarafacial interactions of each π-component.

These three modes of interaction can be achieved in a number of possible geometrical arrangements of the interacting centres. However, let us limit consideration to those interactions which allow for the *maximum* degree of

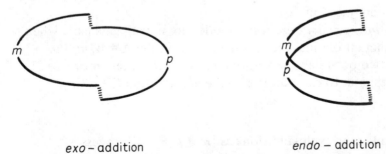

exo – addition   *endo* – addition

FIGURE 3.3
The *exo-* and *endo-* modes of addition in the general $[_\pi m_s + _\pi p_s]$ cyclo-addition process

π-orbital overlap between the two undistorted ethylenes consistent with a highly symmetrical geometrical arrangement of the four carbon atoms. These are shown in Fig. 3.4; they are not necessarily the most favourable interactions, but it is useful to limit discussion to these few cases. The regions of orbital overlap are indicated by the shading.

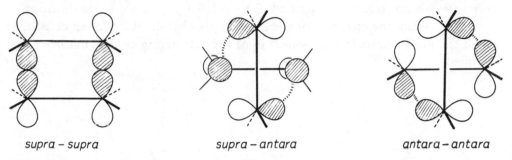

supra – supra   supra – antara   antara – antara

FIGURE 3.4
Possible orbital interactions between two ethylene molecules during cyclo-addition

By using molecular models it may be readily seen that the orbital overlap is the most efficient for the $[_\pi 2_s + _\pi 2_s]$ combination, and the steric inter-actions are less pronounced than in the alternative modes of interaction. The orbital overlap in the *supra-antara* and *antara-antara* geometrical arrangements are improved if one or both of the ethylene molecules is twisted about its C—C axis to that the coplanar relationship of the CH_2—CH_2 atoms is destroyed. It therefore follows that the $[_\pi 2_s + _\pi 2_a]$ and $[_\pi 2_a + _\pi 2_a]$ combinations are less likely, other things being equal, than the $[_\pi 2_s + _\pi 2_s]$ mode in simple unstrained systems.

Problem 3.2 Classify the following reactions and those given in Problem 3.1 by the $[_\pi m_s + _\pi p_a \ldots]$ type of notation.

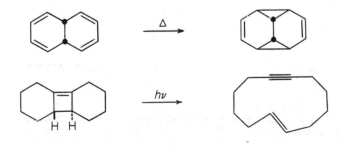

The arrangements of the two olefinic molecules in other $[m + p]$ cyclo-additions according to the four possible topological interactions, $[m_s + p_s]$, $[m_a + p_s]$, $[m_s + p_a]$, and $[m_a + p_a]$, are also readily deduced. These arrangements are always of lower symmetry than the corresponding $[2 + 2]$ cases. The possible spatial arrangements of the two olefins concerned in the proto-type Diels-Alder reaction, Equation (3.5), a $[_\pi 4 + _\pi 2]$ process, are shown in Fig. 3.5. Again, the criterion of the greatest possible orbital overlap consistent with the most symmetrical disposition of the interacting centres has been applied.

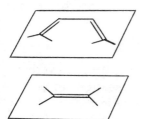

supra – supra

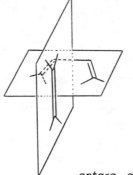

antara – antara

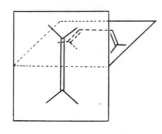

antara – supra

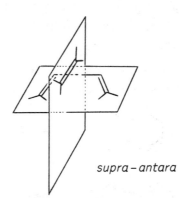

supra – antara

FIGURE 3.5

Possible geometrical arrangements of the two reactants in the prototype Diels-Alder reaction of ethylene with *s-cis*-buta-1,3-diene

74

The main points of interest are:

(i) the $[_\pi 4_s + _\pi 2_a]$ and $[_\pi 4_a + _\pi 2_s]$ processes are not identical;

(ii) the $[_\pi 4_s + _\pi 2_s]$ process offers the best scope for reaction, and the $[_\pi 4_a + _\pi 2_a]$ mode offers the next best alternative;

(iii) only in the $[_\pi 4_s + _\pi 2_s]$ case do the molecules approach in parallel planes; in the other three modes the molecular planes are orthogonal.

We have seen that the stereochemically distinguishable modes of addition on a single olefin component are but two – suprafacial and antarafacial. For a two component $[_\pi m + _\pi p]$ cyclo-addition the *maximum* number of distinguishable modes is therefore 2^2, for a three component $[_\pi m + _\pi p + _\pi q]$ addition it is 2^3, and for an n-component addition it is 2^n. If all of the components are the same (i.e. there is only one olefin involved), then *at least n* of the possible 2^n adducts will be identical. Hence, in the $[_\pi 2 + _\pi 2 + _\pi 2]$ cyclo-addition of three ethylene molecules, Equation (3.6), not one of the modes is distinguishable from the seven others because of the high symmetry and conformational flexibility of the product molecule cyclohexane. For this reaction six possible geometrical arrangements of the interacting centres in three of the modes of interaction are shown in Fig. 3.6. The shading and the broken lines indicate the orbitals that overlap. These arrangements correspond to the boat [(a)–(c)], chair (d), and quasi-chair [(e), (f)] transition state conformations. The arrangements (e) and (f) are, in fact, enantiomeric.

In the boat conformations (a)–(c), the sigma overlap of the shaded π-orbitals at C4 and C5 can only occur if concerted rotations about the C3, C4 and C5, C6 axes take place as indicated. Such rotations, which are of particular significance in discussing electrocyclic reactions, either occur in the same relative direction as in (c), or are opposed as in (a) and (b). These types of concerted rotational motion have been called conrotation and disrotation by Woodward and Hoffmann (1965, 1968, 1969); see Section 3.3(b).

The modes (a), (e), and (f) are, of course, topologically equivalent, as are modes (b) and (d). We have previously seen a type (b) mode in operation in a $[_\pi 2_s + _\pi 2_s + _\pi 2_s]$ process – reaction (3.14). The case (a) and case (c) modes are ruled out in this instance because of the inherent geometrical restraints imposed by the rigid bicyclo[2,2,1] hepta-2,5-diene molecule. The orbital interactions are illustrated in Fig. 3.7. Since reaction (3.14) occurs under thermal, but not photochemical, control we can conclude that $[_\pi 2_s + _\pi 2_s + _\pi 2_s]$

75

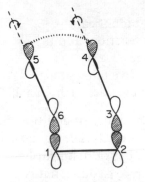

(a) *supra – antara – antara*

(b) *supra – supra – supra*

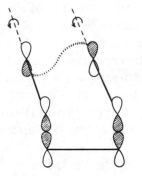

(c) *supra – supra – antara*

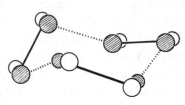

(d) *supra – supra – supra*

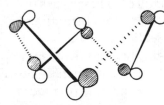

(e) *supra – antara – antara*

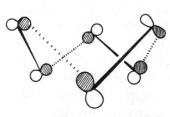

(f) *supra – antara – antara*

FIGURE 3.6
Some of the possible topological interactions and geometrical arrangements of three ethylene molecules undergoing cyclo-addition

processes, when concerted, occur only when all of the participants are in their electronic ground states. This is one example of a more general phenomenon that will be discussed in more detail in the next chapter.

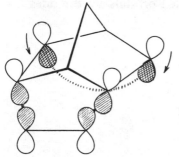

FIGURE 3.7

The $[\pi 2_s + \pi 2_s + \pi 2_s]$ interaction between ethylene and bicyclo[2,2,1]hepta-2,5-diene

Problem 3.3   Suggest a mechanism and deduce the topology of the orbital interactions for the reaction:

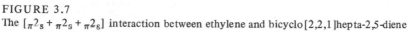

3.3.2   Electrocyclic reactions

An electrocyclic process is defined as the formation of a single bond between the termini of a conjugated polyene ($1\pi \rightleftarrows 1\sigma$), and the reverse reaction, Equation (3.16). Reactions (3.3) and (3.4) are specific examples in which k is 4 and 6 π-electrons respectively. In reaction (3.16) the polyene is shown in the (necessary) all *cis* configuration.

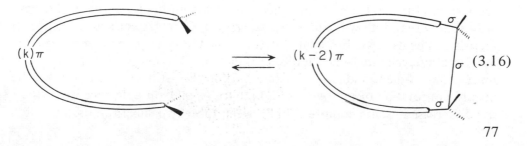

$$(k)\pi \quad \rightleftharpoons \quad (k-2)\pi \qquad (3.16)$$

The cyclization, which clearly involves the overlap of the terminal π-lobes in the polyene, can occur in the physically distinct conrotatory and disrotatory senses, as shown in Fig. 3.8. The substituents A–D are added to illustrate the different configurations in the products. The shaded orbitals are the ones that overlap.

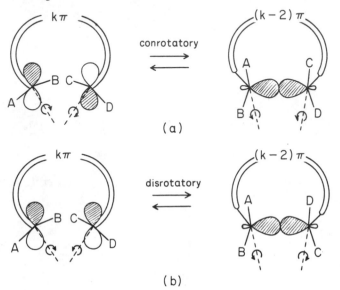

FIGURE 3.8
Possible rotational modes for a general electrocyclic reaction

The conrotatory motion involves an antarafacial interaction between the termini, and disrotation involves a suprafacial interaction between these centres. There are two distinct possibilities for each mode of rotation, and therefore four possible products in all. In many cases, however, the inherent symmetry of the system may not allow such distinction to be made. Even in cases where the two forms of one mode are distinguishable, it does not necessarily follow that both will occur; the geometry of the system and the steric factors can be decisive. For example, the conrotatory ring-opening of *trans*-3,4-dimethylcyclobut-1-ene should, in principle, yield a 1:1 mixture of *trans, trans*-hexa-2,4-diene and *cis, cis*-hexa-2,4-diene (Equation 3.17). However, the inward conrotation of the two methyl groups is unfavourable because of the rapid increase in steric compression between these two substituents, and the

78

free energy of the transition state will be higher than for the other conrotatory process. Reaction (3.17) is found to be completely stereospecific – only the *trans, trans*-diene is formed.

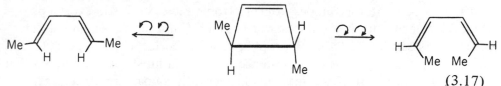

$$(3.17)$$

Geometrical restraints can also impose formidable energy barriers to reaction. In the case of bicyclo[4,1,0]hepta-2,4-diene (i.e. norcaradiene) ring opening to cyclohepta-1,3,5-triene can only occur readily by the single disrotatory mode indicated in Equation (3.18). The alternative disrotatory process and the two conrotatory modes can be ruled out because of their

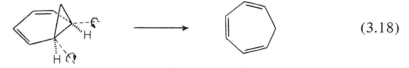

$$(3.18)$$

tendency to introduce severe angle and/or steric strain in the formation of the activated complex because the ultimate triene product must necessarily accommodate one or two *trans*-substituted double bonds. Reaction (3.18), which occurs on thermal activation, is therefore completely stereospecific.

Problem 3.4   Deduce whether conrotatory or disrotatory motions are involved in the following processes. Suggest a structure for the transient intermediate (2).

(i)

(ii)

(iii)

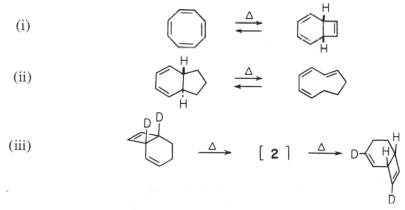

Electronic factors provide the dominant reasons for the choice between conrotation and disrotation, and we shall consider this topic in detail in Chapter 4. However, when the choice is between the two disrotatory modes (or the two conrotatory modes), the electronic factors can still exert a profound influence, but in a rather subtle manner. Consider, for example, the disrotatory scission of the cyclopropyl cation, a species which appears to have, at best, a very transitory existence. Indeed, in most cases it appears that ring scission occurs in concerted sequence with the departure of the leaving group from the cyclopropane ring. The allyl cation is then the 'primary product' (Equation 3.19). The participation of σ-bonds in concerted ionization-rearrangement processes is well-known, as in the pinacol-pinacolone reaction and the Beckmann rearrangement and the present case is no exception.

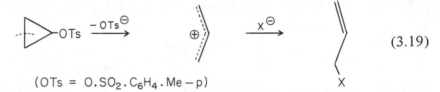

$$(3.19)$$

$$(OTs = O.SO_2.C_6H_4.Me-p)$$

However, the full S_N2 participation by the C2, C3 σ-bond can only occur if the electron density from that bond can buildup on the side of the cyclopropane ring remote from the leaving group. Of the two possible disrotatory modes, therefore, the one shown in Fig. 3.9 is likely to be strongly preferred; experiment indicates that this is so.

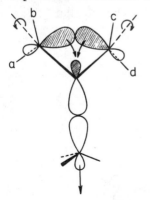

FIGURE 3.9
Preferred mode of disrotation in the ionization-cleavage of cyclopropanes

The electrocyclic ring opening of the cyclopropyl cation can, in a sense, be regarded as the addition of a σ-bond to an unoccupied p-orbital. In a similar vein, the reverse of the general electrocyclic process (Equation 3.16) can be formally regarded as the cyclo-addition of a σ-bond across the termini of the $(k-2)\,\pi$-electron system. To proceed further with the analogy it is necessary to specify the topology of the interaction between σ-bond and π-system. The participating orbitals of σ-bond and π-system can each be acted upon in a suprafacial or an antarafacial manner. The σ-bond is considered to be involved in the *supra* sense if configuration is retained, or inverted, at both of its termini in the course of the reaction. Inversion at one terminus and retention at the other amounts to an *antarafacial* interaction on the σ-bond. The topology of these interactions are illustrated in Fig. 3.10(a). The arrows indicate the orbital lobes which are used in the interaction with the π-system.

Figure 3.10 (b) – (e) illustrates the topology of the interactions between σ-bond and π-system for the electrocyclic ring opening of a cyclobutene (cf. Equation 3.3). We have the usual four possible modes *supra-supra, supra-antara, antara-supra,* and *antara-antara* (cf. Fig. 3.2), and these modes are related to the conrotatory and disrotatory ways of ring cleavage. There are in fact four possible pairs of interactions; in Fig. 3.10(c) and (d) the alternatives which, in so far as the orbital-orbital interactions are concerned are enantiomeric with those shown, and are therefore omitted.

It is seen from Fig. 3.10 that conrotatory cleavage is equivalent to a $[_\sigma 2_s + _\pi 2_a]$ or a $[_\sigma 2_a + _\pi 2_s]$ cyclo-addition, whereas disrotatory cleavage coincides with a $[_\sigma 2_s + _\pi 2_s]$ or a $[_\sigma 2_a + _\pi 2_a]$ process. An important point to note here is the effective placing of the *supra-supra* and *antara-antara* interactions into one category, and the *supra-antara* and *antara-supra* modes into a separate category. The members of the first set each contain an even number of inversions at carbon centres (i.e. 0 or 2), whilst the members of the second set each contain an odd number of inversions (i.e. 1). This is a general result, as will be seen in Section 3.3.3.

The electrocyclic reactions of other systems can be viewed in like manner. For example, the converse of reaction (3.4) may be treated as a $[_\sigma 2 + _\pi 4]$ cyclo-addition.

Problem 3.5   Classify the reactions in Problem 3.4 using the $[_\sigma m_s + _\pi p_s]$ type of notation.

(a)   *supra*   *supra*   *antara*   *antara*

(b) $[_\sigma 2_s + _\pi 2_a]$ (d) $[_\sigma 2_a + _\pi 2_a]$

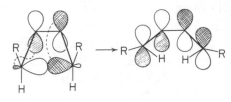

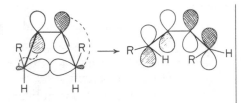

(e) $[_\sigma 2_s + _\pi 2_s]$

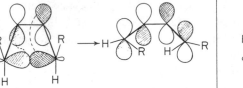

(c) $[_\sigma 2_a + _\pi 2_s]$

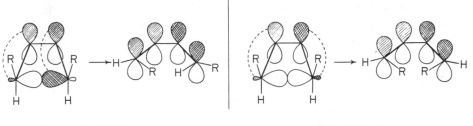

CONROTATION   DISROTATION

FIGURE 3.10
(a) The topology of the possible interactions on a σ-bond; (b) – (e) the inter-relationship between the electrocyclic conversion of cyclobutenes into butadienes and $[_\sigma 2 + _\pi 2]$ cyclo-addition reactions

3.3.3 *Sigmatropic reactions*

A sigmatropic change is one in which a σ-bond, flanked by one or more π-electron systems, migrates in an uncatalysed process to a new position in the molecule (i.e. $1\sigma + m\pi \rightleftarrows 1\sigma + m\pi$); (Woodward and Hoffmann, 1965, 1968, 1969).

Sigmatropic reactions fall into two categories.

(i) Reactions in which the migrating group (Z) is σ-bonded through the *same* atomic centre in reactant and product (commonly Z is the H atom). Such reactions are referred to as $[1, j]$ shifts because Z migrates from C1 to Cj (Fig. 3.11(a)).

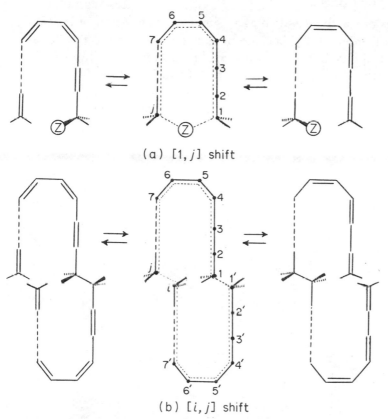

(a) $[1, j]$ shift

(b) $[i, j]$ shift

FIGURE 3.11

Sigmatropic rearrangements of order $[1, j]$ and of order $[i, j]$

(ii) Reactions in which the migrating group is σ-bonded through *different* atomic centres in reactant and product. These are [*i,j*] shifts (Fig. 3.11(b)).

The numbers 1, *i*, and *j* refer to the number of essential interacting centres in the migrating group (i.e. 1 or *i*) and framework system (i.e. *j*) at the transition state. These numbers are always odd for electrically neutral systems containing an even number of electrons, but *i* or *j* will be an even number if the system is electrically charged.

The reaction order [1,*j*] or [*i,j*] is normally independent of whether the π-system(s) are open-chain or part of a cyclic structure. Thus reaction (3.7) is an example of a [1,5] shift and not a [1,2] shift. The Claisen rearrangement (Equation 3.8), is normally classified as a sigmatropic charge of order [3,3], rather than one of order [3, 7], because of the close analogy to the Cope (Equation 3.20) and oxy-Cope (Equation 3.21) reactions. The important point to realize is that the migration of Z from Cl to C*j* occurs directly; the migrating group does not move along the π-system one carbon atom at a time. The transition state of a sigmatropic change is therefore reminiscent of the transition state of a cyclo-addition reaction.

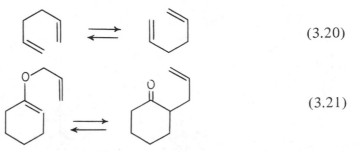

(3.20)

(3.21)

Problem 3.6   Deduce if the following reactions are of order [1,*j*] or [*i,j*]; evaluate the integers *i* and *j*.

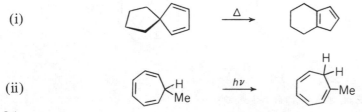

(i)

(ii)

84

(iii)

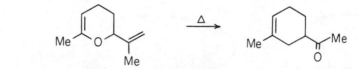

Sigmatropic rearrangements involve the mutual interaction of two components, and since these components individually can be acted upon in a
suprafacial or antarafacial manner, there are but four topologically distinct
modes of migration, as indicated in Fig. 3.12.

Clearly, the intramolecular migration of Z from C1 to Cj must, at the transition state, involve some form of orbital interaction between Z and the
termini of the π-framework system. Sensibly the framework system utilizes
its π-orbitals for this purpose, whereas Z can utilize a π-type or a σ-type
orbital. If Z is a hydrogen atom the only available orbital of sufficiently low
energy is the 1s level (i.e. σ-type orbital), upon which an antarafacial interaction has no physical significance because of its spherical symmetry. For an
H atom migration, therefore, the cases of Fig. 3.12(c) and (d) are identical
respectively with the modes (a) and (b).

A natural consequence of an antarafacial interaction on the Z component
is inversion at the migrating centre, modes (c) and (d). For a carbon atom
this is synonymous with a Walden inversion, and therefore such migration
must, at the transition state, involve the use of a p-type orbital by the carbon
atom concerned. The inversion at the migrating carbon atom can usually
only be detected from the stereochemical nature of the product if the
migrating centre is chiral. Since divalent or trivalent atoms usually can not
support chirality, it is impossible to detect antarafacial interactions in oxygen
or nitrogen atom migrations.

In [1,j] sigmatropic changes the migrating component Z utilizes its own
π-system for the necessary orbital interaction with the framework π-orbitals.
If antarafacial interactions occur they can be detected, as before, by the
transference of chirality from the appropriate centre(s) in the reactant to the
expected centre(s) in the product.

The four possible topological interactions (Fig. 3.12) are not, of course,
equally feasible for any particular sigmatropic reaction since the geometrical
requirements of the system must also be considered. Thus, if the framework
π-system is constrained in a ring then an antarafacial interaction on that
component is usually not possible in the case of [1,j] shifts. Reaction (3.7)

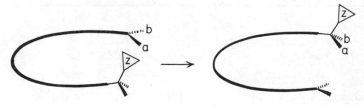

(a) *supra – supra*

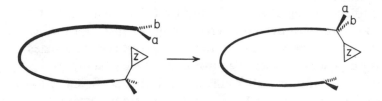

(b) *supra – antara*

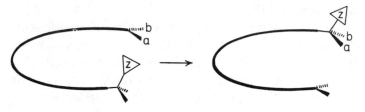

(c) *antara – supra*

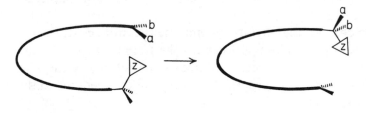

(d) *antara – antara*

FIGURE 3.12

The four possible topological interactions in a $[1,j]$ sigmatropic migration. (The first term represents the interaction on the Z component, the second term the interaction on the π-system) is in this category; the migration of R from one face of the cyclopentadienyl ring to the other face, with concomitant bonding between R and C1 and C5 at all times during the shift, is not possible without a gross distortion of the cyclic π-system. Cases (b) and (d) of Fig. 3.12 are therefore ruled out for reactions of the type (3.7). Indeed, if R is an H atom reaction (3.7) can only proceed by the *supra-supra* pathway (Fig. 3.12(a)). This reaction is observed to be completely stereospecific and occurs under thermal control.

Antarafacial interactions on non-cyclic j components in $[1,j]$ migrations are likewise not possible if j is a small number. Thus, in the case of a $[1,3]$ shift the modes (a) and (c), Fig. 3.12, are physically possible whereas modes (b) and (d) are not. When the value of j is increased the possibility of an antarafacial interaction on the framework π-system is greatly enhanced. The migration shown in Fig. 3.12(b) is feasible for a $[1,7]$ shift if the carbon chain can adopt a gentle spiral conformation so as to facilitate the transfer of Z from the top face at C1 to the bottom face at Cj. These restrictions are less severe for $[i,j]$ shifts, and the interactions (b) – (d) are possible in suitable systems even for relatively small values for i and j.

The orbital interactions for a few sigmatropic changes, one for each of the four possible topological modes are shown in Fig. 3.13.

The seemingly improbable *antara-antara* interaction has been proposed for a Cope rearrangement (Equation 3.22). The geometrical restraints inherent in the fused bicyclic system operate to bring the interacting centres into the correct transition state configuration (cf. Fig. 3.13(d)). This interpretation has, however, been challenged (see p. 194).

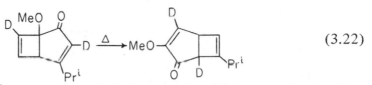

$$(3.22)$$

A sigmatropic change can be regarded as a cyclo-addition reaction in which the σ-bond is added across the termini of the π-system, (Equation 3.23). Thus

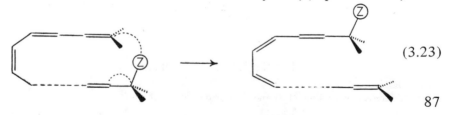

$$(3.23)$$

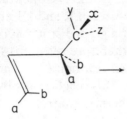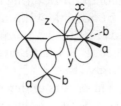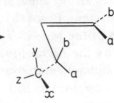

(a) [1,3] *antara–supra*

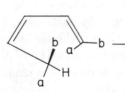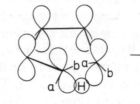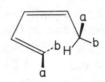

(b) [1,5] *supra–supra*

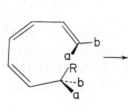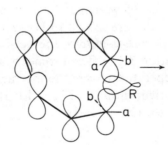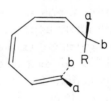

(c) [1,7] *supra–antara*

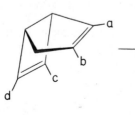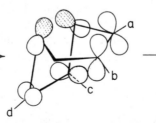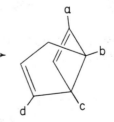

(d) [3,3] *antara–antara*

FIGURE 3.13
Orbital interactions in some [1, *j*] and [*i, j*] sigmatropic shifts

a [1,3] shift is a $[_\sigma 2 + _\pi 2]$ process, a [1,5] shift is a $[_\sigma 2 + _\pi 4]$ process, and a [3,3] sigmatropic change may be classified as a $[_\sigma 2 + _\pi 2 + _\pi 2]$ cyclo-addition reaction.

Let us focus attention, for the sake of brevity, on shifts of order [1,j]. Fig. 3.12 showed the four stereochemical possibilities for the [1,j] migration of a group Z. Closer inspection reveals one additional feature of interest, namely that the products of paths (a) and (b) are enantiomeric, as are the products from (c) and (d). These relationships can be represented as follows:

supra-supra	supra-antara
antara-antara	antara-supra

Since a *supra* interaction on Z results in retention at that centre, and an *antara* interaction leads to inversion, the relationship becomes:

supra (retention)	supra (inversion)
antara (inversion)	antara (retention)

The left-hand column contains the modes in which there is an *even* number of inversions on framework system plus Z (i.e. 0 or 2), whereas the right hand column contains the modes in which the number of inversions is *odd* (i.e. 1). We have seen previously that $[_\sigma 2_s + _\pi 2_s]$ and $[_\sigma 2_a + _\pi 2_a]$ interactions are of the first type, whereas the odd inversions relate to the $[_\sigma 2_s + _\pi 2_a]$ and $[_\sigma 2_a + _\pi 2_s]$ modes. The following inter-relationship therefore holds:

$$[_\sigma 2_s + _\pi 2_s] \left\{ \begin{array}{l} supra\ (retention) \\ \text{or} \\ [_\sigma 2_a + _\pi 2_a] \end{array} \right. antara\ (inversion) \quad \Big| \quad supra\ (inversion) \quad antara\ (retention) \left. \begin{array}{l} \\ \\ \end{array} \right\} \begin{array}{l} [_\sigma 2_s + _\pi 2_a] \\ \\ [_\sigma 2_a + _\pi 2_s] \end{array}$$

Hence, in a [1,j] shift there are four pairs of possible orbital-orbital types of overlap. The situation for the [1,3] process is shown in Fig. 3.14, and it can be seen that the members of each pair, which lead to the same end result, are physically indistinguishable.

89

supra (retention at Z)

antara (inversion at Z)

antara (retention at Z)

supra (inversion at Z)

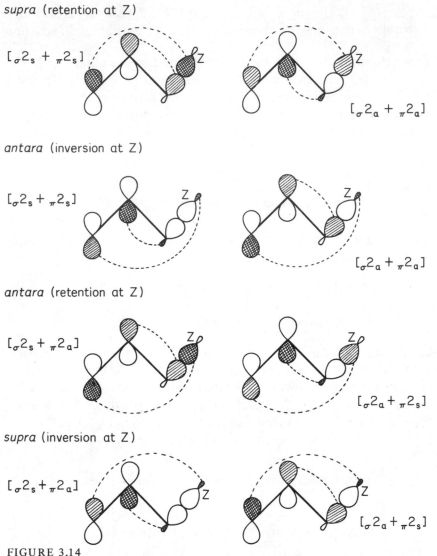

FIGURE 3.14
Topology of the orbital interactions in [1,3] sigmatropic shifts

It is seen that the placing of the *supra-supra* and *antara-antara* interaction modes into one class, and the *supra-antara* and *antara-supra* interactions into a separate class, has general validity. That is, the classification applies not

90

only to electrocyclic and sigmatropic processes, for which proofs have been provided, but also to all other forms of pericyclic reaction. The classification is not trivial; we shall see in Chapter 4 that there is an underlying fundamental importance to these conclusions. For example, all $[2_s + 2_s]$ and $[2_a + 2_a]$ processes require the photochemical excitation of one of the components. In $[2_s + 2_a]$ and $[2_a + 2_s]$ reactions the successful outcome depends on thermal activation. This result, and others that can be similarly derived, is incontrovertible, but there is much controversy surrounding the actual theoretical explanations.

Problem 3.7 (a) Classify the sigmatropic reactions in Problem 3.6 using the $[_\sigma m_s + _\pi p_s \ldots]$ type of notation. (b) Suggest mechanisms for the following reactions:

(i)

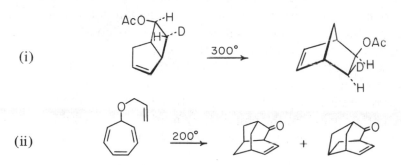

(ii)

3.3.4 Cheletropic reactions

Cheletropic reactions are defined as processes in which two σ-bonds that terminate at a single atom are made (or broken) in a concerted fashion, reaction (3.24); (Woodward and Hoffmann, 1969).

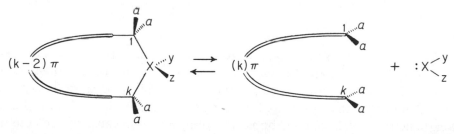

$$(3.24)$$

The major stereochemical features of this process that require discussion are:

(i) The nature of the concerted rotations that must occur about C1 and Ck in order to bring the substituents a into the 'plane' of the polyene molecule as it is formed.

(ii) The relative geometrical dispositions of the polyene and Xyz when the bond-breaking process is complete (forward reaction) or bond-making commences (reverse reaction).

(iii) The nature of the orbitals utilized by Xyz.

In the case of (i) we can predict, because of our previous findings, that the only distinguishable rotation modes are conrotation and disrotation. Each mode has two formal possibilities, and hence there is a maximum of four possible polyenic products when the substituents a are all different. In reaction (3.25), for example, it is clear that the extrusion of sulphur dioxide is accompanied by the outward disrotatory motion of the methyl groups so as to form *trans,trans*-hexa-2,4-diene. The alternative disrotatory process, in which the methyl groups rotate inward, is of higher energy and would have resulted in the *cis,cis*-product. Conversely, the conrotatory motions each would have yielded *cis,trans*-hexa-2,4-diene; reaction (3.25) is therefore highly stereospecific.

$$\text{Me} \begin{array}{c} \text{Me} \\ \overset{\Delta}{\longrightarrow} \end{array} \quad \text{Me} \diagup\!\!\diagup\!\!\diagdown\!\!\diagdown \text{Me} \; + \; SO_2 \qquad (3.25)$$

In case (iii) let us assume that Xyz (e.g. SO_2 in reaction (3.25)) is formed in the singlet ground state; the two electrons are thus placed in a *single* atomic or molecular orbital. Triplet species are excluded simply because their reactions are unlikely to be stereospecific. Consider, for example, the addition of a triplet carbene to an olefinic C=C bond, reaction (3.26). Because of the conservation of spin multiplicity an intermediate (triplet state) diradical is formed.

92

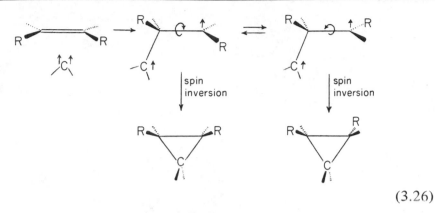

$$(3.26)$$

The diradical has an appreciable lifetime and rotation about the single bonds competes successfully with electron spin inversion. The stereochemical integrity of the original olefin is therefore lost in the formation of the products.

Typical examples of the Xyz molecules that participate in, or are formed by, cheletropic reactions are singlet carbenes, carbon monoxide, nitrogen, and sulphur dioxide. In each case these species can be formally considered to utilize a filled sp^n orbital and an empty p-orbital for bonding purposes on reaction with the polyene molecule; two orbitals are necessary in order to form two bonds to the X atom. Nitrogen is expelled irreversibly in cheletropic processes, but nevertheless the analysis of the hypothetical addition reaction can be used (principle of microscopic reversibility) to gain insight into the stereochemistry of the cheletropic fragmentation. In fact, reaction (3.24) is more readily analysed if viewed from the converse direction. Let us focus attention, for simplicity, on an Xyz species with the structure indicated in Fig. 3.15(a); all of the conclusions reached using this model system will be applicable to the reactions of the actual species mentioned above.

Consider first of all the interactions on the terminal p-atomic orbitals of the polyenyl π-system. These orbitals can be overlapped in the suprafacial (i.e. disrotatory) or antarafacial (i.e. conrotatory) senses. It is clear from Fig. 3.15(b) that the attacking Xyz species will enjoy the maximum degree of orbital penetration of the relevant (shaded) terminal p-π orbitals if it approaches in the direction perpendicular to the polyene plane in the disrotatory mode, or in the polyene plane in the conrotatory mode.

93

(a)

Disrotatory   Conrotatory

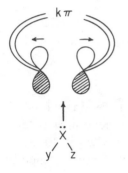

(b)

FIGURE 3.15

(a) Structure of the Xyz component; (b) preferred directions of approach of Xyz to facilitate overlap with the terminal π-lobes of the polyene

There are two possible modes of interaction on the Xyz component. It can utilize its filled sp^2-orbital for σ-type overlap and its empty p-orbital for π-type overlap with the polyenyl π-orbitals, or the role of each of the Xyz atomic orbitals can be reversed. Thus, the sp^2 level can overlap in the π-manner, and the p-atomic orbital in the σ-manner. This possibility, however, will lead to much less effective orbital overlap between the two systems. The various interactions are shown in Fig. 3.16, in which the σ-type overlap is indicated by the parallel solid lines connecting orbitals ($\equiv$) and the π-type overlap by the single broken lines (- - -).

The cheletropic interaction between polyene and Xyz is in fact a sort of double cyclo-addition process because the polyene π-orbitals overlap two orthogonal orbitals on the Xyz species. Each of these interactions should be analysed separately. If we are to use the previous $[_\pi m_s + _\pi p_a]$ type of notation we need now to define a new term to take account of interactions on a single atomic orbital. Woodward and Hoffmann (1969) have reserved the

94

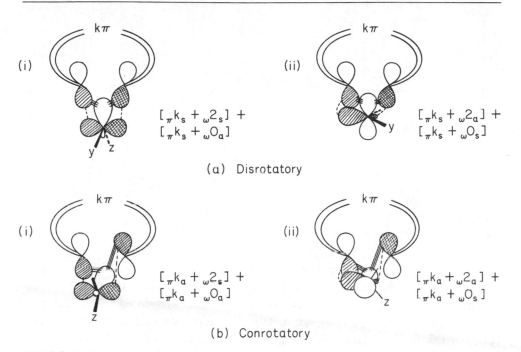

(i)

$k\pi$

$[_\pi k_s + _\omega 2_s] +$
$[_\pi k_s + _\omega 0_a]$

(ii)

$k\pi$

$[_\pi k_s + _\omega 2_a] +$
$[_\pi k_s + _\omega 0_s]$

y   z

y

(a) Disrotatory

(i)

$k\pi$

$[_\pi k_a + _\omega 2_s] +$
$[_\pi k_a + _\omega 0_a]$

(ii)

$k\pi$

$[_\pi k_a + _\omega 2_a] +$
$[_\pi k_a + _\omega 0_s]$

z

z

(b) Conrotatory

FIGURE 3.16
Main interaction modes between the electron deficient Xyz species and the polyene in cheletropic processes

Greek letter ω for this purpose. Such ω orbitals can interact in a suprafacial or antarafacial sense, as shown in Fig. 3.17. Thus a suprafacial interaction on the occupied sp^2-orbital of Xyz is designated $_\omega 2_s$ (where 2 indicates the presence of two electrons), whereas an antarafacial interaction on the unoccupied p-orbital is denoted by $_\omega 0_a$. On this basis the electrocyclic conversion of the cyclopropyl cation into the allyl cation (Equation 3.19) is defined as a $[_\sigma 2_s + _\omega 0_s]$ process if it occurs by the disrotatory mode indicated in Fig. 3.9.

The various types of orbital overlap shown in Fig. 3.16 can be readily classified in this extended nomenclature, as indicated. Thus, in Fig. 3.16(a)(i) the two interactions $[_\pi k_s + _\omega 2_s]$ and $[_\pi k_s + _\omega 0_a]$ are present since the polyene π-system is interacting suprafacially $(_\pi k_s)$ and separately with the sp^2-orbital (suprafacial, and hence $_\omega 2_s$) and p-orbital (antarafacial, and hence $_\omega 0_a$).

95

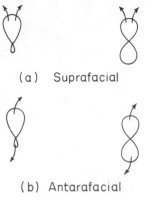

(a)   Suprafacial

(b) Antarafacial

FIGURE 3.17
Interaction topology for ω orbitals

The modes represented in Figs. 3.16(a)(i) and (b)(i) are usually referred to as *linear cheletropic reactions* since the polyene-Xyz system is arranged symmetrically. Figs. 3.16(a)(ii) and (b)(ii) illustrate *non-linear* cheletropic processes, which are of lower symmetry. The sequence of events in these two types of reaction are dramatically apparent when comparison is made between the positions of the various nuclei in the reactants and in the products. A somewhat simplified picture is given in Figs. 3.18(a) and (b) which correspond respectively to the linear cheletropic interaction of Fig. 3.16(b)(i) and the non-linear interaction of Fig. 3.16(b)(ii). In the linear process the Xyz species is expelled along the major axis of the system, whereas in the non-linear fragmentation while X departs along the general axis, the atoms y and z are displaced through 90° as indicated. In both examples the atom X remains at all times within the general molecular plane.

In a similar analysis of the case indicated by Fig. 3.16(a)(i) it can be shown that X is displaced out of the general molecular plane while y and z additionally describe an arc of 90°. However, the Xyz nuclei at all times remain in a plane that bisects the polyene system, so that the change is of the linear cheletropic type. Here the topology of the interactions on the orbitals of Xyz are, of course, identical to the alternative linear pathway in which X remains in the general molecular plane (cf. Fig. 3.18(a)), but the additional translational displacements on y and z does ensure a more efficient bonding contact between polyene and Xyz when the disrotatory mode is in operation.

96

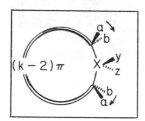 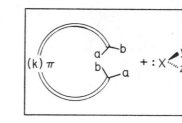

(a)

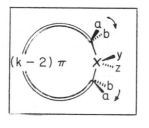 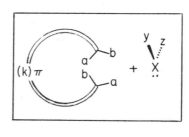

(b)

FIGURE 3.18
Atomic displacements during cheletropic reactions with conrotation; (a) linear, (b) non-linear

It was shown previously that $[2_s + 2_s]$ and $[2_a + 2_a]$ interactions should be classified together (even inversions), whereas $[2_s + 2_a]$ or $[2_a + 2_s]$ interactions form a separate category (odd inversions). The various possible cheletropic processes may be similarly grouped together, Table 3.1, assuming a constant value for k for the whole set of interactions.

TABLE 3.1
Selection rules for cheletropic reactions

(i) even inversions for $[_\pi k + _\omega 2]$	disrotatory-linear
odd inversions for $[_\pi k + _\omega 0]$	conrotatory-non-linear
(ii) odd inversions for $[_\pi k + _\omega 2]$	disrotatory-non-linear
even inversions for $[_\pi k + \omega 0]$	conrotatory-linear

In Chapter 4 it will be seen that whatever mode operates under a particular set of reaction conditions depends not only upon the molecular geometry, but also upon the actual numerical value of k. Thus the molecular geometry may militate against the conrotatory motion, but the value of k then exerts a decisive influence over the choice between linear and non-linear modes. However, it should be pointed out that at the present time no experimental procedure is available which allows distinction to be made between linear and non-linear cheletropic reactions so that, in this area at least, the interpretations are of a purely theoretical nature.

Problem 3.8   The following cheletropic reactions have been investigated. The activation enthalpies ($\Delta H^{\ne}$) of the two processes are equal to within experimental error (*c.* 30·5 kcal mole^{-1}), whereas the activation entropies differ substantially: for (i) $\Delta S^{\ne} = +7 \pm 3$ cal deg^{-1} mole^{-1}, and for (ii) $\Delta S^{\ne} = -18 \pm 5$ cal deg^{-1} mole^{-1}. Give reasons, based on the different topologies of the two reactions, for the differences in the activation parameters (NB. $\Delta G_2^{\ne} - \Delta G_1^{\ne} \simeq 10$ kcal mole^{-1}).

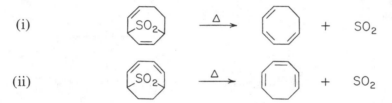

(i)

(ii)

3.3.5   *Other pericyclic reactions*

It seems scarcely necessary to consider the various stereochemical features of other types of pericyclic reaction since the general procedures have been covered exhaustively in this Chapter. In Chapter 4 it will be seen that all pericyclic reactions can be classified within the framework of the π, σ, ω notation, and thereby can be divided into two groups, namely those in which the total inversions are even, and those in which the total inversions are odd. The choice between the two groups is not a free one, but depends upon the actual number of electrons involved in the pericyclic change. This in turn controls whether the process occurs under thermal control (all participants in their electronic ground states) or photochemical control (one participant in the first electronic excited state).

The concept of the conservation of orbital symmetry 4

The basic tenet of the Woodward-Hoffmann theory is that orbital symmetry is conserved in concerted pericyclic reactions. Their initial papers (1965) utilized a frontier orbital argument. These ideas were developed by Longuet-Higgins and Abrahamson (1965) who used the somewhat more rigorous group theoretical approach, and both of these types of analysis were extended by Woodward and Hoffmann (1965, 1969) to cover the whole range of pericyclic reactions. Their results on the conservation of orbital symmetry were embodied in a single statement – the general Woodward-Hoffmann rule.

One central point should emerge from the later sections in this chapter and from Chapters 5 and 6, and that is the complete agreement between the general Woodward-Hoffmann rule and the whole body of the experimental results. The rule pre-dates much of the experimental data obtained on pericyclic reactions so that it does have important predictive value. The essential correctness of the rule is therefore not in question, but its theoretical basis has been the subject of much controversy. The main theoretical explanations that have been advanced are discussed in this chapter and in Chapter 5.

The general Woodward-Hoffmann rule and its application to organic pericyclic reactions will be discussed first in this chapter, but only briefly because a much wider account is to be found in Chapter 6. Of the various theoretical approaches, the frontier orbital method will be considered first because of its conceptual simplicity, and this will be followed by the more formal orbital symmetry arguments. Chapter 5 contains the theories based on the assumption that the transition states of pericyclic reactions enjoy aromatic stabilization. This general arrangement of the theoretical material has been adopted because it allows for ideas to be developed in logical sequence and with the simpler concepts considered first. It also happens to roughly reflect the chronological order in which the various theoretical developments took place.

4.1 The general Woodward-Hoffmann rule for pericyclic reactions

A ground state pericyclic change is symmetry-allowed when the total number of $(4q + 2)_s$ and $(4r)_a$ components is odd; the converse applies to photo-pericyclic reactions.†

The terms $(4q + 2)$ and $(4r)$ refer to the numbers of interacting electrons of the reaction components, and q and r may individually assume values in the series 0, 1, 2, 3 . . . Hence the $(4q + 2)$ term refers to those components containing 2, 6, 10, . . . electrons, and the $4r$ term to those containing 0, 4, 8, 12 . . . electrons. The subscripts s and a refer to suprafacial and antarafacial interactions respectively.

The conrotatory ring-opening of cyclobutenes, which we have previously classified as $[_\pi 2_s + _\sigma 2_a]$ or $[_\pi 2_a + _\sigma 2_s]$ processes, are at once seen to be allowed reactions. Both components contain 2 electrons and are therefore $(4q + 2)$ components. We are only concerned with the $(4q + 2)$ components acting in a suprafacial manner, and hence the $_\sigma 2_a$ and $_\pi 2_a$ terms are ignored. In each case this leaves one, an odd number, of $(4q + 2)_s$ terms; the reaction is therefore allowed under thermal control. In contrast, electrocyclic reactions involving $[_\pi 2_s + _\sigma 2_s]$ or $[_\pi 2_a + _\sigma 2_a]$ interactions, which typify the disrotatory cleavage of cyclobutenes, contain an even number of $(4q + 2)_s$ terms (i.e. 2 or 0). The reactions are forbidden under thermal control but since the rule is reversed in the case of first excited-state processes, these modes may occur under photochemical activation of the cyclobutene.

We saw earlier that the $[_\pi 2_s + _\pi 2_s + _\pi 2_s]$ cyclo-addition reaction has been observed to occur under thermal control (see Fig. 3.7). The number of $(4q + 2)_s$ components is odd (i.e. three), so that the above general rule agrees with this result.

Reaction (4.1), an example of a [1,7] sigmatropic hydrogen shift, must for steric reasons involve a $[_\pi 6_s + _\sigma 2_s]$ interaction (see p. 85). The terms are both of the $(4q + 2)_s$ type, and the rule therefore predicts that only the excited-state process is energetically favourable. In fact no thermochemical

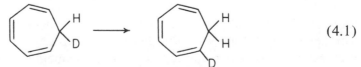

(4.1)

† In view of more recent developments, the expression 'symmetry-allowed' is perhaps unfortunate and 'energetically preferred' seems more appropriate.

suprafacial [1,7] hydrogen shifts have come to light, although many such (allowed) photochemical reactions are known. Instead, the thermolysis of cycloheptatrienes results (among other processes) in [1,5] sigmatropic migrations of the $[_\pi 4_s + _\sigma 2_s]$ type; such migrations are in agreement with the general Woodward-Hoffmann rule.

As a final example and guide to the use of the general rule, consider the sequence of reactions (4.2) discovered by Kraft and Koltzenburg (1967). The first step, the photochemical addition of butadiene to benzene, gives an adduct

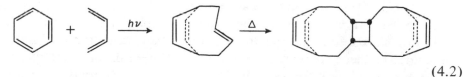

$$(4.2)$$

that must have resulted from a $[_\pi 4_s + _\pi 4_s]$ reaction. The second stage, which is essentially a [2 + 2] cyclo-addition across the termini of the reactive *trans*-ethylenic double bonds, occurs spontaneously. The stereochemistry of the final product leaves no doubt that a $[_\pi 2_s + _\pi 2_a]$ reaction is involved. Both reaction stages are allowed by the general rule; in the first case we have an odd number of $(4r)_a$ components, and in the second reaction there is an odd $(4q + 2)_s$ term.

4.2   The frontier orbital approach

Most chemists are weaned on the idea of valency electrons when first intro-duced to the chemical reactions of simple species like, C, N, O, Na or Cl. These electrons, of course, occupy the highest filled electronic level(s) in such species and, when chemical reaction occurs, these electrons are transferred into the molecular bonding and non-bonding levels. In discussing the chemical reactivity of molecules it is again the properties of the most energetic elec-trons that are considered. Thus, for example, the interpretation of the reactions of ammonia and of amines usually contains reference to the 'non-bonding' electron pairs; these may be referred to as the frontier electrons since they suffer the greatest perturbation on interaction with the empty acceptor orbitals of the attacking reagent. The frontier electrons of an unsaturated delocalized system, such as butadiene, reside in the highest occupied π-molecular orbital (i.e. ψ_2), the so-called frontier orbital or HOMO (highest occupied molecular

101

orbital). In the case of photochemically excited butadiene the frontier orbital or HOMO is ψ_3, since this now contains the most energetic electron. In ground-state butadiene the ψ_3 orbital is unoccupied, and is referred to as the lowest unoccupied molecular orbital (i.e. LUMO). The HOMO levels have electron donor properties, whilst the LUMO levels can accept electrons. The basis of the frontier orbital analysis of concerted pericyclic reactions is the assumption that these processes take place at the position and in the direction of maximum overlap between the HOMO and LUMO of the reacting species (Fukui, 1971). If the reacting species possesses a singly occupied molecular orbital (SOMO), it is assumed to play the part of the HOMO or of the LUMO, or of both, since it has some electron donor and some electron acceptor character. The theory developed by Fukui is different in some details to the approach adopted by Woodward and Hoffmann (1965) in their original paper on electrocyclic processes, in that it emphasizes the importance of the LUMO-HOMO interaction.

Consider the thermochemical electrocyclic conversion of cyclobutene into butadiene (Fig. 4.1). The relevant interactions are between the π-HOMO and σ-LUMO or the π-LUMO and σ-HOMO levels. It can be seen that the in-phase overlap between the members of each pair (Fig. 4.1, shaded orbital lobes) leads directly to expected conrotatory mode for the ring opening. This representation also nicely illustrates the process to be of the $[_\sigma 2_s + _\pi 2_a]$ or

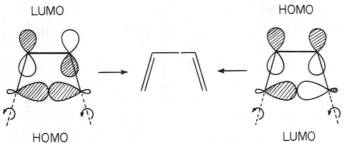

LUMO   HOMO

HOMO   LUMO

FIGURE 4.1

The preferred (conrotatory) mode of the HOMO-LUMO interaction in the thermochemical ring opening of cyclobutene

$[_\sigma 2_a + _\pi 2_s]$ type (cf. Fig. 3.10(b)). An equivalent representation is the replacement of the shaded and unshaded orbital lobes with one containing + and − signs to represent the signs of the wave functions. The shading notation will

102

generally be used when it is desired to give a clearer idea of the topology of the orbital interactions.

In the photochemical cyclobutene-butadiene inter-conversion the excitation energy is used for the $\pi \rightarrow \pi^*$ transition. Both π and π^* are SOMO levels, denoted respectively by $(SOMO)_1$ and $(SOMO)_2$. The relevant interactions are then between $(SOMO)_1$ and the σ-HOMO level, and between $(SOMO)_2$ and the σ-LUMO level, as indicated in Fig. 4.2. The $(SOMO)_2$ and σ-HOMO, or the

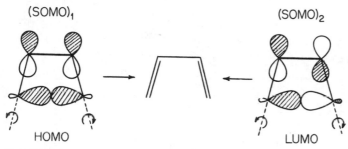

FIGURE 4.2
The preferred (disrotatory) mode of SOMO-HOMO and SOMO-LUMO interactions in the photochemical ring opening of cyclobutene

$(SOMO)_1$ and σ-LUMO interactions are ignored because of the widely disparate energies of these pairs of orbitals as compared with those discussed above; more effective interactions occur between orbitals of similar energy.

The frontier orbital method is capable of extension to include for all pericyclic reactions. The analysis of a few representative 'allowed' pericyclic processes is given in Fig. 4.3. Note that the transition state of the [3,3] sigmatropic rearrangement is likened to the intimate interaction of two allyl radicals; the strongest bonding interactions will be between the non-bonding (SOMO) levels of these species. In many cases there are alternative HOMO-LUMO interactions, but these have not been illustrated in the figure.

Problem 4.1   Show for the reactions given in Fig. 4.3 that the frontier orbital method leads to the same predictions as the general Woodward-Hoffmann rule.

The frontier orbital method has also been used to explain the unusual specificity in certain Diels-Alder $[_\pi 4_s + _\pi 2_s]$ reactions; where distinction can be made only one of the two possible *supra-supra* modes of addition occurs

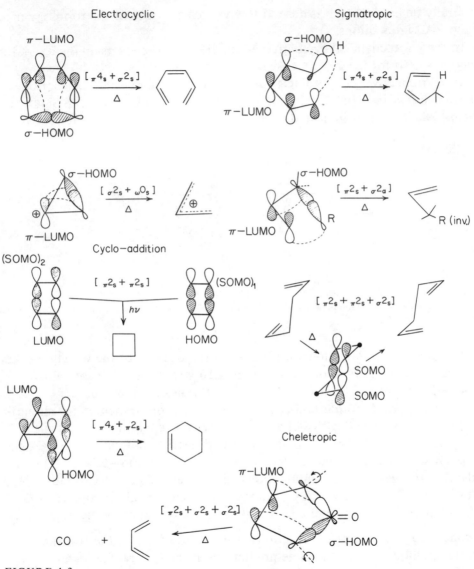

FIGURE 4.3
Frontier orbital analysis of some allowed pericyclic reactions

under the usual experimental conditions. The dimerization of cyclopentadiene, which yields the *endo*-adduct rather than the *exo*-adduct, Equation (4.3)

104

furnishes the best known example of this type of behaviour. The *exo*-compounds are often thermodynamically more stable than their *endo*-counterparts and in some cases are apparently formed exclusively. However, careful analysis of these reactions has shown that the *endo*-compounds are

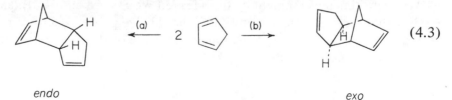

(4.3)

endo   *exo*

the kinetically controlled products (i.e. formed in the reaction with the lower activation energy) but dissociation and recombination, particularly at higher temperatures, eventually leads to a build-up of the more stable isomer (thermodynamic control). One of the HOMO-LUMO interactions for the *endo*-contact (Woodward and Hoffmann, 1965) is shown in Fig. 4.4 in comparison with one of the interactions for the *exo*-addition. In the endo-addition there

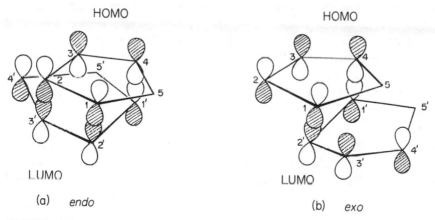

FIGURE 4.4
One of the HOMO-LUMO interactions for (a) the *endo*-addition, and (b) the *exo*-addition of two molecules of cyclopentadiene

is an extra attractive interaction between diene and dienophile which is necessarily absent in the *exo*-mode because the relevant atomic centres (respectively C2 and C3') are then too far apart. Although this attractive

105

interaction is only a second order perturbation, as it does not lead to bond formation between C2 of the diene and C3' of the dienophile, it nevertheless is thought to be sufficient to lower the activation energy for the *endo* approach.

An interesting development of this idea led Woodward and Hoffmann to predict that $[_\pi 6_s + _\pi 4_s]$ cyclo-additions should give predominantly the *exo*-adduct. This arises because of the repulsive nature of the secondary interactions for the *endo*-transition state. Subsequent experimental work confirmed this prediction.

Problem 4.2 For the $[_\pi 6_s + _\pi 4_s]$ cyclo-addition between hexatriene and butadiene show:

    (i) that the reaction is allowed under thermal activation by the general Woodward-Hoffmann rule;

    (ii) that the secondary orbital interactions are repulsive (i.e. destabilizing) for the *endo*-transition state geometry.

These secondary interactions should be considered at C2 and C5 of the triene (not C3 and C4 because of the poor orbital overlap between these sites and C2 and C3 of the diene).

The frontier orbital treatment of charged even-electron systems is also relatively straightforward, and odd-electron neutral systems (i.e. radicals) can be analysed without difficulty as well. In the case of radicals the important level for the component containing the odd electron will be the SOMO, whereas for the neutral even-electron component one must consider both the HOMO and LUMO levels. Since the SOMO-HOMO and SOMO-LUMO interactions between the two components must necessarily lead to opposite predictions for the stereochemical behaviour of the system, one may reasonably conclude that the pericyclic reactions of radicals will not be stereospecific. However, this assumes that the SOMO-HOMO and SOMO-LUMO interactions to be equally important, whereas one of the interactions may predominate depending upon the relative energy of the SOMO level. Hence in some situations there might be a slight preference for one of the two possible interaction modes, and stereoselectivity could then result. A similar conclusion is available from the appropriate state correlation diagrams (Longuet-Higgins and Abrahamson, 1965; see Section 4.3). Unfortunately the available experimental data does not bear upon this point (see also Table 5.1).

From the foregoing discussion it appears that the frontier orbital method is at once a simple, concise, and accurate method for assessing the stereochemical outcome of pericyclic reactions. Furthermore, it is a method that is equally applicable to symmetrical and to unsymmetrical systems. There are some disadvantages in the theory, however. Firstly, it is necessary to derive the general phase characteristics of the HOMO and LUMO levels. Hückel molecular calculations can be used for this purpose, but there are available a number of approximate methods, for example the electron-in-a-box model, which are usually satisfactory even if they are more difficult to apply to more complex systems. Nevertheless, frontier orbital analysis is quicker and more simple than the formalized correlation diagram approach, and with a little practice one can intuitively arrive at the correct relative phase relationships in the HOMO and LUMO levels.

The second objection to the method is more serious. A basic assumption in the theory is that the electron density at the various positions in the frontier orbital are related to the reactivity at those positions. Although this assumption is valid, albeit fortuitously so, for the above types of alternant hydrocarbons, it fails completely in the case of non-alternant hydrocarbons (see p. 24) and for some hetero-atomic systems (Dewar, 1969, 1971). Consider, for example, the [1,5] sigmatropic shift of Z in reaction (4.4). The transition state for the

$$\text{(4.4)}$$

reaction was assumed by Woodward and Hoffmann (1965) to resemble the intimate interaction of a cyclopentadienyl radical and $Z\cdot$. The SOMO level for the odd non-alternant π-radical is in fact doubly degenerate (see p. 31), and the members of this pair inevitably differ in their symmetry properties. Thus opposite predictions follow from the separate interaction of these molecular orbitals with the SOMO of $Z\cdot$. From experiment, however, it is known that reaction (4.4) occurs under thermal control by the $[_\pi 4_s + _\sigma 2_s]$ pathway. The topology of the migration is therefore identical to the analogous sigmatropic shift of Z in the acyclic pentadienyl system, reaction (4.5), and the acyclic model can often be used to assess sigmatropic rearrangements in cyclic systems provided that the limitations in the method are realized.

Fukui's representation of $[1,j]$ shifts is somewhat different, and the relevant interactions are between σ-HOMO and π-LUMO (Fig. 4.3). It is immaterial whether the π-system is connected at only one or both of its termini of the

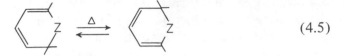

$$(4.5)$$

σ-HOMO system. Therefore, the picture of the $[1,5]$ hydrogen shift shown in Fig. 4.3 could equally well be applied to the analogous rearrangement in cyclopentadiene, so that there is apparently no conflict between the acyclic and cyclic models. This representation, however, only circumvents the immediate problem and does not bear up to close scrutiny. The difficulty is that at the transition state of the above $[1,5]$ shift when the fully delocalized π-system has been set up, the molecular orbital is not one that is a recognizable solution for a six-atom cyclic interaction. In other pericyclic processes, frontier orbital analysis reveals a type of orbital interaction that can lead directly to a recognizable molecular orbital in the product molecule. For example, in the $[_\pi4_s + _\sigma2_s]$ electrocyclic reaction this orbital is ψ_3 of the hexatriene molecule.

Both the Woodward-Hoffmann and Fukui frontier orbital analyses lead to the same results as the general Woodward-Hoffmann rule, and both therefore correctly predict the topology of pericyclic processes. Although there are serious objections to this approach, nevertheless it is a very useful mnemonic device for illustrating the stereochemistry of the orbital interactions that occur in pericyclic changes as predicted by the general Woodward-Hoffmann rule.

One additional feature that distinguishes the frontier orbital method from orbital symmetry analysis is its ability to separately analyse triplet state processes (Fukui, 1971) in photochemical reactions. However, it is notably difficult in excited state reactions, even if they are stereospecific, to be sure of concertedness. Certain stereospecific photochemical cyclo-addition reactions, hitherto thought to be concerted, have recently been re-interpreted as radical cage recombination reactions. The triplet states of many unsaturated molecules† are lower in energy than the corresponding singlet states because

---

† Notably aromatics and carbonyl compounds; the triplet states of simple olefins are much more elusive because of the occurrence of cross-over points between singlet and triplet manifolds. Olefinic triplet states nevertheless are substantially less energetic than the excited singlets.

of differences in electron correlation. In triplet reactions the species may be much longer-lived than their singlet counterparts as the rate of crossing to the ground state is lower because of the required spin-orbit coupling. Hence triplets are usually less selective and are more susceptible to bi-radical pathways than are the analogous reactions involving singlets; triplet reactions are not considered further in this volume.

4.3   Orbital symmetry and correlation diagrams

The arguments used by Woodward and Hoffmann (1969) are based on the symmetry properties of orbitals. Initially they employed the frontier orbital approach, as outlined above, but subsequently developed Longuet-Higgins and Abrahamson's method (1965) which utilized a group theoretical analysis. It is not in our interests, and neither is it necessary, to apply Group Theory in its full rigour; in particular we shall use the simplified system of nomenclature developed previously (see p. 14).

The principle of orbital symmetry conservation is readily explained by means of orbital correlation diagrams. The basic idea is that if a molecule that is undergoing a pericyclic change has one or more elements of symmetry, then the molecular wave function will have corresponding symmetry. Moreover if the reactant, the transition state, and the products in the reaction have these symmetry elements in common, the molecular wave function will maintain its symmetry throughout the course of the reaction. Likewise, the wave functions of the individual molecular orbitals must also display consistent behaviour with respect to the symmetry element(s). Hence, an orbital wave function that is symmetric with respect to the element in the reactants must change continuously so that it is also symmetric with respect to the same element in the transition state and in the products, although the positions of the nuclei are altered along the reaction pathway. By this means it is possible to correlate individual molecular orbitals of the reactants with those of the products.

The general rules for the construction of correlation diagrams have been mentioned previously (see p. 10). There are six important points to bear in mind in this context.

  (i) The relative positions of the atomic centres in the reactants, in the transition state, and in the products must be defined.

(ii) The appropriate symmetry elements (there may be more than one) are delineated. These elements must bisect bonds formed or broken in the chemical change, and must be present throughout the course of the reaction if they are to be of practicable value. If no such element exists it is not possible to construct a meaningful correlation diagram.

(iii) The relevant molecular orbitals in the reactants and an equal number in the products are then deduced. The chosen orbitals are those which are most profoundly affected by the process of reaction, and are inevitably linked to those atomic centres where a change in hybridization occurs, or where the bonding affiliations to neighbouring atoms is altered. The σ-framework molecular orbitals are usually ignored in this first-order treatment although bond-elongations or bond-contractions, which affect the energies of these levels, inevitably occur during the reaction. These energy changes are assumed to be smaller than those consequent upon the main bond reorganization process.

(iv) The chosen molecular orbitals are classified as symmetric (S) or antisymmetric (A) with respect to the defined symmetry element(s). If there are two important symmetry elements then the classification must refer to both and must always be in the same sequence – first to element 1 and then to element 2. It is important to realize that the *composite* symmetry label, say SA, which arises when two elements are employed, is not the same if the letters are reversed; $SA \neq AS$. If an orbital is neither symmetric nor antisymmetric relative to the element, then the fully delocalized orbital must be invoked (see p. 15).

(v) The number of levels of a particular symmetry in the reactants must equal precisely the levels of the same symmetry in the products. If this condition does not apply the chosen symmetry element is of no practical value.

(vi) Levels of the same symmetry are correlated taking care not to violate the non-crossing rule (see p. 11). This inevitably means that the lowest energy reactant level of S symmetry will correlate with the lowest energy product level of S symmetry. The lowest levels of A symmetry correlate, and so on. The presence of such correlations are best shown graphically.

110

4.4   Symmetry control of pericyclic reactions

Let us now consider an actual pericyclic change, and put the above rules and conditions into practice. We shall concentrate on electrocyclic reactions and cyclo-additions, although the ideas are readily extended to include for all types of pericyclic change. The electrocyclic conversion of cyclobutene into buta-1,3-diene is a convenient starting point, reaction (4.6).

$$\text{(4.6)}$$

We will assume that the carbon framework of both molecules is planar, and furthermore that planarity is maintained in the transition state. The butadiene is considered to be formed in the s-cis-conformation.

There are three main symmetry elements:

(i)   a twofold axis which bisects the cyclobutene bonds 1-2 and 3-4 and the butadiene 2-3 bond, here designated as a C_{2y} axis (see Fig. 4.5(a)).

(ii) A mirror plane of symmetry orthogonal to the molecular planes, which we shall call a σ_{yz} plane (see Fig. 4.5(b)).

(iii) A mirror plane which coincides with the molecular planes (σ_{xy}).

The element σ_{xy} is rejected because, among other reasons, it does not bisect bonds formed or broken. It is readily seen that if the electrocyclic change (Equation 4.6) occurs by conrotation the C_{2y} axis is present at all times; in the case of disrotation the symmetry element is the σ_{yz} plane. These features are shown in Fig. 4.5.

The C3–C4 σ-bond of the cyclobutene is cleaved and the C1–C2 π-bond is rearranged in the electrocyclic change. The associated molecular orbitals and their antibonding counterparts (i.e. σ, σ^*, π, and π^*) suffer large changes in their energy, and must therefore be considered. The process results in the formation of the π-orbitals in the product molecule. Because of condition (iv), above, these must be regarded as the fully delocalized π-molecular orbitals ($\psi_1 - \psi_4$; see p. 28). The various molecular orbitals are shown in Fig. 4.5 along with their symmetry properties relative to the elements C_{2y} and to σ_{yz}. It is immediately noted that for the element C_{2y} we have the correct pairing of S and A levels in reactant and product. The same holds true for the mirror plane σ_{yz} so that the correct correlation diagrams can be completed as shown.

111

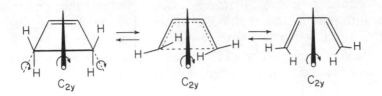

(a) Conrotation

Level / Symmetry   Symmetry / Level

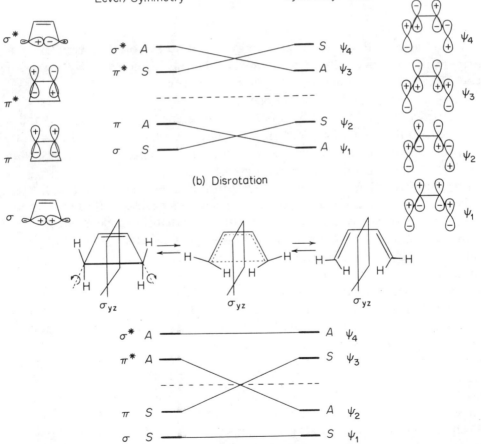

(b) Disrotation

FIGURE 4.5
Symmetry elements and orbital correlation diagrams for the cyclobutene-butadiene interconversion

If reaction (4.6) is conducted under thermal control the electrons will, of course, only populate the bonding levels of both reactant and product molecules. Since we have limited our consideration to the fate of but four electrons, then the electronic configuration of the cyclobutene may be written as $\sigma^2\pi^2$. The superscripts refer to the number of electrons in each orbital. The corresponding ground-state configuration for butadiene is $\psi_1^2\psi_2^2$.

Inspection of Fig. 4.5 reveals that the complete correlation $\sigma^2\pi^2 \rightarrow \psi_1^2\psi_2^2$ occurs only in the conrotatory mode. The conrotatory process is said to be 'symmetry allowed' under thermal control. This accords with the experimental findings; the thermal disrotatory cleavage of cyclobutenes is unknown.

Although the correlation $\sigma^2\pi^2 \rightarrow \psi_1^2\psi_2^2$ is absent in the disrotatory mode, inspection of Fig. 4.5(b) reveals the presence of the excited state correlation $\sigma^2\pi\pi^* \rightarrow \psi_1^2\psi_2\psi_3$.† In effect this means that if one of the cyclobutene π-electrons is excited so that it enters the π^* level, which is in fact the lowest energy electronic transition available to the molecule, then disrotatory scission, if it occurs before the excitation energy is dissipated, yields butadiene also in its first excited state. The process is said to be photochemically 'allowed'. The same correlation is not available in the conrotatory mode so that it is a 'symmetry-forbidden' process under photochemical control.

In practice the ethylenic type $\pi \rightarrow \pi^*$ transition occurs at rather high energy which results in some experimental difficulty in preparative scale reactions. On the other hand the analogous $\pi \rightarrow \pi^*$ transition for butadiene (i.e. $\psi_2 \rightarrow \psi_3$) requires a lower radiation energy which is within the scope of most laboratory photochemical reactors that employ the mercury arc. In consequence, it is the converse of reaction (4.6) that is usually observed in the light induced process, and there has been ample experimental verification of the predicted disrotatory cyclization of butadienes to cyclobutenes. These interpretations, although correct from the stereochemical viewpoint, are not correct in physical detail. It is known that the product cyclobutene is generated in its *ground state,* and that the implied correlation $\psi_1^2\psi_2\psi_3 \rightarrow \sigma^2\pi\pi^*$ is not possible on simple energy grounds. Discussion of this and related points are deferred until later (see pp. 125 and 136).

---

† Rapid radiationless transitions virtually depopulate all of the upper excited states prior to chemical reaction. The only excited states that normally require consideration are the lowest single or triplet states. Unless specifically mentioned to the contrary, it is assumed here that we are dealing with spectroscopic singlet states (see also p. 108).

We saw in Chapter 3 that conrotation was equivalent to a $[_\sigma 2_s + _\pi 2_a]$ or a $[_\sigma 2_a + _\pi 2_s]$ cyclo-addition and that disrotation corresponded to a $[_\sigma 2_s + _\pi 2_s]$ or a $[_\sigma 2_a + _\pi 2_a]$ process. Using this terminology the above results are summarized in Table 4.1.

TABLE 4.1
Rules for the electrocyclic interconversion of cyclobutene and butadiene

Δ	$h\Delta$
$[_\sigma 2_s + _\pi 2_a]$	$[_\sigma 2_s + _\pi 2_s]$
$[_\sigma 2_a + _\pi 2_s]$	$[_\sigma 2_a + _\pi 2_a]$

The general Woodward-Hoffmann rule is, of course, in complete agreement with the data presented in Table 4.1 because the general rule itself was formulated on the basis of such results.

The terms 'symmetry allowed' and 'symmetry forbidden' are perhaps somewhat misleading since in fact the rules are not obligatory. An allowed process is one in which the activation energy is *likely* to be attainable under normal experimental conditions; the forbidden reaction is *likely* to be characterized be an exceptionally high energy of activation. The symmetry arguments do not take account of the more subtle features of molecular architecture or of the possibility of alternative reactions, whether they be concerted or not, or indeed of any special stability or instability of reactants or products which can have an important bearing upon the actual value of the activation energy.

Let us proceed now to the construction of the energy state correlation diagram. This diagram correlates molecular electronic ground states and excited states rather than the individual orbitals. The symmetry of an energy state is dependent upon the product of all of the individual symmetries of the electronic motion in the orbitals comprising that state. The total state symmetry is deduced by making use of the inter-relationships: $(S) \times (S) = S$; $(A) \times (S) = (S) \times (A) = A$; $(A) \times (A) = S$. In effect the value $(+1)$ is assigned to (S) and (-1) to (A), thus: $(+1)^2 = +1 = S$; $(+1)(-1) = -1 = A$; and $(-1)^2 = +1 = S$.

It follows from the above that states of A symmetry can result only if there are an odd number of unpaired electrons occupying orbitals of A symmetry. Electron pairs must always denote an S term to the overall symmetry function whether they occupy an orbital of S symmetry or of A symmetry. Hence the ground states of cyclobutene and of butadiene (respectively $\sigma^2\pi^2$ and $\psi_1^2\psi_2^2$) are both of S symmetry. The first excited states ($\sigma^2\pi\pi^*$ and $\psi_1^2\psi_2\psi_3$) are of A symmetry, in either mode, because of the symmetry reversal between the π and π^* and ψ_2 and ψ_3 levels in each case.

The partially complete state correlation diagrams are given in Fig. 4.6. In the conrotatory mode we can correlate the ground state levels ($\sigma^2\pi^2 \rightarrow \psi_1^2\psi_2^2$) because of our previous findings (Fig. 4.5(a)). However, since it is also known that the first excited states ($\sigma^2\pi\pi^*$ and $\psi_1^2\psi_2\psi_3$) do not correlate in this mode, they must each correlate directly with higher energy antisymmetric levels. The problem is to determine the electron configuration in these higher levels. From an inspection of Fig. 4.5(a) it may be seen that since $\psi_1^2 \rightarrow \pi^2$, $\psi_2 \rightarrow \sigma$, and $\psi_3 \rightarrow \sigma^*$, the required cyclobutene excited state is $\sigma\pi^2\sigma^*$. Likewise, since $\sigma^2 \rightarrow \psi_2^2$, $\pi \rightarrow \psi_1$ and $\pi^* \rightarrow \psi_4$ the butadiene excited state that correlates with the cyclobutene first excited state has the configuration

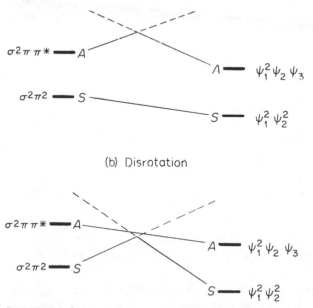

(a) Conrotation

$\sigma^2\pi\pi^*$ —— A

$\sigma^2\pi^2$ —— S

A —— $\psi_1^2\psi_2\psi_3$

S —— $\psi_1^2\psi_2^2$

(b) Disrotation

$\sigma^2\pi\pi^*$ —— A

$\sigma^2\pi^2$ —— S

A —— $\psi_1^2\psi_2\psi_3$

S —— $\psi_1^2\psi_2^2$

FIGURE 4.6
Partial energy state correlation diagrams for the electrocyclic cyclobutene-butadiene interconversion

$\psi_1\psi_2^2\psi_4$. The complete symmetry state diagram is shown in Fig. 4.7(a) for the conrotatory motion, due account having been taken of the non-crossing rule (see p. 11). The disrotation state correlation diagram may be completed in

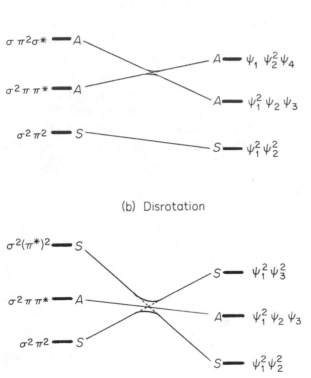

(a) Conrotation

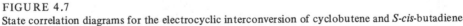

(b) Disrotation

FIGURE 4.7
State correlation diagrams for the electrocyclic interconversion of cyclobutene and S-cis-butadiene

like manner, but in this case different higher excited states must be invoked. As noted earlier, however, the details of these photochemical correlations are not valid (see pp. 125 and 136).

The main advantage of state correlation diagrams is that all of the information is at once apparent. The 'forbidden' processes ($h\nu$ conrotatory, Δ disrotatory) are characterized by formidable electronic energy barriers,

116

whereas in the 'allowed' reactions (Δ conrotatory, $h\nu$ disrotatory) there is a smooth correlation of the relevant states of each molecule.

A further well-known electrocyclic process is the interconversion of cyclohexa-1,3-dienes and hexa-1,3,5-trienes, of which reaction (4.7) is the prototype. As in the cyclobutene-butadiene transformation, reaction will

$$(4.7)$$

occur under thermal or photochemical control, and the stereochemical consequences are different. If we again assume planarity of the carbon framework of reactant, transition state, and product the important symmetry elements are once again the C_{2y} twofold axis (conrotation) and the σ_{yz} mirror plane (disrotation).

In this instance we need scarcely construct the correlation diagram. The relevant orbitals to consider are the delocalized π-orbitals of the hexatriene ($\psi_1 - \psi_6$), the delocalized π-molecular orbitals of the hexadiene ($\chi_1 - \chi_4$) and σ and σ^* for the bond that is cleaved. The levels $\chi_1 - \chi_4$ will have *precisely* the same symmetry properties as the butadiene π-levels (cf. Fig. 4.5), and the σ and σ^* levels also have the same characteristics as deduced previously. The lowest hexatriene level (ψ_1) is the typical 'streamer' orbital (i.e. $\pm\pm\pm\pm\pm\pm$) which is of A symmetry with respect to C_{2y} and of S symmetry with respect to the mirror plane σ_{yz}. The remaining π-levels ($\psi_2 - \psi_6$) follow the usual alternation pattern in their symmetries. The results are summarized in Table 4.2.

The bonding levels of S symmetry are equal in number in reactant and

TABLE 4.2
Orbital correlation table for the cyclohexadiene-hexatriene interconversion

		Bonding levels		Antibonding levels	
		hexatriene	cyclohexadiene	hexatriene	cyclohexadiene
Conrotation (C_{2y})	A	$\psi_1\psi_3$	χ_1	ψ_5	$\chi_3\sigma^*$
	S	ψ_2	$\sigma\chi_2$	$\psi_4\psi_6$	χ_4
Disrotation (σ_{yz})	A	ψ_2	χ_2	$\psi_4\psi_6$	$\chi_4\sigma^*$
	S	$\psi_1\psi_3$	$\sigma\chi_1$	ψ_5	χ_3

product *only* in the disrotatory case ($\psi_1 \rightarrow \sigma$, $\psi_3 \rightarrow \chi_1$) as are, of course, the levels of A symmetry ($\psi_2 \rightarrow \chi_2$). Disrotation is therefore symmetry allowed under thermal control.

The imbalance of bonding S levels between reactant and product, as in the conrotatory mode, is very characteristic of thermally forbidden processes. Since, however, $\psi_1 \rightarrow \chi_1$, $\psi_2 \rightarrow \sigma$, $\psi_3 \rightarrow \chi_3$ and $\psi_4 \rightarrow \chi_2$, or specifically $\psi_1^2\psi_2^2\psi_3\psi_4 \rightarrow \sigma^2\chi_1^2\chi_2\chi_3$, we have a correlation between first excited states and conrotation is the preferred mode under photochemical control. Again, although these correlations give the correct stereochemical answers, they are not in fact valid (see pp. 125 and 136).

The results to date are summarized in Table 4.3, which indicates the alternating sequence of allowed and forbidden processes (*supra-antara* or *antara-supra* versus *supra-supra* or *antara-antara*) with an alternation in the number of participating electrons. The generality of Table 4.3 will be further illustrated

TABLE 4.3
Selection rules for electrocyclic reactions

Δ	$h\nu$
$[_\sigma2_s + _\pi2_a]$	$[_\sigma2_s + _\pi2_s]$
$[_\sigma2_a + _\pi2_s]$	$[_\sigma2_a + _\pi2_a]$
$[_\pi4_s + _\sigma2_s]$	$[_\pi4_s + _\sigma2_a]$
$[_\pi4_a + _\sigma2_a]$	$[_\pi4_a + _\sigma2_s]$

by considering one or two cyclo-addition reactions. Nevertheless, it should be apparent to the reader with an eye for sequences that a $[_\pi6_s + _\sigma2_s]$ electrocyclic reaction, as in reaction (4.8) for example, will be forbidden under

$$(4.8)$$

thermal control, and allowed under photochemical control. Likewise the general $[_\pi m_s + _\sigma2_s]$ case is thermally allowed if $m = 4n$ and forbidden if $m = (4n + 2)$ where $n = 0, 1, 2, 3 \ldots$. When $m = 0$ (i.e. $m = 4n$, $n = 0$) the electrocyclic reaction effectively involves the addition of a σ-bond to an unoccupied atomic p-orbital (see p. 81), as in the ring scission of the cyclopropyl cation (Equation 4.9). In the ω symbolism (see p. 95) the reaction

118

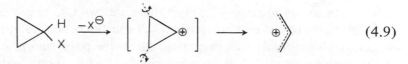

$$\tag{4.9}$$

(4.9) is classified as one of order $[_\sigma 2_s + _\omega 0_s]$ or $[_\sigma 2_a + _\omega 0_a]$, which are allowed processes under thermal control. The analogous electrocyclic scission of the cyclopropyl anion (Equation 4.10) is found to be symmetry allowed for

$$\tag{4.10}$$

conrotation under thermal activation (i.e. $[_\sigma 2_s + _\omega 2_a]$ or $[_\sigma 2_a + _\omega 2_s]$) or disrotation under photochemical control (i.e. $[_\sigma 2_s + _\omega 2_s]$ or $[_\sigma 2_a + _\omega 2_a]$). Formal correlation diagrams can be constructed for all of these cases.

Problem 4.3   Utilize orbital symmetry theory to suggest a mechanism whereby 3,7,7-trimethylcycloheptatriene is thermally equilibrated with its 2,7,7- and 1,7,7-isomers. (*Clue:* Consider consecutive electrocyclic and sigmatropic processes.)

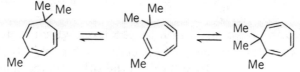

The simplest cyclo-addition reaction is the dimerization of ethylene (Equation 4.11). In Chapter 3 (p. 73) it was shown that the parallel

$$\tag{4.11}$$

approach of the two ethylenes is equivalent to the $[_\pi 2_s + _\pi 2_s]$ interaction. An antarafacial interaction on one, or both, of the molecules requires that the approach be orthogonal. Because of the high symmetry of the system the *supra-antara* and *antara-supra* modes are identical. Correlation diagrams for the $[_\pi 2_s + _\pi 2_s]$ addition are to be found in the literature (Woodward and Hoffmann, 1965, 1969). We will concentrate here on the other two modes of addition.

119

In the *antara-antara* case (Fig. 4.8) there are two C_{2v} axes – one bisects the molecular axes of the two ethylenes (C_{2z}) and the other lies in the xy plane (which is a horizontal plane perpendicular to the page) and at $45°$ to the y and z co-ordinates (C_{2xy}) such that it bisects the two σ-bonds that are being formed. The *antara-supra* mode is of lower symmetry, and the only useful element is the C_{2z} axis. There are no symmetry planes for the system because of the non-planar nature of the first-formed product molecule.

The various important molecular orbitals are shown in Fig. 4.8. These take cognisance of the requirement (see p. 110) that *all* orbitals must either be symmetric or antisymmetric with respect to the symmetry elements. The fully delocalized orbitals are therefore necessary to the *antara-antara* combination.

At relatively large distances apart the bonding interaction between the two ethylenes will, of course, be minimal. The *AS* and *AA*, and the *SS* and *SA* levels are therefore degenerate. Likewise the σ-level pairs, *SS* and *AS* and also *SA* and *AA*, are degenerate if it is assumed that lateral (across ring) interactions are negligible. In the *antara-supra* mode the lower symmetry forces one to consider the localized π-molecular orbitals; the bonding and antibonding levels are again in degenerate pairs.

In the *antara-antara* cyclo-addition the *AS* level, which is an attractive interaction between the two ethylenes, *decreases* in energy to become the bonding *AS* σ-level, σ_2. The *AA* π-level on the other hand, increases in energy because of the repulsive interaction and is transformed into σ_4^*. The lack of correlation between ground states ($\chi_1^2\chi_2^2$ and $\sigma_1^2\sigma_2^2$) means that the thermo-chemical $[_\pi2_a + {}_\pi2_a]$ cyclo-addition is symmetry forbidden; this accords with Table 4.3. Since, however, the first excited states are correlated (e.g. $\chi_1^2\chi_2\chi_3 \rightarrow \sigma_1\sigma_2^2\sigma_4^*$; the other possible first excited olefin states all correlate with more energetic levels in the product) the photochemical reaction is allowed. The correlation diagram is very similar to that for the $[_\pi2_s + {}_\pi2_s]$ cyclo-addition.

In the *antara-supra* mode of addition there is the expected correlation of bonding levels ($\pi_1^2\pi_2^2 \rightarrow \sigma_1^2\sigma_2^2$) for the allowed $[_\pi2_s + {}_\pi2_a]$ thermochemical reaction. However, the diagram also reveals a correlation of first excited state levels ($\pi_1^2\pi_2\pi_4^* \rightarrow \sigma_1\sigma_2^2\sigma_4^*$ or $\pi_1\pi_2^2\pi_3^* \rightarrow \sigma_1^2\sigma_2\sigma_3^*$) indicating allowed pathways for the photochemical reaction. This observation well illustrates the inherent danger in the construction and use of correlation diagrams. It is much safer to assume a reaction to be forbidden when a correlation diagram indicates

120

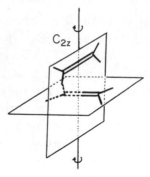

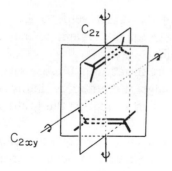

antara – antara   antara – supra

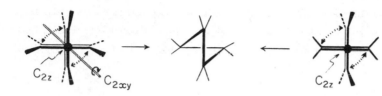

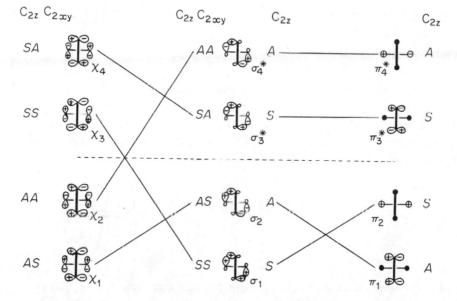

FIGURE 4.8

Orbital correlation diagrams for the $[_\pi 2_a + _\pi 2_a]$ and $[_\pi 2_s + _\pi 2_a]$ dimerizations of ethylene

that this is so, than it is to accept an allowed process at face value. The error here essentially arises because of the low symmetry of the system at hand, the assumption of degeneracy between the various pairs of levels, and the lack of sophistication in the method of analysis. There are in fact much more serious and fundamental objections to the correlation diagram method, which will be considered presently. It is appropriate here, however, to rectify the faults in Fig. 4.8 for the *antara-supra* mode.

One obvious point requiring explanation is the means whereby the essentially localized π-orbitals $\pi_1 - \pi_4^*$ become the delocalized σ-molecular orbitals $\sigma_1 - \sigma_4^*$. Consider, for example, the fate of the π_1-level. As the reaction progresses this orbital will interact or mix with other π-levels, provided they have the correct symmetry (i.e. A). The π_4^*-orbital is ideal for this purpose, and Equation (4.12) indicates the details of the correlation $\pi_1 \rightarrow \sigma_2$. In a similar way it can be shown that π_2 mixes in π_3^* to give the σ_1-level. In both

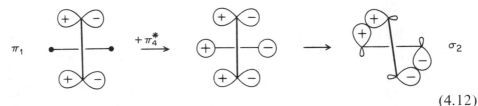

$$(4.12)$$

of these cases the high energy unoccupied antibonding levels (π_3^* or π_4^*) are mixed in such that an energy lowering (bonding) interaction results. The effect of mixing in π_1 into π_4^* (or π_2 into π_3^*), on the other hand, leads to destabilizing (antibonding) interactions, for example, Equation (4.13) which illustrates the formation of the σ_4^*-level. These are just specific cases of a

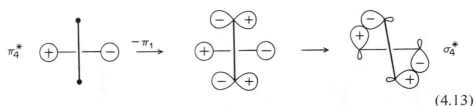

$$(4.13)$$

general phenomenon: if two atomic orbitals overlap two new (molecular) orbitals are formed, one of which is bonding and the other antibonding. As far as the electrons in the lower energy atomic orbital are concerned the interaction is a stabilizing one; for the electrons in the more energetic atomic

122

orbital, however, the interaction is destabilizing. The total net effect is one of stabilization only if the original component orbitals possess three electrons (or less) between them. This is certainly true for reactions (4.12) and (4.13).

For the *antara-supra* combination it is possible to construct a more realistic correlation diagram than that shown in Fig. 4.8 by using the appropriate delocalized π-molecular orbitals mentioned above (Caserio, 1971). The general details of Table 4.3 are therefore correct, and further correlation diagram checks are available for $[_\pi 4 + _\pi 2]$ cyclo-addition reactions (Fig. 3.5) for all but the $[_\pi 4_s + _\pi 2_a]$ case which lacks important symmetry.

Problem 4.4 Suggest a symmetry allowed pathway to account for the following chemical transformation.

4.5   Limitations in the orbital symmetry method

The orbital symmetry method and the use of correlation diagrams is really only applicable to those pericyclic systems that possess symmetry. Strictly speaking, therefore, the electrocyclic ring fission of *cis*-3,4-dimethylcyclo-butene to give *cis,trans*-hexa-2,4-diene (Equation 4.14) cannot be assesed by these methods because a single symmetry element is not present in reactant,

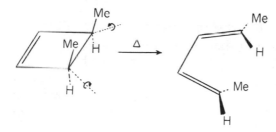

(4.14)

transition state, and product. There are very many similar cases; indeed, most of the known pericyclic reactions lack important symmetry, and this includes *all* of the sigmatropic changes of order [1,*j*] and virtually all of the shifts of order [*i,j*]. These cases can be treated by a modified form of orbital analysis

123

(the frontier orbital method) as was seen earlier (Section 4.2), or by the analytical method developed by Woodward and Hoffmann (1969), one facet of which is illustrated in Equations (4.12) and (4.13).

In cases where the lack of symmetry is due entirely to the presence of substituents, as in Equation (4.14), Woodward and Hoffmann have argued that the presence of the substituents should be ignored since it is the local orbital symmetry that is important, and not the gross molecular symmetry.† This would seem to be a reasonable argument, particularly in view of the fact that reaction (4.14) is highly stereospecific and follows the pathway predicted by orbital symmetry theory. Although this type of argument by analogy has been very important in the development of chemistry in general and in organic chemistry in particular, nevertheless it is not a quantitative method and hence should be treated with a certain amount of reservation. Orbital symmetry theory is not a uniformly applicable method because even the local symmetry may not (indeed, in many cases it certainly is not) conserved throughout the whole course of the reaction. The symmetry element may be absent in the transition state, or in the intervening phases of the conversion of reactants into products, because of a departure from the assumed geometry of reaction centres.‡ If this is the case then the validity of the correlation diagram is in question because an implicit assumption in the method is that the molecular orbitals for the intermediate phases must show the same symmetry behaviour as the molecular orbitals of the reactants and products. The disappearance of the symmetry label brings an element of discontinuity into a process that has to be continuous for the orbital symmetry interpretation to be valid.

The presence of hetero-atoms also causes difficulty. In the Woodward-Hoffmann approach the hetero-atom is replaced by the isoelectronic CH_n unit; $=N-$ is replaced by $=CH-$, $=O$ is replaced by $=CH_2$, $-NH_2$ and $-OH$ are both replaced by $-CH_3$. The system is then treated as a hydrocarbon with the highest possible inherent symmetry, and the stereochemical consequences of a particular pericyclic reaction are then deduced from orbital symmetry

† A similar argument has been employed to explain the weak intensities ($\epsilon_{max} \sim 15$) of the $n \to \pi^*$ electronic absorption bands of aliphatic aldehydes and ketones. Only in the case of formaldehyde is the transition symmetry forbidden.

‡ Many spectroscopic electronic transitions of organic molecules are rigorously forbidden on symmetry grounds, but a large number of them in fact are observed. Indeed, some have large extinction coefficients because nuclear vibrations can destroy the otherwise perfect symmetry of the relevant species.

analysis. There will clearly be a lack of proper symmetry in most of these cases, and the objections outlined above are particularly relevant here. In addition, it should be remembered that the presence of the hetero-atom is likely to affect appreciably the value of the activation energy of the concerted reaction, and also allows for the possibility of new reactions.

The construction of correlation diagrams is tedious, and in some cases quite onerous because of the difficulty in visualizing the orientation of the various atomic centres and their relationship to the symmetry element. Apart from this it is quite easy to make errors in the construction of the diagrams, and even properly constructed diagrams can give false information. Consider, for example, Fig. 4.7 (b); the conclusion to be drawn from this diagram is that the first excited states of reactant and product are correlated. That is, electronic excitation of butadiene if followed by disrotatory cyclization, gives electronically excited cyclobutene directly (Equation 4.15). We have already seen that this is the normal direction in which the photochemical reaction

$$\text{(structure)} \xrightarrow[\text{(a)}]{h\nu} \left(\text{structure}\right)^* \xrightarrow[\text{(b)}]{\text{disrotation}} \left(\square\right)^* \qquad (4.15)$$

proceeds since the converse ring-opening process is experimentally more difficult to arrange.

Reaction (4.15) involves the conversion of excited singlet butadiene, which is $c.$ 132 kcal mole^{-1} more energetic than the molecule in its ground state, into excited singlet cyclobutene, which has an analogous energy excess of $c.$ 164 kcal mole^{-1}. Since the ground state of cyclobutene is about 20 kcal mole^{-1} higher in energy than the ground state of butadiene, simple calculation reveals that reaction (4.15b) is endothermic by about 52 kcal mole^{-1} (i.e. ~220 kJ mole^{-1}). The activation energy, of course, will be greater than this and will be much too large for reaction to be accomplished within the lifetime of the excited butadiene molecule. Reaction (4.15) is therefore not at all probable.

From experiment one merely knows that the photochemical cyclization of butadiene starts from an excited singlet state and terminates at the ground state of the cyclobutene; appropriate labelling indicates the cyclization to be stereospecific. What intervenes between start and finish is not clear, but it is certainly not excited singlet cyclobutene. What seems more likely is that at

125

some intermediate phase along the energy profile connecting excited singlet butadiene and excited singlet cyclobutene a cross-over to the ground state energy surface occurs, which presumably involves a radiationless transition. At this point the thermally activated molecule, which is in the nuclear con-figuration corresponding to the disrotatory transition state between butadiene and cyclobutene, can proceed along the energy surface to furnish the product or return to re-form butadiene. Oosterhoff and van der Lugt (1969) are responsible for this interpretation, and their detailed calculations reveal that the crossing occurs from a *symmetric* excited state (rather than the anti-symmetric level portrayed in Fig. 4.7(b)) which has a convenient energy minimum in the region of the energy maximum for the electronic ground state. The initial photo-excitation to the symmetric excited state is forbidden, and the excited molecule enters this surface by way of the antisymmetric excited state level; the whole process is represented in Fig. 4.9.

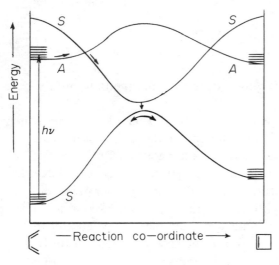

FIGURE 4.9
Relative changes in energy during the conversion of butadiene into cyclobutene by the photochemical method

As a general principle Oosterhoff and van der Lugt have deduced that if a given mode for a thermochemical electrocyclic reaction is unfavourable because of the presence of a high potential barrier, there will be another potential surface of the same symmetry which has an energy minimum not far above this barrier. The photo-induced reaction may profit from this energy minimum to bring about the electrocyclic transformation that is the converse of the given mode. In effect this principle, although differing in the details of interpretation, comes to the same conclusions as the Woodward-Hoffmann orbital symmetry theory. It also accords with the conclusions of Zimmermann and of Dewar (see Chapter 5) who employed somewhat different theoretical approaches. Of particular interest and significance is the development by Dougherty (1971) of Dewar's PMO approach as a general theory for photo-pericyclic reactions (see p. 136).

The inconsistency in the details of photochemical transformations are not peculiar to electrocyclic reactions alone, but are relevant to other photo-pericyclic reactions as well. For example, calculation shows that reaction (4.16) is also highly endothermic, and hence the product cannot be formed in the

$$\text{I} + \left(\text{I}\right)^* \longrightarrow \left(\square\right)^* \tag{4.16}$$

excited singlet state. A similar situation presumably applies here also as in the case of the photo-induced butadiene-cyclobutene interconversion. Once again, the conclusions of the Woodward-Hoffmann theory are perfectly valid, although the theoretical interpretations are not entirely self-consistent. There are further problems in photochemical reactions associated with the reliable interpretation of the experimental results, notably on whether or not the observed reactions are actually concerted (see p. 108).

Alternative rationalization - the aromaticity of pericyclic transition states

5

Several methods, alternative to the treatments outlined in the previous chapter, have been put forward for the rationalization of pericyclic reactions since the original publications of Woodward and Hoffmann first appeared. We will concentrate here on only two of these methods because they have achieved a greater currency than the others: they feature the concept of aromaticity.

5.1   The Zimmerman Method

The concept of the Möbius strip was explained earlier (see p. 55). The basis of the Zimmerman analysis is an extension of this idea. A cyclic polyene is defined as a Hückel system if its basis molecular orbital (i.e. the lowest filled π-level $-\psi_1-$ as in the case of benzene, for example) contains zero or an even number of phase dislocations. Möbius systems possess an odd number of phase dislocations in the basis molecular orbitals. In accordance with the rules predicting aromaticity for these systems, which results from the application of the Hückel molecular orbital theory, it may be inferred that since cyclic conjugation also arises in the transition states of pericyclic reactions, the following conclusions apply:

(a) *Hückel systems are of lower energy where there are (4n + 2) participant electrons;*
(b) *Möbius systems are energetically preferred when the number of participant electrons is 4n.*

The rules are for thermochemical reactions, and are precisely reversed for the first excited state photochemical processes.

Consider first the electrocyclic reactions of butadiene. The basis molecular orbital (i.e. ψ_1, $\pm\pm\pm\pm$) readily comes to mind, and it can be seen that there

128

are no phase dislocations in the disrotatory mode (Fig. 5.1(a)), whereas there is one out of phase overlap in the conrotatory ring closure (Fig. 5.1(b)). Since there are four participant electrons (a $4n$ system), the Möbius-like transition state will be preferred and ring closure should occur by the conrotatory mode. A similar analysis applies to the converse, ring-opening, process (Fig. 5.1(c)).

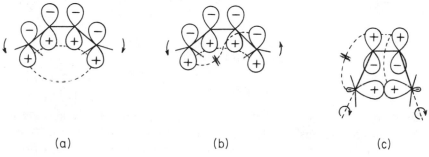

(a)   (b)   (c)

FIGURE 5.1
Hückel and Möbius systems in the butadiene-cyclobutene interconversion; (a) Hückel, (b) and (c) Möbius

Extension of these ideas to include the cyclohexadiene-hexatriene system, in which there are $(4n + 2)$ participating electrons, is straightforward.

Problem 5.1   Analyse the cyclohexadiene ⇌ hexatriene interconversion by the Zimmerman method. What is the interaction (i.e. Hückel or Möbius) at the transition state of the thermochemical and photochemical reactions?

The three possible topological interactions in $[_\pi 2 + _\pi 2]$ cyclo-addition reactions are shown in Fig. 5.2; again the basis molecular orbitals of the ethylene components are considered. In the *supra-supra* and the *antara-antara* combinations there are no out of phase orbital overlaps (or two if the signs are reversed on one ethylene component). In the *supra-antara* mode there is one out of phase overlap. Since there are four electrons involved, the Möbius type interaction (i.e. *supra-antara*) should be preferred; the other combinations should therefore be possible under photochemical control. These results accord with the previous findings of orbital symmetry theory.

The *supra-supra* interaction in cyclo-addition reactions is particularly easy to analyse by the Zimmermann method, and a formal diagram of the orbital interactions is not at all necessary to the analysis. Consider the $[_\pi 6 + _\pi 4]$ reaction (5.1), which hitherto has not been observed. The face to face inter-

129

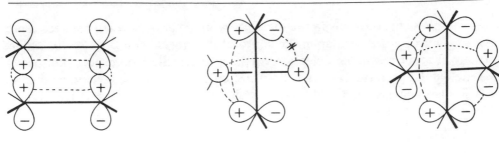

supra – supra   supra – antara   antara – antara
                       antara – supra

FIGURE 5.2
Hückel and Möbius systems in the dimerization of ethylene

action of the two π-systems is the only mode that is geometrically and sterically feasible, and for the basis molecular orbitals this means no phase dislocations. Since there are 10 electrons involved in the change the transition

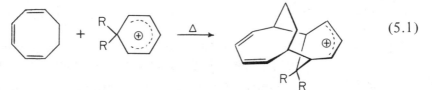

(5.1)

state is of the $(4n + 2)$ Hückel-type. The reaction is allowed, but of course
may not occur if alternative processes are preferable energetically (e.g.
elimination of R^+ to give the benzenoid compound C_6H_5R).

The appropriate correlation diagrams can also be constructed for the
Hückel and Möbius closures in pericyclic processes where the system main-
tains some symmetry, and the method is capable of extension to include for
unsymmetrical systems (Zimmerman, 1966, 1971). The molecular orbital
energies of Hückel- and Möbius-type cyclic polyenes are readily derived from
the simple circle mnemonic discussed earlier (see pp. 43 and 55).

Various other pericyclic reactions are analysed in Fig. 5.3 using the
Zimmerman method. Cases (a) and (b) represent respectively the linear and
non-linear (see Fig. 3.16, p. 95) cheletropic reactions of an acyclic polyene
with singlet carbene. The polyene contains m π-electrons; the carbene, of
course possess two frontier electrons which are placed in the sp^2-hybrid
orbital, the p-orbital being empty.

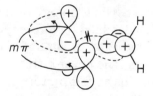

Disrotation   Conrotation

(a)

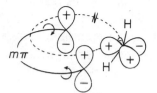
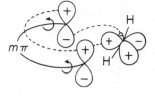

Disrotation   Conrotation

(b)

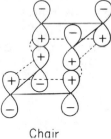
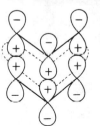

Chair   Boat

(c)

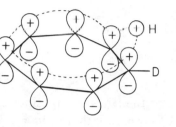

(d)

FIGURE 5.3
(a), (b) Cheletropic, and (c), (d) Sigmatropic processes analysed by the Zimmerman method

In the linear approach (a) the carbene orbitals are interacting in a suprafacial manner. The topology of the interaction with the polyene orbitals can be suprafacial, which therefore requires a disrotatory twisting about the terminal bond axes, or antarafacial which can result only if the conrotatory mode applies. The linear disrotatory process involves a Hückel interaction, whereas the linear conrotatory reaction has a Möbius transition state. Hence if $(m + 2)$, that is the total number of participant electrons, is equal to $(4n+2)$ the Hückel-type disrotatory closure will be preferred. If $(m + 2) = 4n$, then the conrotatory (Möbius) closure is predicted. Hence butadiene should undergo a linear cheletropic reaction with singlet carbene (or similar electron deficient species – e.g. SO_2) with disrotatory closure, whereas the analogous reaction of hexatriene requires the operation of the conrotatory mode.

In the non-linear approach (b) the carbene orbitals are interacting in an antarafacial manner, and the polyene orbitals can interact either suprafacially or antarafacially as before. The disrotatory process this time relates to a Möbius system, and the conrotatory process to a Hückel system. The non-linear cheletropic reaction with conrotation will be preferred for the case $(m + 2) = (4n + 2)$, and with disrotation for the case $(m + 2) = 4n$. These conclusions are in full agreement with those obtained using the general Woodward-Hoffmann rule.

The final examples in Fig. 5.3, cases (c) and (d), respectively represent the orbital analysis for the Cope reaction (5.2), and the suprafacial[1,7] hydrogen shift in reaction (5.3). The basis molecular orbital interactions in (c) and (d)

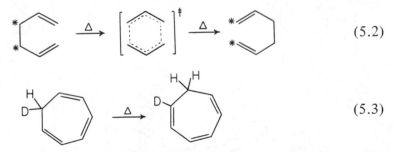

$$(5.2)$$

$$(5.3)$$

indicates that both systems are of the Hückel-type since there are no phase dislocations. In only case (c), however, are there $(4n + 2)$ electrons intimately involved in the change, and hence in reaction (5.2) the transition state is resonance stabilized; in reaction (5.3) it is not. The suprafacial[1,7] hydrogen shift should occur only under photochemical control, which agrees with our previous findings and with the results of experimental work. The straight-forward (i.e. first order) application of either the Zimmerman approach or of the general Woodward-Hoffmann rule does not permit distinction between the two transition states of case (c). From experiment it is known that the four-centre, chair-like transition state is preferred, and Woodward and Hoffmann have indicated that extended Hückel molecular orbital calculations also predict this type of behaviour. The six-centre, boat-like, transition state could be regarded, in an extension of the Zimmerman model, as two separate Hückel systems. The transition state is essentially bicyclic although net bonding between C2 and C5 exists in neither reactant nor product. This arrangement is less favourable than the $(4n + 2)$ alternative – the four-centre case, and hence the reaction should be stereospecific.

The relatively few examples cited above are sufficient to show that the Zimmerman method is at once ingenious, simple to apply, informative, and apparently accurate. It has the occasional advantage over the general Woodward-Hoffmann rule, but on the whole is a less widely used procedure, particularly since the Woodward-Hoffmann rule has built into itself such decisive predictive power. Unlike the frontier orbital method, however, the Zimmerman procedure requires no knowledge of the higher molecular orbitals of the system under consideration. An interesting, though somewhat obvious, feature of the method is that the same result is obtained whichever of the various molecular orbitals of the reacting molecule(s) are chosen for the analysis. The reason is simply that changing the molecular orbital has the effect of introducing an additional *even* number of out of phase overlaps; if there were originally an odd number of such dislocations in the system, then the *total* number of dislocations still remains odd.

Problem 5.2   For the butadiene $\rightleftharpoons$ cyclobutene interconversion show that the transition state for conrotatory closure has an odd number of out of phase orbital overlaps regardless of whether ψ_1, ψ_2, ψ_3 or ψ_4 is chosen as the basis set. Show that the *supra-supra* cyclo-addition of two ethylenes has an even number of out-of-phase overlaps for each of the three possible combinations of π and π^* orbitals for the two components.

Problem 5.3   Analyse reactions (3.13), (3.14), (4.3a), (4.5) with $Z = H$ and (4.9) by the Zimmerman procedure.

It was stated at the outset that the Zimmerman method is based on the Hückel molecular orbital theory criterion of whether or not a given transition state is aromatic. Dewar has criticized this approach *because* of the theoretical basis, which is regarded as a very much less reliable guide to aromaticity than either the Pople SCF molecular orbital treatment or the perturbation molecular orbital method (see p. 46). Certainly the Hückel approach does not sufficiently emphasize the instability ('anti-aromaticity') of planar conjugated $4n$ π-electron monocyclic systems when the value of n is small (i.e. 1 or 2), and over-emphasizes the resonance energies of $(4n + 2)$ systems when n is larger than about 3 or 4. Nevertheless, although the two procedures are based on somewhat different criteria for aromaticity, in operation they are very closely similar and indeed give rise to identical predictions. It does seem that the Zimmerman approach has not been given the credit that it deserves. The alternative approach developed by Dewar must, however, be considered seriously, particularly since its natural extensions provide the most satisfactory rationale of photo-pericyclic reactions of all of the various theories that have achieved currency at the present time.

5.2   The Dewar approach

In a recent book Dewar (1969) has given a general account of the perturbation molecular orbital (PMO) approach and its relevance in discussions on physical-organic chemistry. Of particular interest is one application which provides a general theory of pericyclic reactions (Dewar, 1969, 1971). The PMO treatment in this context has but one central concept, namely the potential aromaticity of pericyclic transition states (see p. 61), and may be generalized into a single definitive rule:

Thermal pericyclic reactions take place via aromatic transition states; conversely, the photochemical reactions take place through excited forms of anti-aromatic transition states.

This generalization has been called *Evans' Rule* after M. G. Evans who first proposed the basic idea (1939), in connection with the Diels-Alder reaction, that aromatic transition states were favoured energetically.

Some of the essential properties of aromatic, non-aromatic, and anti-aromatic hydrocarbons have been considered earlier (see p. 41); basically these differences may be attributed to the assignment of positive, zero, and

134

negative resonance energies to the respective molecular systems. A set of simple rules defining aromaticity are therefore necessary, and these have been provided by Dewar (see pp. 51–57):

(a) *Replace all hetero-atoms by C atoms with the equivalent number of* $p(\pi)$-*electrons*

(b) *Delete all* essential *single and* essential *double bonds from the structure under consideration.*

(c) *The phases of the atomic orbitals are chosen to minimize phase dislocations. A Hückel system* (H) *is one in which all of the atomic orbitals overlap in phase (or there is an even number of dislocations). Anti-Hückel* (A-H) *systems have one (or an odd number) of phase dislocations.*

(d) *Aromatic systems have positive resonance energies* (+), *whereas antiaromatic systems have negative* (−) *resonance energies. It is assumed that there are no first-order differences between* σ-π *and pure* π-*delocalized systems.*

(e) *Conjugated monocyclic hydrocarbons of the type* $(CH)_N$ *may then be classified as follows:*

Ring size (N)	Neutral molecule	Cation	Anion
$4n$	− H, + A-H	...	...
$4n + 1$	zero	−H, + A-H	+H, − A-H
$4n + 2$	+H, − A-H	...	...
$4n + 3$	zero	+H, − A-H	−H, +A-H

This way of tabulating the various points in the Dewar theory is somewhat cumbersome. In predicting the preferred transition states for monocyclic pericyclic reactions the only information that is really required is the number of participant electrons. Since we are concerned here only with *even* electron systems, whether they be charged or electrically neutral, the total number of electrons is therefore $4n$ or $4n + 2$. A concise summary of the Dewar theory is then given by:

Preferred topology	Number of electrons	
	Δ	$h\nu$
Hückel	$4n + 2$	$4n$
Anti-Hückel	$4n$	$4n + 2$

135

When it is realized that a Hückel transition state involves zero or an even number of inversions and that an anti-Hückel transition state has an odd number of inversions, then the direct and complete correspondence of the Dewar theory and general Woodward-Hoffmann rule (p. 100) is clearly apparent.

These rules are simple and straightforward to use. Consider the case of azulene (1); no matter how the valence bond structures are drawn, the central bond always appears as a single bond, that is an *essential* single bond. Delection of this bond, rule (b), yields cyclodecatetraene (2), which must be a Hückel-type polyene because it has an untwisted $p\pi$-system, rule (c). Molecule (2) is also aromatic since it possesses $(4n + 2)$ $p\pi$-electrons, rules (d) and (e), and hence it is a +H hydrocarbon.

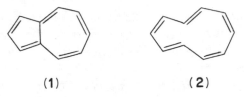

(1)   (2)

Consider now the electrocyclic processes depicted in Fig. 5.1. Case (a) clearly involves a −H type transition state, whereas in cases (b) and (c) the interactions are of the + A-H type. Accordingly, the electrocyclic interconversion of butadiene and cyclobutene should occur by the lower energy conrotatory pathway if the process is concerted. In the first excited state processes, because of the reversal of Evans' Rule, the disrotatory mode should be strongly preferred.

Consider Fig. 5.2; it is at once apparent that the *supra-supra* and *antara-antara* interactions should lead to transition state complexes of high energy since they are of the −H type. The concerted thermochemical dimerization of two ethylenic molecules should therefore proceed by way of *supra-antara* or *antara-supra* interactions (if geometrically possible) because they provide pathways to the low energy + A-H transition state. Conversely, the first excited state photochemical cyclo-addition should occur by either *supra-supra* or *antara-antara* modes because once again we have a + A-H transition state available (i.e. the excited form of a −H transition state).

It is appropriate here to mention the extension of the PMO method for the qualitative rationalization of photo-pericyclic reactions, particularly since

various points in the Woodward-Hoffmann theory have been criticized. However, it should be stressed that the PMO method in no way challenges the
stereochemical predictions of the Woodward-Hoffmann theory, but gives a
more reasonable account of the mechanism of the photo-pericyclic change.

The application of PMO theory to photo-pericyclic reactions has been discussed by Dougherty (1971), and he draws attention to the consequences of
the breakdown in the Born-Oppenheimer (BO) approximation in certain
excited state processes. The BO approximation assumes that nuclear motions
are very slow compared with the speed of electronic transitions, so that
effectively the nuclei behave as if they were fixed in space (cf. Franck-Condon
principle). Since electronic motions are thus independent of nuclear motions,
then the potential energy *versus* reaction co-ordinate curves for the ground
state and first-excited state processes should roughly parallel one another.
However, the relative energies of the bonding wells (i.e. the hollows in the P.E.
surface corresponding to reactant and product) are reversed on the excited
state surface so that the transition state on this surface moves from one side
of the reaction co-ordinate to the other.

Photo-pericyclic reactions that fit this simple picture can be analysed in
much the same way as ground state reactions. In Dougherty's terminology
these include X-type reactions, which are processes that take place entirely
on the excited state surface and generate excited state products. The electronic
relaxation of these products to the ground state should produce detectable
luminescence.

When the energy separation between the two surfaces is small it is possible
that nuclear motion will mix the two states so that for a given total energy
and nuclear configuration it is not possible to assign the system to either
state. This then is a breakdown in the BO approximation, and in such regions
a single molecular structure cannot be drawn (cf. probability distribution
representation of orbitals). However, the BO 'hole' provides a mechanism for
the system to relax radiationlessly into the ground state, through that
geometry, as excitation energy is converted into chemical potential on the
ground state surface.

The argument then is that since the majority of photochemical reactions do
not have direct thermal analogues, then the two electronic surfaces will not
parallel each other and the BO approximation is likely to breakdown at some
point along the reaction co-ordinate. Whenever there is no first-order stabiliz-

ation of the activated complex on the ground state surface (i.e. anti-aromatic transition state), the PMO analysis reveals that there will be a depression in the excited state surface near this region because of the *aromatic* stabilization of the system with this electronic and nuclear configuration (cf. p. 126). Photochemical reactions in this situation will tend to proceed through the associated BO hole; these are classified as N-type and G-type reactions. The N-type photochemical reactions are essentially complete when the system reaches a non-bonding ground state and are characterized by non-bonded (usually radical) intermediates. They are not considered in this volume. G-type reactions end in a bonding ground state configuration as is the case for photo-pericyclic reactions. The reverse situation, namely processes in which reactants in a bonding ground state configuration are transformed into electronically excited products by way of an anti-aromatic transition state, such that chemi-luminescence is observed, are also G-type processes.

In summary, the PMO method when extended to photochemical reactions of the G-type predicts a reversal of aromatic properties from ground state to excited state. This justifies the set of rules for photochemical pericyclic reactions given above. Dougherty's analysis also reveals dangers in the use of orbital and state correlation diagrams for assessing photo-pericyclic reactions because the breakdown in the BO approximation leads to a destruction of symmetry.

It is worth noting here that the Dewar approach also allows one to analyse the alternative reaction processes. The [2 + 2] cyclo-addition reaction, for example, need not be concerted but could proceed via a diradical (or zwitter-ionic) intermediate (Equation 5.4). The transition state here is isoconjugate with butadiene (a non-aromatic molecule), which has a lower energy than the anti-aromatic cyclobutadiene, and hence the activation energy should not be unreasonably high in suitably substituted systems. Tetrafluoroethylene, for example, is known to dimerize by just such a diradical mechanism.

$$\text{diagram} \tag{5.4}$$

A clear-cut distinction is available in the Dewar approach between the alternative geometries for the Cope reaction (Fig. 5.3(c)). The chair-like transition state is isoconjugate with benzene, and should be substantially

138

lower in energy than the boat-like transition state which, being isoconjugate with butalene (3), is doubly anti-aromatic. Although the preference for the chair-like geometry has received ample experimental verification, the Dewar treatment does seem to over-emphasize the difference in the activation energies. From experiment the boat-like transition state geometry is known to form without especial difficulty when geometrical features make the attainment of the chair arrangement impossible. Such reactions appear to be concerted, but might well be worth re-investigation.

(3)

In the cheletropic reactions (a) and (b) of Fig. 5.3 it is clear that there must be an odd number of interacting atomic centres if the acyclic polyenes are neutral molecules. This ring contains $(m + 1)$ members, but also $(m + 2)$ electrons. Hence, in order to use the Dewar scheme, it is necessary to equate these systems with their isoelectronic polyenyl *anions*. Thus, if $m = 4n$ the isoelectronic anion has a ring containing $(4n + 1)$ members, whereas if $m = (4n + 2)$ the polyenyl anion has $(4n + 3)$ conjugated atoms. From rule (d), above, it then follows that the linear cheletropic reaction (Fig. 5.3(a)) with disrotation is favourable only for the $(4n + 1)$ case (i.e. +H type). This corresponds to those reactions in which the olefinic component has $4n$ π-electrons. For $(4n + 2)$ π-electron olefins, the low energy pathway for the linear cheletropic reaction is when the conrotatory mode is operative (i.e. + A-H type). The non-linear approach (Fig. 5.3(b)) requires that $4n$ π-electron olefines react by the conrotatory mode (+H type), and $(4n + 2)$ π-electron olefins by the disrotatory mode (+ A-H type). These predictions have exact correspondence with those from both the Woodward-Hoffmann theory and the Zimmerman approach.

Other pericyclic changes are likewise readily analysed using the Dewar procedure. Consider, for example, the concerted elimination of hydrogen from a dihydrobenzene; there are two possibilities, Equations (5.5) and (5.6). The

(5.5)

139

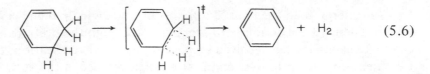

$$(5.6)$$

1,4-elimination (Equation 5.5) should be the more favoured process (transition state isoconjugate with a substituted benzene rather than a cyclobutadiene), and experiment has shown there to be a marked difference in the mechanisms of 1,4- and 1,2- eliminations of these types. Reactions of the first type are generally thought to be concerted.

As a final set of examples of the use of the Dewar concept of pericyclic changes, consider the situation in [1,j] shifts. Reaction (5.7) illustrates the transition state for a suprafacial [1,5] hydrogen migration. Since it is isoconjugate with benzene (essential double bond ignored), the activated complex should not be particularly energetic, and in fact concerted reactions of this type are very well known. The alternative [1,3] and [1,7] shifts on the other hand, respectively reactions (5.8) and (5.9), each must be characterized by a

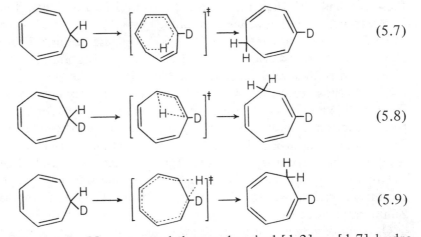

$$(5.7)$$

$$(5.8)$$

$$(5.9)$$

−H type transition state. No concerted thermochemical [1,3] or [1,7] hydrogen migrations are known for monocyclic olefins. When, however, the migrating group is other than hydrogen, the possibility of inversions (i.e. antarafacial interaction) at the migrating centre must be considered. Likewise, when the polyene is not constrained within a cyclic framework of atoms, the possibility of inversion at the migration terminus also arises. A single inversion has

140

the effect of converting a + H system into a − A-H system, and a − H transition state into a + A-H one. Thus, [1,3] and [1,7] shifts are favoured only if such inversions can occur readily; examples are known but they are relatively few at the present time.

Photochemical [1,*j*] shifts are likewise readily analysed. If the interactions are assumed to be entirely *supra-supra*, then the low energy pathways are for [1,3] and [1,7] migrations (i.e. excited forms of anti-aromatic systems).

Problem 5.4   Analyse the following reactions by the Dewar procedure:

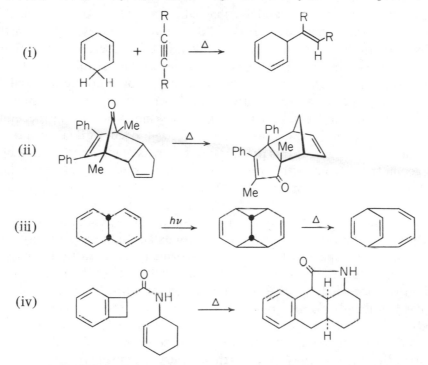

It should be evident, therefore, that the analytical method developed by Dewar is conceptually simple, is straightforward in its application, even to unsymmetrical systems, and has as its basis a more satisfactory theory. It suffers from one disadvantage, however, when compared with the general Woodward-Hoffmann rule. It cannot be used so readily as a predictive theory; all of the various possible reaction processes have to be separately analysed,

141

and the possible low energy pathway(s) then deduced. In the case of the general Woodward-Hoffmann rule the likely topology for a pericyclic change is given directly by the rule, and the stereochemistry of the process is at once evident. Both methods therefore have great merit, and will be used interchangeably from this point on.

Even in retrospect, it is still astonishing to learn that no concerted processes have been discovered that represent clear-cut violations of the Woodward-Hoffmann rule. An immense amount of experimental work has been concentrated in this area since 1965, and so it can be said with justification that the Woodward-Hoffmann formulation has achieved a place as one of the great unifying principles of organic chemistry. This should become evident from the results discussed in the next chapter. It is as well to remember, however, that the vast majority of organic reactions occur by stepwise mechanisms, and hence the Woodward-Hoffmann and related theories should not be invoked too liberally, and without adequate grounds. Likewise, it is worth stressing again that 'forbidden' processes are nothing of the kind. A reaction proceeding by way of an anti-aromatic transition state might well occur at a faster rate than its aromatic analogue, if this preferred pathway is made unattainable by steric or geometric factors. Alternatively, even under apparently ideal circumstances, the preferred (i.e. concerted) pathway may not be obtained, for a stepwise mechanism may have a lower energy requirement. This then is the crux of the matter – even concerted processes almost always have an energy of activation, and the various theories herein discussed do not in any way give a quantitative estimate of its magnitude. Normally the activation energy of the preferred concerted pathway will be appreciably lower than those of the alternative concerted processes which proceed via anti-aromatic transition states unless, as already pointed out, other factors intervene. The evaluation of activation energies by means of molecular orbital calculations has been achieved; although understandably the results are somewhat crude at the present time, these approaches are nevertheless very promising.

In conclusion, it would be as well to examine for points of divergence among the various analytical procedures discussed in this and in the previous chapter. A search for such divergences is likely to prove unrewarding, yet there is one area in which total harmony is lacking. This concerns the possibility of pericyclic reactions of odd-alternant π-radicals. Consider, for example, the hypothetical electrocyclic change (Equation 5.10). The various predictions

$$\langle\!\!\!\!\cdot \longrightarrow \left[\langle\!\!\!\!\cdot\,\right]^{\ddagger} \longrightarrow \cdot\!\triangleleft \qquad\qquad (5.10)$$

are summarized in Table 5.1; included also are the results of Dewar's MINDO/2 calculations (Dewar and Kirschner, 1971).

There have been no reports of definitive experimental work on reactions of this type. Such studies are likely to be faced with formidable experimental

TABLE 5.1
Predictions concerning the mechanism¶ and stereochemistry of reaction (Equation 5.10)

Method	Thermal	Photochemical
1. Frontier orbital§	non-concerted	non-concerted
2. Orbital or state correlation diagram#	non-concerted	conrotatory*
3. General Woodward-Hoffmann rule†	conrotatory	disrotatory
4. Zimmerman‡	non-concerted	non-concerted
5. Dewar-Evans‡	non-concerted	non-concerted
6. MINDO/2	disrotatory**	?

¶ Non-concerted is taken also to indicate lack of stereospecificity.
§ Result assumes equal importance of the opposed SOMO-HOMO and SOMO-LUMO interactions (see p. 106).
# See Longuet-Higgins and Abrahamson (1965).
* Disrotatory for the second excited state which is only very slightly higher in energy than the first (assuming the proposed sequence of excited state levels is in fact correct).
† This refers to a rider to the rule (itself based on extended Hückel calculations) which states: 'odd electron systems generally conform to the pattern for even electron systems containing one more electron', Woodward and Hoffmann (1969).
‡ Non-aromatic transition states.
** Calculated activation energy is appreciably larger than that for the ring-opening of the cyclopropyl cation.

problems, not the least of which is the known tendency for radicals (particularly unreactive radicals) to add reversibly to π-bonds and hence facilitate *cis*, *trans*-isomerization. If evidence favouring a stereospecific concerted transformation does come to light, the data is likely to be kinetic rather than stereochemical in origin. For the present, however, the behaviour of these $(4n + 3)$, and the homologous $(4n + 1)$, π-radicals must remain an open question. The remainder of this book will be devoted to the consideration of even-electron systems only.

The organic chemistry of pericyclic reactions   6

In the previous chapters it should have become abundantly clear that concerted pericyclic reactions are promoted either by thermal activation or by photochemical activation, and are almost always highly stereospecific. It is fair to say that in a large number of cases the photochemical reactions have not been investigated with sufficient thoroughness to be sure they are in fact concerted. Stereospecificity in a process is not an unambiguous criterion for concertedness. Implicit to a concerted reaction is the intervention between reactants and products of a *single* transition state; this 'species' has a lifetime of the order of the period of a vibration (*c.* 10^{-13} s). It is possible that in a stepwise reaction the *intermediates* may also, in certain circumstances, have exceedingly short kinetic lifetimes. If such a process is also stereospecific, as may well be the case, then the dinstinction between concertedness and non-concertedness becomes blurred, and may not be open to simple experimental tests.

Increasing numbers of reactions although stereospecific have been shown to proceed in a stepwise manner. Many of these processes utilized photochemical activation or metal catalysis to promote the chemical transformation, so that the interpretation of some of the other reactions in these categories in terms of the Woodward-Hoffmann rules may yet require review.

For convenience the various pericyclic processes will be discussed according to reaction type, and each category is subdivided according to the numbers of participant electrons. The coverage is not intended to be exhaustive,† nor even representative, because for the most part the examples have been drawn from the relatively simple and straightforward pericyclic transformations known at

† The in-breadth coverage of the area is to be found in several comprehensive reviews: Woodward and Hoffmann (1969) Gill (1968), Miller (1968), Gilchrist and Storr (1972), and references cited therein. For thermal unimolecular processes see Frey and Walsh (1969).

the present time. More complex systems are occasionally discussed not only to highlight the diversity of these processes, but also to illustrate the occurrence of particular topological features.

6.1 Electrocyclic reactions

6.1.1 *2-electron processes*

This corresponds to the electrocyclic ring-opening of the cyclopropyl cation; the preferred reaction pathways should involve $[_\omega 0_s + _\sigma 2_s]$ or $[_\omega 0_a + _\sigma 2_a]$ interactions, (Equation 6.1). In simple unfused ring systems the evidence for disrotatory scission comes from kinetic measurements (see below). The stereochemical test is not available because of the interception of the allyl cation by a counter-ion, (Equation 6.2). However, when the cyclopropyl cation is part of a bicyclic system, for example (1), it is found that electrocyclic cleavage occurs readily even when the number n has the small value of 3 or 4. In these circumstances the conrotatory mode, which would yield the unstable *trans-*

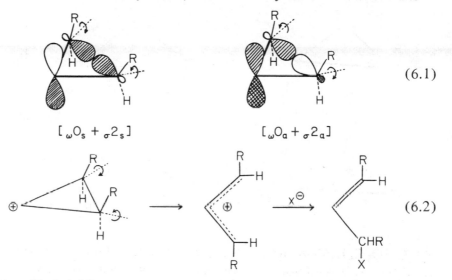

$$[_\omega 0_s + _\sigma 2_s] \qquad\qquad [_\omega 0_a + _\sigma 2_a]$$

$$(6.1)$$

$$(6.2)$$

allyl cation (2), is inhibited and ring-opening should be extremely slow (if concerted) contrary to experimental observations. Disrotation is therefore observed (as predicted) since the much more stable *cis*-allyl cation (3) is the product.

145

The most convincing evidence for the high stereospecificity of these processes comes from the rate data of solvolytic reactions. In certain of these
reactions there is good evidence that the departure of the leaving group X
(where X⁻ is halide or *p*-toluenesulphonyl anion) and ring-scission is concerted
(see also p. 80). Thus reactions (6.3) are inevitably much faster than the

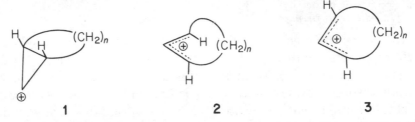

| 1 | 2 | 3 |

reaction (6.4) in which the anchimerically assisted ionization of X⁻ is inhibited
because the inward disrotation of the more bulky substituents R raises the
activation energy for the *cisoid* reaction. Thus, for example, for the case

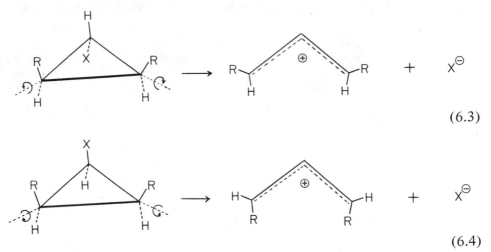

$$(6.3)$$

$$(6.4)$$

$X = O.SO_2C_6H_4Me\text{-}p$ and $R = Me$, the *cis*-tosylate (Equation 6.4) is solvolysed (i.e. AcOH-NaOAc) 4500 times more slowly than its *trans*-isomer
(Equation 6.3).

In certain circumstances the inward rotation of the substituent groups
becomes the only possible mode of disrotation. Consider the epimeric chlorides
(4) and (5). In both cases the cleavage of the bridging σ-bond must be attended

146

by the *outward* rotation of the bridgehead H-atoms in order that the *cis*-allyl cation (**6**) is formed rather than the highly strained *trans*-cation (**7**). The *endo*-chloride (**4**) is solvolysed (AcOH-NaOAc) readily at 125° since anchimeric assistance for the ionization is geometrically possible. The *exo*-chloride (**5**), however, remains unchanged, under identical conditions, in 700 h.

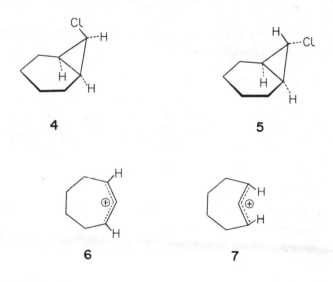

4   **5**

6   **7**

When the bridging ring is somewhat larger the *inward* rotation of the bridgehead H-atoms becomes sterically feasible, and anchimerically assisted ionization for the *exo*-halide becomes available. Thus, solvolysis of the *exo*-bromide (**8**) gives *trans*-cyclo-oct-1-en-3-ol (Equation 6.5).

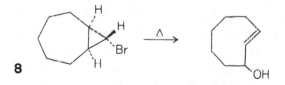

8   (6.5)

These solvolytic reactions are useful means for ring expansion. The cyclo-propane ring is formed readily by the addition of a halogeno-carbene across the termini of the double bond in a cyclo-alkene. With a monohalogeno car-bene a mixture of *endo*- and *exo*-halogenobicycloalkanes is formed, only one

147

of which will usually be solvolytically reactive. It is expeditious, therefore, to utilize a dihalogenocarbene, (Equation 6.6).

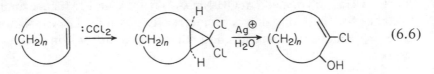

$$(6.6)$$

The analogous ring expansions of 3-membered heterocycles has also been observed, for example Equation (6.7).

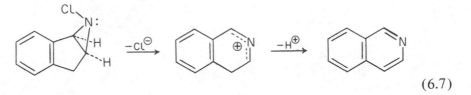

$$(6.7)$$

6.1.2   4-electron processes

Direct observation of the electrocyclic cleavage of the cyclopropyl anion has been reported for one case, (Equation 6.8); the observed conrotatory mode is the predicted thermochemical pathway. An isoelectronic system has provided

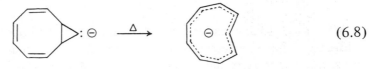

$$(6.8)$$

the definitive results in this area. The *cis*- and *trans*-aziridine diesters (9) and (10) undergo conrotatory fission at 100° to form the dipolar 4π-electron intermediates indicated in Equation (6.9). These interconvert more slowly at the reaction temperature than they are intercepted by dimethylacetylene dicarboxylate in $[_\pi 2_s + _\pi 4_s]$ cyclo-addition processes. The stereochemistry of the initial electrocyclic change follows from the nature of the cyclo-adduct finally produced; (9) → (11) and (10) → (12). The alternative conversions (9) → (12) and (10) → (11) must result from electrocyclic reactions of the type $[_\omega 2_s + _\sigma 2_s]$ or $[_\omega 2_a + _\sigma 2_a]$, that is disrotatory cleavage. These are the preferred photochemical pathways, and they have also been observed for this system.

148

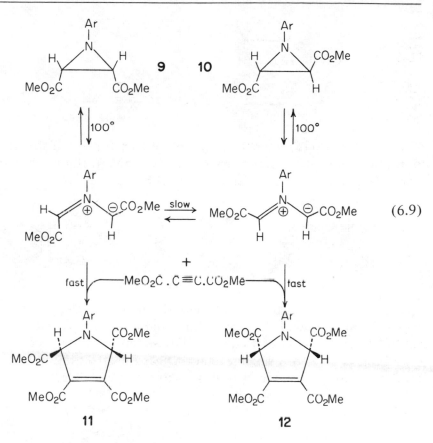

(6.9)

The few other iso-electronic systems that have been studied have also furnished the expected results.

The butadiene-cyclobutene electrocyclic interconversions are predicted to occur thermochemically by way of $[_\sigma 2_s + _\pi 2_a]$ or $[_\sigma 2_a + _\pi 2_s]$ interactions, which again involves a conrotatory motion about the relevant bond axes. Since usually butadienes are thermodynamically more stable than their cyclobutene valence isomers, it is the ring fission process that is normally observed. Many of these reactions can be put into a general form as in reactions (6.10) and (6.11), where A and B typically are Cl, Me, C_6H_5, Ar, and CO_2Me. The isomeric cis,cis-compounds are not usually obtained in reaction (6.11), and on simple steric grounds they would not be expected. In the case of the deuter-

149

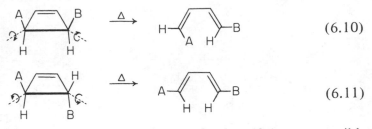

(6.10)

(6.11)

iated cyclobutene (**13**), there is a slight preference for one of the two possible conrotatory modes; this secondary kinetic isotope effect arises because of the shorter length of C–D bonds relative to C–H bonds.

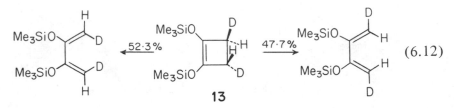

(6.12)

Although the *cis*-fused cyclobutenes (**14**) and (**15**) suffer conrotatory thermochemical σ-bond cleavage without undue difficulty, reactions (6.13) and (6.14), the stability of such molecules is considerably increased if the second ring is smaller. A small second ring has the effect of raising the ground state energy of the cyclobutene, thus making it more labile, while at the same

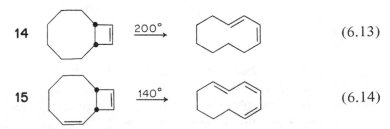

(6.13)

(6.14)

time the concerted conrotatory cleavage is inhibited because of the higher activation energy now needed to develop the *transoid* double bond in the activated complex. Thus molecules of the type (**16**) are cleaved to (**17**) only at rather elevated temperatures. Non-concerted mechanisms presumably operate, and it is to be expected that if the substituents X and Z are able to delocalize charge, or an odd electron, then rather milder conditions might be sufficient to effect the cleavage. Likewise, mild conditions might suffice in

150

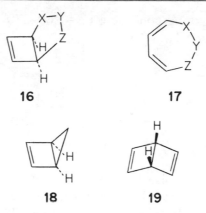

16   **17**

18   **19**

the cleavage of highly strained cyclobutenes (e.g. **18** and **19**), particularly if the product of the reaction is of very low energy (**19** gives benzene). In actual fact the conversion of (**18**) into cyclopentadiene involves the *allowed* $[_\pi 2_s + _\sigma 2_a]$ *reverse cyclo-addition* process, (Equation 6.15), so that generalizations should be made with some caution.

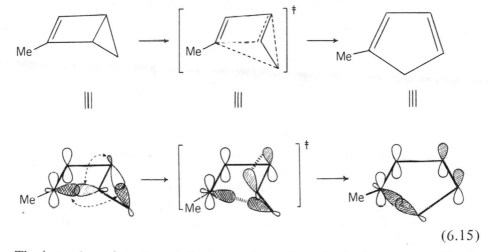

(6.15)

The interplay of steric and electronic factors are nicely demonstrated in the thermolyses of compounds (**20**) and (**21**). The *trans*-compounds (**21**), for which conrotation is geometrically possible, are cleaved to the isomeric butadienes at 90–110° (E_a = 27–29 kcal mole^{-1}; 113–122 kJ mole^{-1}). In contrast, the reaction of the *cis*-compounds (**20**) at the same rate ($k_1 \sim 10^{-4}$ s^{-1})

requires much more vigorous conditions ($T = 260\text{--}270°$; E_a = 42–45 kcal mole^{-1}, 176–189 kJ mole^{-1}).

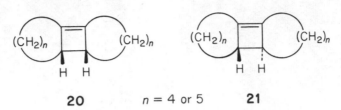

20   n = 4 or 5   **21**

The pentadienyl cation is isoelectronic with butadiene, and has also been shown to follow the predicted stereochemical pathway for electrocyclic closure, (Equation 6.16). Irradiation of the ketone (**22**; R = H) yields the *cis*-isomer of (**23**; R = H); the predicted $[_\sigma 2_s + _\pi 2_s]$ or $[_\sigma 2_a + _\pi 2_a]$ disrotatory

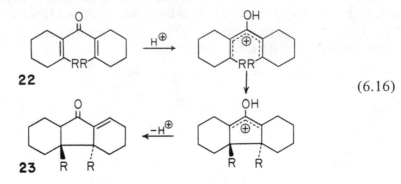

(6.16)

cyclizations are thought to be involved. Likewise, irradiation of 1,1′-bicyclo-hexenyl furnishes (**20**: n = 4), as expected. Even better evidence for the validity of the Woodward-Hoffmann rules for photochemical electrocyclic reactions is given by Equation (6.17). Here the reactant acyclic butadiene suffers from no geometrical restraints, and yet the thermodynamically less stable cyclobutene isomer is formed as required by the theory. In the

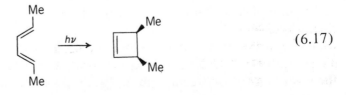

(6.17)

majority of the photochemical butadiene → cyclobutene processes that have been observed, the geometries of the reactants were such that *only* the predicted disrotatory pathways were possible, for example Equation (6.18).

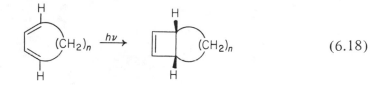

$$(6.18)$$

However, in the case $n = 5$ the monocyclic *cis,trans*-diene is also known, and it furnishes the *trans*-fused bicyclic system on irradiation, and the *cis*-fused cyclobutene on thermal activation; both transformations are as predicted.

The $[_\sigma 2_s + _\pi 2_s]$ electrocyclic photochemical cyclization is important from the preparative viewpoint. The interesting but labile compounds Dewar benzene (**19**) and cyclobutadiene have been prepared by such means, Equations (6.19) and (6.20). The anti-aromatic cyclobutadiene is too reactive to be isolated, but is conveniently trapped as the tricarbonyliron(0) complex from which it can be later regenerated under oxidative conditions, for example by using cerium (IV) salts.

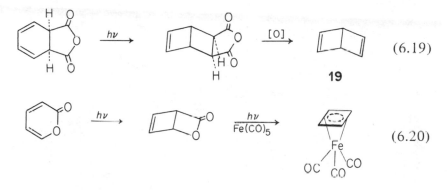

$$(6.19)$$

$$(6.20)$$

6.1.3   *6-electron processes*

The hexatriene-cyclohexadiene interconversion is the prototype reaction for this category. The thermochemical cyclizations, for example Equations (6.21)–(6.23), confirm the predicted $[_\sigma 2_s + _\pi 4_s]$ or $[_\sigma 2_a + _\pi 4_a]$ pathway. The last example illustrates the operation of both of the possible disrotatory modes.

153

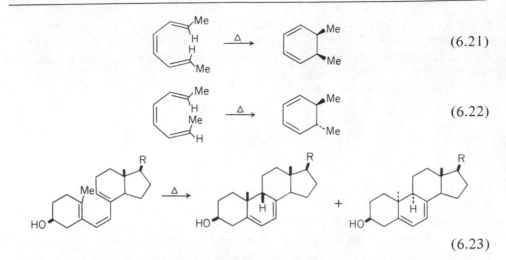

$$(6.21)$$

$$(6.22)$$

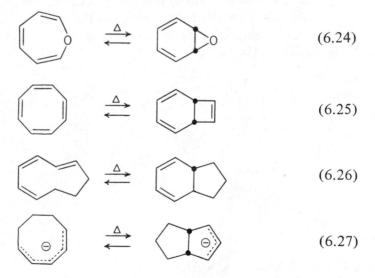

$$(6.23)$$

The valence isomerization of the hexatriene moiety when embedded in a cyclic array of atoms is also well known, Equations (6.24)–(6.27).

$$(6.24)$$

$$(6.25)$$

$$(6.26)$$

$$(6.27)$$

The valence isomerization of cyclo-octatetraene (Equation 6.25) has been shown by Huisgen *et al.* to be the first step in the interesting thermal rearrangement of bromocyclo-octatetraene into *trans*-β-bromostyrene. The illustrative (Equation 6.28) reaction course is for the analogous 1,4-dibromo-compound.

154

The key step is the ionization of the allylic bridgehead bromine atom, which receives anchimeric assistance from the strategically placed π-lobes of the cyclobutene double bond. The recombination of the ion pair is therefore stereospecific, and the final conrotatory cleavage of the cyclobutene ring furnishes the *trans*-β-bromostyrene exclusively.

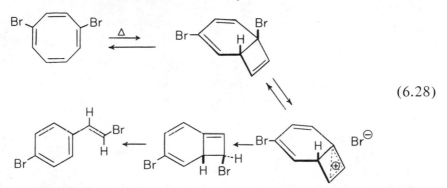

(6.28)

The position of the disrotatory cycloheptatriene-norcaradiene equilibrium (cf. Equation 6.24; $>O = >CXY$) is very dependent on the C7 substituents X and Y. Electron withdrawing π-substituents (e.g. CN) appear to be essential for the stabilization of the norcaradiene valence isomer. Valence isomerization in the azocine series is also structure dependent. Thus (24) is wholly converted into (25) in the cases $n = 3$ or 4, whereas with $n = 5$ the equilibrium is only established at $100°$, and when $n = 6$ only (24) is present.

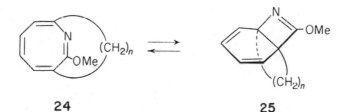

24   25

The photochemically allowed $[_\sigma 2_s + _\pi 4_a]$ or $[_\sigma 2_a + _\pi 4_s]$ pathways are also well documented, for example Equation (6.29). The cleavage processes are also known, and if these processes are followed by recyclization under purely thermal control, then *cis-trans* isomerizations have been observed, e.g. Equation (6.30). A similar reaction sequence has been proposed for the photoisomerization of *trans*-9,10-dihydronaphthalene to the *cis*-isomer, in which case the interesting 10π-electron molecule cyclodecapentaene (i.e. [10]-annulene) is an intermediate. The 9,10-dihydronaphthalenes are labile compounds, and exposure to oxygen is sufficient to effect their oxidation to

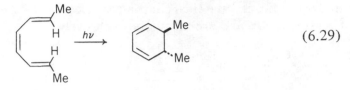

$$(6.29)$$

naphthalene. Similarly simple 9,10-disubstituted naphthalenes are degraded to 1,5- and 2,6-disubstituted naphthalenes unless the 9,10-substituents are linked to form a cyclical bridge. Several propellanes, as they are called, are now known.

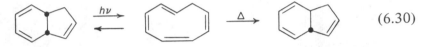

$$(6.30)$$

The different stereochemical features of thermal and photochemical $[_\sigma 2 + _\pi 4]$ processes are nicely summarized in the reactions of [16]-annulene, (Equation 6.31). The cyclizations occur at the termini of the *trans,cis,trans*-hexatriene units of the [16]-annulene structure.

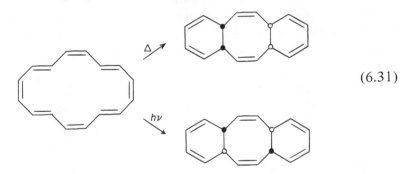

$$(6.31)$$

6.1.4 *8-electron and higher order processes*

Very few reactions in this category have come to light. The thermal isomerization of 9,9-dimethylbicyclo[6,1,0]nonatriene (**26**) yields the expected *trans*-8,9-dihydroindene (**27**); first step conrotatory, second step disrotatory, (Equation 6.32). Rather less clear-cut results are obtained for other compounds in this series, including the parent hydrocarbon of (**26**). The photochemical

156

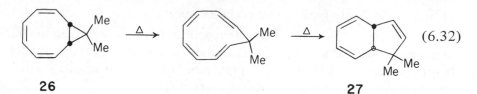

26   **27**   (6.32)

isomerization of (**28**) has been reported to give [16]-annulene (double disrotation).

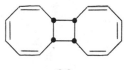

28

The thermal electrocylic closure of 8-electron systems has also been observed, Equations (6.33) and (6.34); the initial products have the expected stereochemistry and can be isomerized further to bicyclic molecules by disrotatory closure across the termini of the hexatriene systems. Reactions (6.35) and (6.36) are related processes to those discussed above.

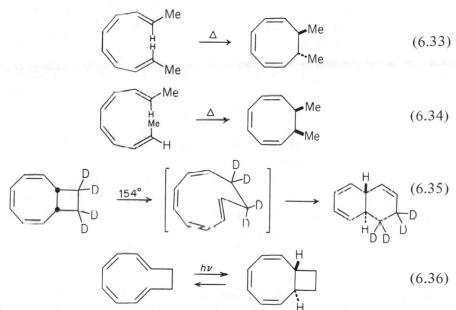

(6.33)

(6.34)

(6.35)

(6.36)

157

6.1.5   *Metal-catalysed electrocyclic reactions*

Quite a number of metal-catalysed pericyclic reactions are known in which the topology of the reactions parallel that expected for the uncatalysed photo-chemical, rather than the thermal, processes. A few electrocyclic reactions fall into this category, for example Equation (6.37).

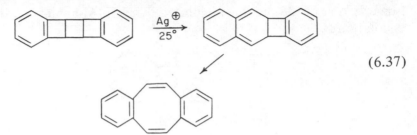

$$\text{(6.37)}$$

In the majority of these cases, however, it is clear that the 'thermally allowed' processes cannot operate because of geometric restraints. The function of the metal atom or ion might then be simply to reduce the activation energy of the geometrically possible transformation, which could occur by a step-wise mechanism. The ultimate chemical test of this non-concerted pathway would be the isolation or detection of a σ-bonded organo-metallic intermediate. This is by no means an easy task, particularly since the metal is often effective at the catalytic level of concentration. In the absence of chemical proof to the contrary, it is therefore tempting to assume that all metal-catalysed processes are concerted. Each of the various theories is capable of extension to include for the in-phase interaction of the metal-substrate molecular orbitals, and in each case one can obtain a theoretical match for the experimental observations. However, further experimental work has shown in a few cases that the reactions are not concerted, for example in some of the Fe(0) and Rh(I) catalysed [1,3] hydrogen shifts. There is circumstantial evidence that the Ag^+ ion (although a d^{10} system is yet an efficient catalyst for certain electrocyclic and reverse cyclo-addition processes) reacts with the substrate to form argento-carbonium ions (Paquette, 1971). It seems unlikely, therefore, that the Woodward-Hoffmann theory will find uniform application in this area.†

† For a discussion of the possible role of orbital symmetry relationships in metal catalysed pericyclic reactions see Pettit *et al.* (1969), Mango (1969), and Schrauzer (1968).

6.2   Cyclo-additions reactions

6.2.1   *2-electron processes*

The formation of a bridged ion (e.g. **29**) by the capture of a proton by a π-bond must certainly be an example of an $[_\omega 0_s + _\pi 2_s]$ reaction. There are many processes, including the reactions of saturated hydrocarbons with protons in highly acidic media, that could be regarded as proceeding by way of related non-classical ions.

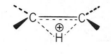

29

6.2.2   *4-electron processes*

The reactions in this category are 4-centre 4-electron processes. The related 3-centre 4-electron process involved in the addition of singlet carbenes to olefinic π-bonds, is discussed under cheletropic reactions.

The number of examples of $[2_s + 2_a]$ reactions, the predicted thermochemical pathway, is relatively small. The second step of reaction (4.2) has been interpreted as a $[_\pi 2_s + _\pi 2_a]$ cyclo-addition, and the thermal isomerization of bicyclo[1,1,0]butanes, for example, reactions (6.38) and (6.39), have been likewise regarded as $[_\sigma 2_s + _\sigma 2_a]$ retro cyclo-additions. The high temperatures

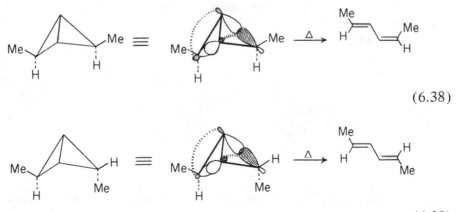

(6.38)

(6.39)

required for reactions (6.38) and (6.39) has been put down to unfavourable steric factors rather than to the occurrence of a non-concerted stepwise mechanism. Reaction (6.15) has previously been mentioned as an example of a $[_\sigma 2_s + _\sigma 2_a]$ process.

The loss of CO_2 from β-lactones (Equation 6.40) is often stereospecific, as is the loss of $HN{=}C{=}O$ from β-lactams; both may be formally regarded as $[_\sigma 2_s + _\sigma 2_a]$ retro cyclo-additions. In the cleavage of 1,2-dioxetans, however,

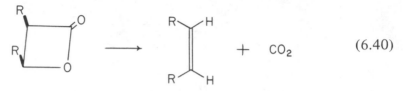

$$\text{(6.40)}$$

one of the carbonyl fragments is formed in an excited state (chemiluminescence), and the reaction presumably involves the $[_\sigma 2_s + _\sigma 2_s]$ mode, (Equation 6.41). In the majority of the known examples of $[2 + 2]$ reactions stepwise

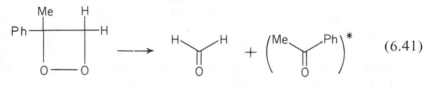

$$\text{(6.41)}$$

mechanisms are known to operate (e.g. Equation 6.42), presumably because the concerted $[2_s + 2_a]$ pathway is difficult to realize and the substituents may be capable of stabilizing the diradical or dipolar intermediate. The stereospecificity of such non-concerted reactions then depends on the relative lifetimes of the intermediates.

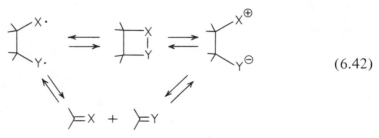

$$\text{(6.42)}$$

In the known cases of photochemical $[2 + 2]$ reactions one of the systems, of necessity, is always a π-component. This arises because σ-components are not good absorbing chromophores from the experimental standpoint; examples of $[_\pi 2_s + _\pi 2_s]$ processes are given by reactions (6.43) and (6.44). In several instances the dimerization of simple olefins requires photosensitiz-

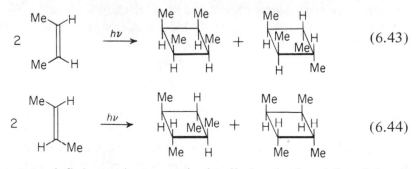

(6.43)

(6.44)

ation, triplet state olefinic species are undoubtedly involved and thereby diradical intermediates can form. Non-concerted photochemical [2 + 2] reactions are common and in several cases the sensitizer (usually a ketonic C=O function) resides in the same molecule as the olefinic π-bond. These dimerizations have a considerable synthetic importance.

The unsensitized conversion of norbornadiene into quadricyclane (Equation 6.45), long regarded as the classical example of a $[_\pi 2_s + _\pi 2_s]$ reaction, has now been re-interpreted in terms of a non-concerted mechanism. Other examples of possible concerted $[_\sigma 2_s + _\pi 2_s]$ reactions are shown in Equations (6.46) and (6.47).

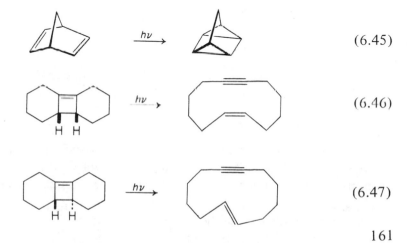

(6.45)

(6.46)

(6.47)

161

6.2.3   6-electron processes

The six-electron cyclo-addition and reversion processes are by far the most common of all pericyclic changes. This is largely due to the fact that $[2_s + 4_s]$ processes are both geometrically and energetically favourable. Within this category falls the well-known Diels-Alder reaction, for which no more than a very brief survey can be given here.†

The prototype Diels-Alder reaction is that between buta-1,3-diene and ethylene which generates cyclohexene [e.g. see Equation (3.5)]. Many structural variations are possible on both components, with the most scope for elaboration apparently resting with the π^2-system, or dienophile. Although structural variations of the π^4-component (or diene) are well-documented, these are a bit limited by the need for this system to be a good electron donor and not too sterically hindered (i.e. the s-cis-conformation must be attainable). The most efficient dienophiles characteristically have a particularly electron-deficient π-bond, or one that is strained, or is part of an anti-aromatic π-system, (30)–(38). Strained σ-bonds are capable of reacting in a similar manner, although it is not clear with cyclopropanone (39), for example, if the reactions

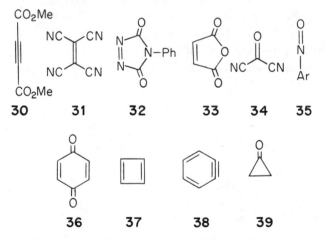

are concerted. A few typical Diels-Alder (6.48)–(6.52) and retro Diels-Alder (6.53)–(6.57) reactions (see Kwart and King, 1968) are given as illustrative examples, and the preferred endo-addition is seen in reactions (6.48)–(6.50).

† For leading reviews see: Huisgen et al. (1964), Wassermann (1965), Hamer (1967), Carruthers (1971), Onishchenko (1964), Seltzer (1968), and Kwart and King (1968).

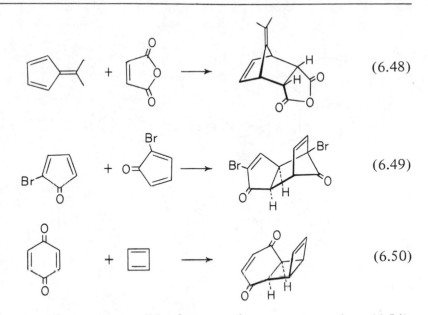

(6.48)

(6.49)

(6.50)

Many of these reactions are reversible, for example compare reactions (6.54) and (4.3). However, the formation of a molecule of particularly low energy [e.g. Equations (6.53), (6.56), and (6.57)] makes the equilibrium constant so large that the process becomes essentially irreversible.

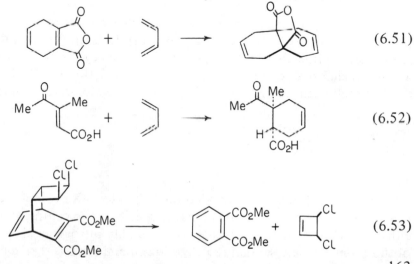

(6.51)

(6.52)

(6.53)

163

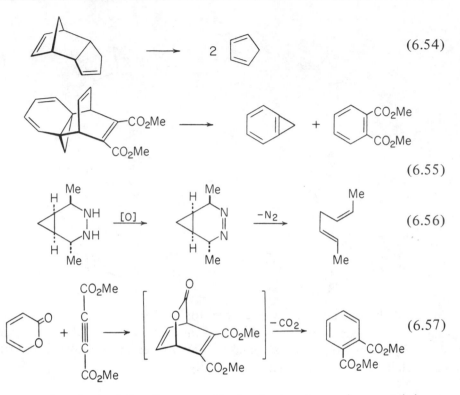

(6.54)

(6.55)

(6.56)

(6.57)

A structural variant of the dienes are the isoelectronic species containing only three framework atoms, (Equation 6.58); Huisgen (1963, 1964). Although, in principle, the XYZ molecule can be negatively charged (e.g. allyl anion), in almost all of the known examples of reaction (6.58) this system is an electrically neutral dipolar species, and the reactions are commonly

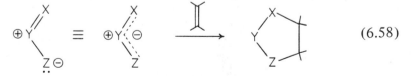

(6.58)

referred to as 1,3-dipolar cyclo-additions. The atoms X, Y, and Z are commonly C, N, or O, and various combinations are possible. The central atom Y can be either *sp*-hybridized, in which case it is invariably nitrogen and XYZ is linear, or this atom can be essentially *sp²*-hybridized and XYZ is then a bent molecule.

If the central sp^2-hybridized atom is carbon, the 1,3-dipolar molecule must then have a net deficiency of two electrons, and it will be exceptionally reactive. The known species of this type are α,β-unsaturated carbenes and nitrenes, for which other types of reaction are available, including a tendency towards internal rearrangement of the group R [in XC(R)Z] from the carbon atoms to either X or Z (depending upon which of these two atoms possesses only six electrons).

The formation of the two new σ-bonds is unlikely to be equally advanced in the transition states of 1,3-dipolar cyclo-additions because of the highly unsymmetrical nature of the cyclic array of participating atoms. Nevertheless, in most cases these reactions appear to be concerted, and they have proven valuable in heterocyclic synthesis. A few examples are shown in Equations (6.59)–(6.64). Reaction (6.63) marks one of the earliest proofs not only of

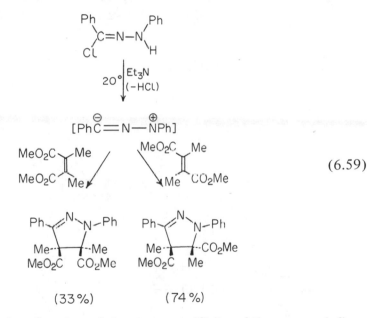

(6.59)

(33%)　　　　(74%)

molozonide formation, but also of the stereospecificity of the ozone-olefin cyclo-addition. This interpretation of such results has, however, recently been challenged. Reaction (6.64) illustrates both 1,3-dipolar and retro 1,3-dipolar cyclo-addition reactions in a single sequence. The retro reaction is fairly uncommon at present.

165

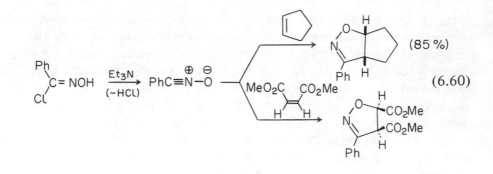

$$(6.60)$$

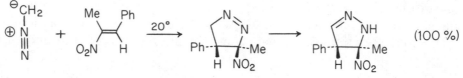

$$(100\%)$$

$$(6.61)$$

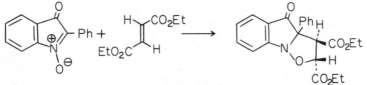

$$(6.62)$$

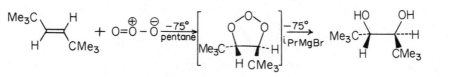

$$(6.63)$$

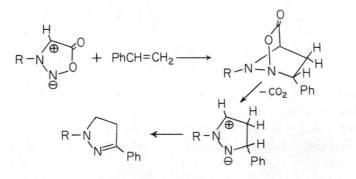

$$(6.64)$$

There is an additional problem in [2 + 4] cyclo-additions concerning the relative orientations of the two components when both are unsymmetrical. Orientation effects are almost always observed in Diels-Alder reactions, and there exists a simple method for predicting the outcome of a given reaction. Consider, for example, the reactions of the dienes (40) and (41) with the olefin (42). The various possible transition state orientations are (43) and (44) for diene (40), and (45) and (46) for diene (41). The *ortho* and *para* orientations (44) or (45) are strongly preferred, and the major products are derived from

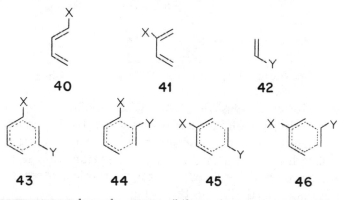

these arrangements, perhaps because of the extra conjugative interaction of the substituents with the 6-electron system when so placed. The major reaction pathway is yet further promoted by the presence of a Lewis acid catalyst (e.g. $ZnCl_2$, BF_3, $AlCl_3$, $SnCl_4$, etc.), presumably through an increase in the polar character of the transition state. Compare for example the ratio of the products obtained in the uncatalysed and $AlCl_3$-catalysed reaction (Equation 6.65).

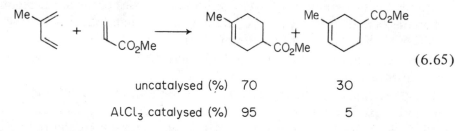

(6.65)

uncatalysed (%)	70	30
$AlCl_3$ catalysed (%)	95	5

The Lewis acid catalysts are also useful for increasing the rates of Diels-Alder reactions. This enables some reactions to be carried out at much lower temperatures, or other rather slow reactions to be performed under reasonable experimental conditions. The *endo*-specificity is often also increased in these catalysed processes, (Equation 6.66). Reasonable predictions can also be made on the orientations in 1,3-dipolar cyclo-additions.

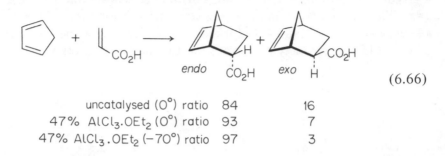

$$\text{endo} \qquad \text{exo} \tag{6.66}$$

uncatalysed (0°) ratio	84	16
47% AlCl$_3$.OEt$_2$ (0°) ratio	93	7
47% AlCl$_3$.OEt$_2$ (−70°) ratio	97	3

The transition states in Diels-Alder and in 1,3-dipolar cyclo-additions are isoconjugate respectively with benzene (or a substituted benzene to be precise) and cyclopentadienyl anion (or the appropriate hetero-aromatic system). Aromatic stabilization is also available for cationic transition states provided that the six electrons are delocalized over seven atomic centres. Few examples are known, but reaction (6.67) is in this category.

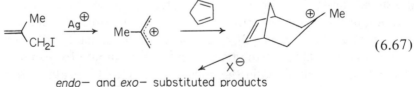

$$\tag{6.67}$$

endo− and *exo−* substituted products

Interesting two-component cyclo-addition processes occur in the reactions of ketenes (and of other systems containing cumulated double bonds) with olefins.† A typical example is given by the reaction of ketene with cyclopentadiene, (Equation 6.68). It is notable that the 6-membered ring, the normal Diels-Alder product, is not formed.

These reactions may be regarded as involving four or six electrons, so that the allowed pathways should be as follows: (i) [$_\pi 2_s + _\pi 2_a$], (ii) [$_\pi 2_s + _\pi 2_s + _\pi 2_s$], (iii) [$_\pi 2_s + _\pi 2_a + _\pi 2_a$], or (iv) [$_\pi 2_s + _\pi 4_s$]. In each case we are limited by the

† For leading reviews see: Ulrich (1968), Fischer (1964), Taylor (1967), and Baldwin and Ford (1969).

168

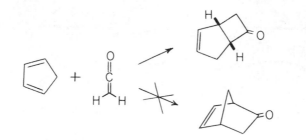

$$(6.68)$$

assumption that the olefin interacts in the geometrically realizable $_\pi 2_s$ mode. In terms of the orbital analysis, only the type (i) interaction is distinctly different from the others and it is the pathway favoured by Woodward and Hoffmann (1969). Their analysis emphasizes the electrophilic character of the central sp-carbon atom of the ketene, and this property is expressed in the extreme valence bond structure (47), which finds analogy with the vinylium cation (48). In other words the ketene has a low-lying acceptor orbital $\pi_{C=O}^*$ which is orthogonal to the bonding $\pi_{C=C}$-level (49). For the vinylium cation the acceptor orbital is the localized p-orbital on the sp-carbon atom. Woodward and Hoffmann conclude that it is the presence of these orbitals that gives

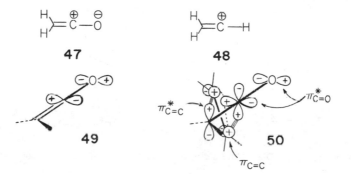

added weight to the orthogonal olefin $\pi_{C=C}$-HOMO-ketene $\pi_{C=C}^*$-LUMO interactions, since additional attractive HOMO-LUMO interactions are then possible, (50). The alternative LUMO-HOMO interaction (olefin $\pi_{C=C}^*$ and ketene $\pi_{C=C}$) does not yield additional stabilization, but the mixing of these two levels is regarded as less important. The lower steric requirement of the ketene sp-carbon atom relative to the sp^2-carbons of simple olefins, is another feature

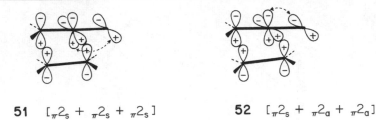

51 $[_\pi 2_s + _\pi 2_s + _\pi 2_s]$ **52** $[_\pi 2_s + _\pi 2_a + _\pi 2_a]$

in favour of the $[_\pi 2_s + _\pi 2_a]$ interaction in these systems. The other three analyses (ii)–(iv) are equally attractive, and (ii) and (iii) have the virtue of con-ceptual simplicity, (51) and (52). In effect, however, either of these inter-actions is equivalent to the $[_\pi 2_s + _\pi 4_s]$ mode because in each case there is an in-phase overlap of six atomic orbitals (i.e. all are Hückel systems). In a sense the 1,2-diene may be regarded as a normal (i.e. 1,3-diene) Diels-Alder com-ponent except that one of the double bonds is folded back on itself. The direct equivalence between the simple Diels-Alder $[_\pi 2_s + _\pi 4_s]$ reaction and the ketene-olefin cyclo-addition is illustrated in Fig. 6.1. This analysis is due to Dewar.

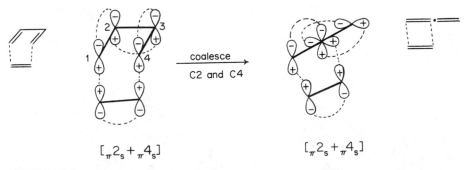

coalesce
C2 and C4

$[_\pi 2_s + _\pi 4_s]$ $[_\pi 2_s + _\pi 4_s]$

FIGURE 6.1
Correspondence between the Diels-Alder olefin-diene reaction and the olefin-ketene reaction as $[_\pi 2_s + _\pi 4_s]$ processes

The reaction of a substituted ketene with cyclopentadiene produces a cyclobutanone in which the bulkiest substituent is in the *endo*-configuration,

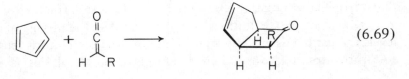

(6.69)

for example reaction (6.69). Both the Woodward-Hoffmann and the Dewar transition state geometries are capable of rationalizing the stereospecificity of this reaction; the Dewar formulation is simpler and is shown in Fig. 6.2. The major steric interactions exist between the ketene substituents R or H and the H atom at C2 of the diene; clearly the H–H interaction is of lower energy, and the preferred conformation is as shown. This leads directly to the *endo*-product.

A number of cumulene-olefin cyclo-additions appear to be non-concerted, notably when hetero-atoms are present and the 1,4-dipolar zwitterionic intermediates are likely to be stabilized. Reaction (6.68), although concerted, shows some of this character since the isomeric cyclobutanone is not produced. The presence of hetero-atoms is not essential to a stepwise mechanism.

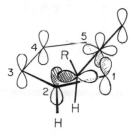

FIGURE 6.2
The topology of the monosubstituted ketene-cyclopentadiene interaction

Thus in the dimerization reactions of allenes, or in their cyclo-addition reactions to olefins, non-concerted pathways appear to be favoured. The allene dimers are always of the head-to-head, tail-to-tail, type which suggests that 1,4-diradical intermediates are formed in these reactions. The stereo-specific addition that may attend these and related reactions may merely be an indication of the lack of conformational flexibility of the diradical intermediates because of steric crowding.

The alternative $[_\pi 2_a + _\pi 4_a]$ thermochemical pathway has been invoked tentatively in a few cases, as have the $[_\pi 2_s + _\pi 4_a]$ and $[_\pi 2_a + _\pi 4_s]$ interactions in certain intramolecular photochemical isomerizations. None of these interpretations are without some form of ambiguity, but usually because of incomplete experimental data.

171

6.2.4   8-electron and higher order processes

Relatively few reactions in this category have come to light, and detailed mechanistic studies tend to be lacking. The interpretation of these processes in terms of the general Woodward-Hoffmann rule may yet prove to be incorrect in several cases. For this reason this section is given but brief coverage.

[4 + 4] cyclo-addition reactions are well known, but have been observed only in photochemical reactions for which the $[_\pi 4_s + _\pi 4_s]$ pathway is available. Stereochemical information is frequently lacking, and non-concerted pathways have not usually been excluded. An example of a reaction of this type is given by the first step of reaction (4.2).

Only one or two [6 + 2] reactions have yet been discovered. The transformation (Equation 6.70) possibly involves a $[_\pi 6_s + _\pi 2_s]$ interaction in the first step followed by a reverse cyclo-addition of the $[_\sigma 2_s + _\sigma 2_s + _\sigma 2_s]$ type in the second step. Chlorosulphonyl isocyanate reacts with cycloheptatriene (Equation 6.71) to yield three cyclo-adducts, apparently by formal $[_\pi 6_s + _\pi 2_a]$ and $[_\pi 2_s + _\pi 2_a]$ processes. However, it seems more likely that the 1,4-dipolar species (53) is an intermediate in the change.

$$(6.70)$$

 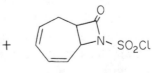

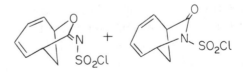

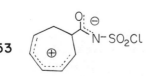

53

$$(6.71)$$

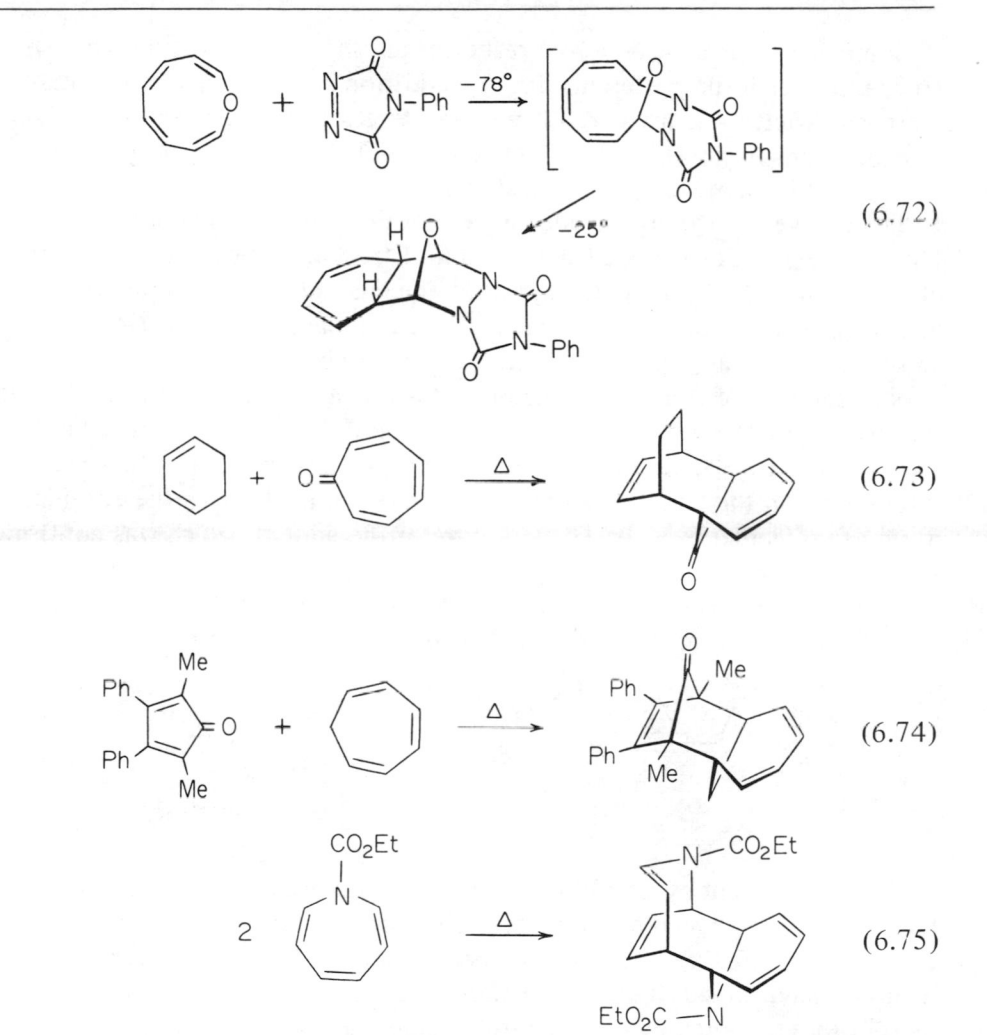

(6.72)

(6.73)

(6.74)

(6.75)

The ten-electron cases are represented by [6 + 4] and [8 + 2] processes. The former now appear to be well characterized, but the [8 + 2] reactions are comparatively rare and the known examples are ambiguous. An [8 + 2] cyclo-addition is possibly involved in reaction (6.72). The initial adduct, shown to be present at lower temperatures, underwent a further electrocyclic transformation with disrotation. Again, however, the available evidence does not rule out a 1,4-dipolar intermediate (cf. 53).

Some examples of $[_\pi 6_s + _\pi 4_s]$ reactions are shown in Equations (6.73)–(6.75), in which the preference for *exo*-addition is clearly apparent. This stereospecificity was predicted from considerations based on the secondary perturbations in the HOMO-LUMO and LUMO-HOMO interactions (see p. 105), and other examples are also known.

The twelve-electron cyclo-additions have the three formal possibilities, [6 + 6], [8 + 4], or [10 + 2]. Irradiation of tropone yields a [6 + 6] dimer; although the $[_\pi 6_s + _\pi 6_s]$ pathway should be characterized by a relatively low activation energy, there is no evidence that the reaction is concerted. The other twelve electron cases are likewise not documented.

No examples of fourteen electron cyclo-additions have come to light, but one sixteen electron case is known, (Equation 6.76). Of the two predicted pathways, $[_\pi 14_a + _\pi 2_s]$ or $[_\pi 14_s + _\pi 2_a]$, the one involving an antarafacial interaction on the $_\pi 2$ component appears most unlikely from the consideration of molecular models. The structure of the adduct, which was confirmed by single crystal X-ray crystallographic analysis, indicates the assigned $[_\pi 14_a + _\pi 2_s]$ pathway to be correct. The antarafacial interaction on the heptafulvalene molecule is possible because of its twisted shape.

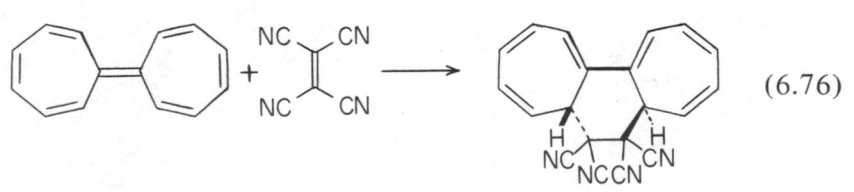

(6.76)

Two component cyclo-additions of higher order have yet to be discovered. Except in a few special cases the activation parameters, notably the entropy of activation, are likely to provide insurmountable barriers to reaction. Indeed, it should have already become obvious from the examples quoted in this section that the entropy considerations demand that at least one, and frequently both, of the olefinic π-systems should be constrained within a cyclic framework of atoms. In this way the interacting termini are held sufficiently close for the appropriate time for reaction to proceed at an observable rate. With increases in the extent of the π-systems other factors must be considered, not the least of which is the possibility of realizing the electron delocalization in the transition state. Although it is not necessary for all of the atoms in each of the two components to assume a co-polanar relationship with the other atoms of its own set, nevertheless severe departures from co-planarity can only disrupt the necessarily extensive through conjugation by orbital-orbital overlap. In many projected high order cyclo-addition reactions, therefore, it may be confidently expected that only the concerted cyclo-additions of a lower order will be observed, or the reactions will occur by a stepwise mechanism.

6.2.5 *Multicomponent cyclo-additions*

The vast majority of organic reactions involve, at the transition state, the cleavage of only one bond and/or the formation of one bond. Since, for all but the most highly exothermic chemical processes, the degree of bond-breaking at the transition state is usually quite well advanced, it is also generally true that the degree of formation of the new bond is not so well advanced. Because the two processes do not perfectly complement each other, an energy of activation is almost always necessary. In three-component cyclo-additions, where three bonds are cleaved and three formed in the rate determining step, it may be anticipated that the activation energies will be higher than those of the comparable two-component cyclo-additions. The entropy of activation is also of crucial importance, and results in another demarcation in the rates of related two- and three-component processes. The cyclic trimerization of three molecules of ethylene, for example, is so improbable (because each molecule has to be in the correct nuclear configuration with sufficient energy for sufficient time) that the reaction rate is negligible. Accordingly, it is found to be necessary to embed at least two of the three components in a single molecule, and frequently this molecule will have additional geometrical restraints that restrict conformational flexibility.

Among multicomponent cyclo-addition reactions, the [2 + 2 + 2] case is by far the most common, and the *supra-supra-supra* mode is encountered most frequently, Equations (6.77), (6.78). The $[_\sigma 2_s + _\sigma 2_a + _\pi 2_a]$ interaction, also a predicted mode, appears to be involved in the degenerate isomerization of snoutene (Equation 6.79). The awkward $_\sigma 2_a$ interaction is facilitated by the

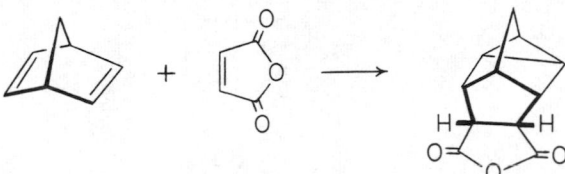

$$(6.77)$$

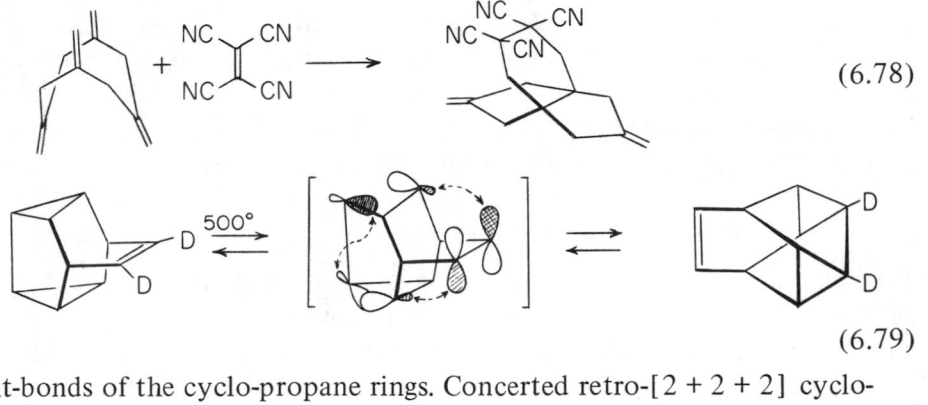

(6.78)

(6.79)

bent-bonds of the cyclo-propane rings. Concerted retro-[2 + 2 + 2] cyclo-additions are relatively uncommon, probably because of the higher than usual activation energy necessary to promote these reactions. Most of the known cases involve the formation of low molecular weight molecules of high thermo-dynamic stability, Equations (6.80) and (6.81), but this in itself is no guarantee of success. For example, the thermolysis of ethylene oxalate, (54), most prob-ably occurs by a stepwise mechanism judging by the complexity of the pro-duct mixture, and triprismane (55) is remarkably stable in view of the fact

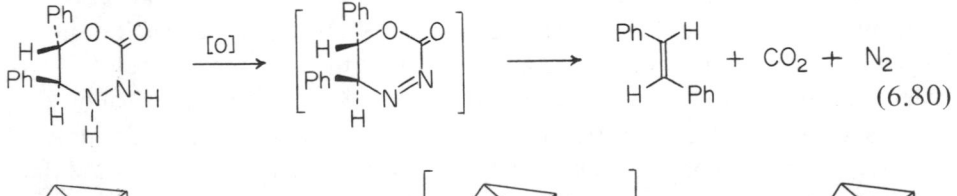

(6.80)

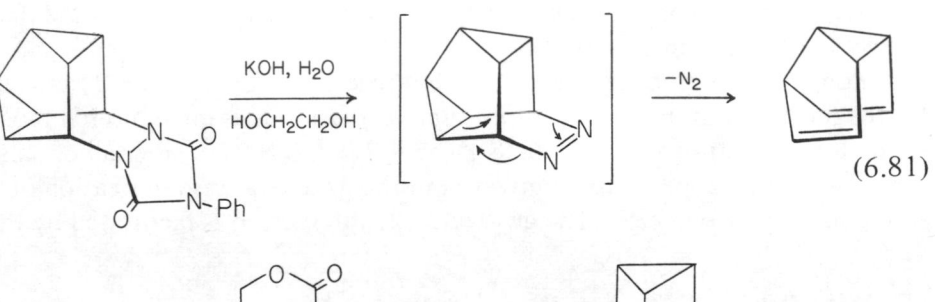

(6.81)

54

55

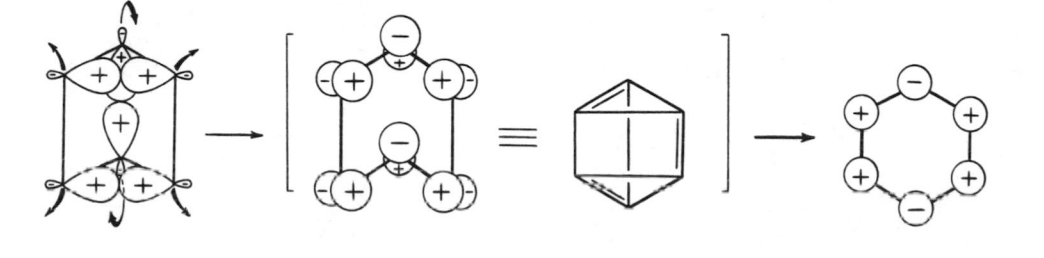

55

that its conversion into benzene is exceptionally exothermic. The stability of (55) is explained in the Evans-Dewar theory by the anti-aromaticity of the transition state for the cycloreversion $[_\pi 2_s + _\pi 2_a + _\pi 2_a]$ process; in orbital symmetry terms the reaction would involve the correlation of a bonding σ-level of (55) with one of the degenerate antibonding π-levels of benzene. A summary of these conclusions is conveniently expressed in the diagram of the orbital interactions for the conversion of (53) into benzene.

Multicomponent reactions of higher order are almost unknown, and the few cases that have been reported might well not be concerted.

An interesting reaction, for which there are only one or two known examples, is the bis-terminal addition of an acetylene to two π-bonds. The process may be formally regarded as a $[_\pi 2_s + _\pi 2_s + _\pi 2_s + _\pi 2_s]$ cyclo-addition, and reaction (6.82) is an example.

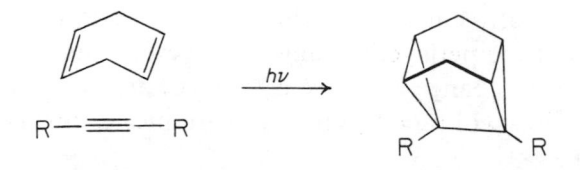

$$(6.82)$$

Certain apparently low order cyclo-additions could equally well be regarded as disguised multicomponent processes. Consider, for example, reaction (6.83); the transition state could be likened to the $[_\pi 2_s + _\pi 4_s]$ cyclo-addition between a pentadienyl cation and an olefin, (56). The alternative $[_\pi 2_s + _\pi 2_s + _\sigma 2_s + _\pi 2_s + _\pi 2_s]$ pathway (57) seems equally attractive. Several other reactions have this sort of duality in interpretation.

177

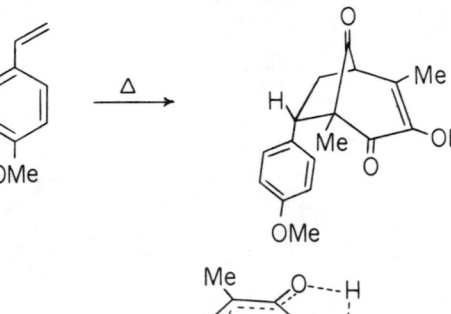

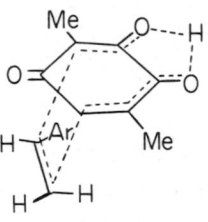

(6.83)

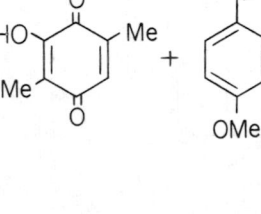

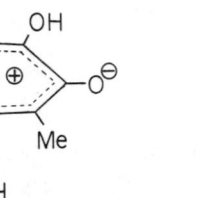

56   57

Metal-catalysed multicomponent cyclo-addition reactions are not considered here because the interpretation of the mechanisms of these reactions is still highly controversial.

6.3 Sigmatropic reactions

Sigmatropic reactions are of order $[1,j]$ or of $[i,j]$. The values $(1+j)$ or $(i+j)$ give the numbers of interacting atomic nuclei. When these values are even, then they are also equal to the numbers of electrons delocalized in the transition states of the pericyclic changes. However, when $(1+j)$ or $(i+j)$ is odd, the sigmatropic change will have cationic or anionic character, and the participant electrons will then be one less (cationic) or one greater (anionic) than these values.

There are limitations on the possible types of sigmatropic change. For $[1,j]$ shifts, in general j can assume any integer value above unity ($j = 2, 3, 4$ ...). For $[i, j]$ shifts, on the other hand, either i or j or both must have an odd integer value (by definition $i, j > 1$). Thus $[2,4]$ shifts are not a real possibility because the relevant delocalized transition state can not be constructed. Instead one arrives at an electrocyclic or cyclo-addition process rather than a

178

sigmatropic change. However, the fact that a sigmatropic change is a formal possibility does not guarantee its chemical feasibility; other processes can intervene. The [2,5] sigmatropic shift in a cationic system, for example reaction (6.84), has apparently not been observed. The electrophilic addition (Equation 6.85) might well be the preferred pathway in the majority of cases.

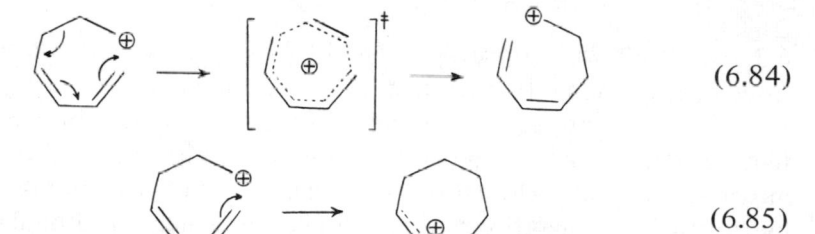

$$(6.84)$$

$$(6.85)$$

6.3.1 *[1,j] shifts*

6.3.1.1 *2-electron processes* The three centre [1,2] shift in an electron deficient species (carbonium ion, carbene, nitrene, or nitrenium ion) essentially involves a $[_\omega 0 + _\sigma 2]$ interaction, (Equation 6.86). The transition state

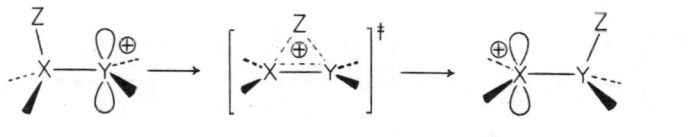

$$(6.86)$$

$$Y = -\overset{\oplus}{C}R_2, -\overset{..}{C}R, -\overset{\oplus}{N}R, -\overset{..}{N} \text{ etc.}$$

is isoconjugate with the cyclopropenium ion, a Hückel-type aromatic system. The physically indistinguishable $[_\omega 0_s + _\sigma 2_s]$ and $[_\omega 0_a + _\sigma 2_a]$ interactions are the predicted low energy pathways; only the migration with retention of configuration at Z is geometrically possible. The predicted pathway has been amply verified for the appropriate systems (Z = alkyl). In the carbonium ion reactions in which the loss of the leaving group and the migration of the alkyl group are concerted (Equation 6.87) (anchimeric assistance), it has also been found in suitable cases that the expected inversion of configuration occurs at the migration terminus. Finally, it should be noted that the bridged species itself may be an actual intermediate if further charge delocalization can occur within the group Z; the notable cases are when Z is aryl.

179

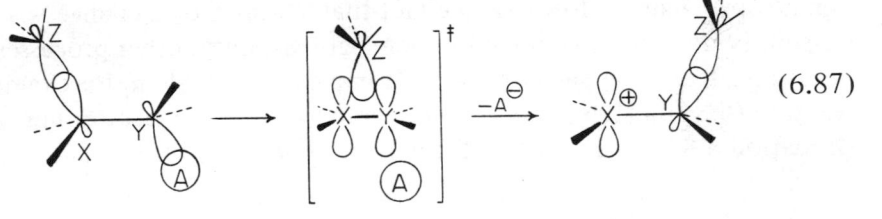

$$(6.87)$$

6.3.1.2 *4-electron processes*   The [1,2] shift by way of a four electron three-centre anionic transition state is an example of an $[_\omega 2 + _\sigma 2]$ reaction. A *supra-antara* interaction is required for electronic stability, and geometry requires that the inversion occurs at the migrating group rather than at the migration terminus, (Equation 6.88). This is, of course, impossible for a hydrogen atom migration and for alkyl groups the poor orbital overlap and extreme crowding in the transition state makes the shift exceedingly unlikely. Such migrations all appear to occur by a stepwise mechanism, for example the Stevens rearrangement (Equation 6.89) in which radical intermediates are implicated.

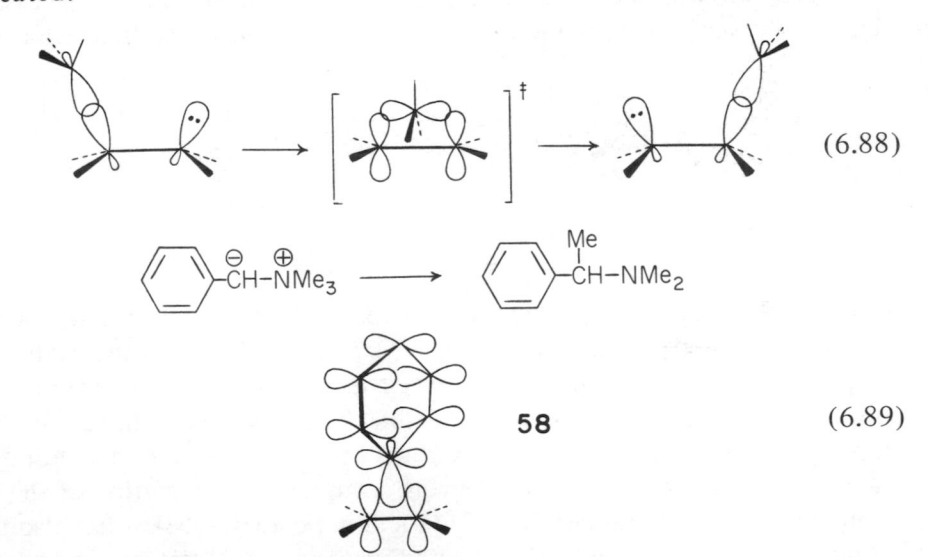

$$(6.88)$$

$$(6.89)$$

58

The [1,2] migration of aryl groups is more complex because the migrating centre can utilize both its sp^2-orbital and the orthogonal p-π orbital (**58**); see for example Phelan, Jaffé, and Orchin (1967).

It may be similarly deduced that thermochemical [1,3] shifts should occur by the *supra-antara* pathway since the *antara-supra* process is not geometrically possible. The theory predicts an inversion at the migrating centre, and again H-shifts are thus precluded. Only one or two alkyl migrations have been observed, reaction (6.90) being the classical example, and the expected inversion at the migrating centre takes place. Steric effects are likely to limit the generality of these processes, and where stabilizing substituents are present, radical mechanisms are likely to be observed.

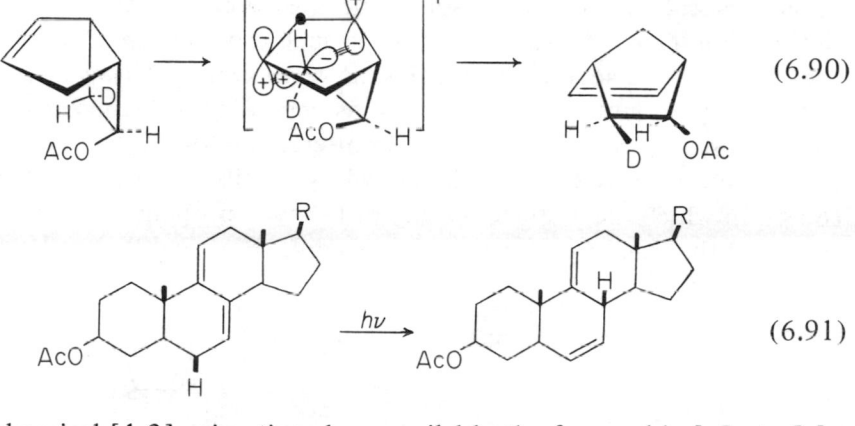

(6.90)

(6.91)

Photochemical [1,3] migrations have available the favourable $[_\sigma 2_s + _\pi 2_s]$ pathway, and several light-induced sigmatropic changes could be so interpreted. Reaction (6.91) is an example.

The need, because of geometric considerations, for the inversion to occur at the migrating centre also extends to the five-centre [1,4] shifts. The $[_\omega 0_s + _\pi 2_s + _\sigma 2_a]$ and $[_\omega 0_s + _\pi 2_a + _\sigma 2_a]$ interactions are therefore to be expected. Reaction (6.92) is a good example of a [1,4] shift in a cationic system, and it can be seen that the above requirements are fulfilled.

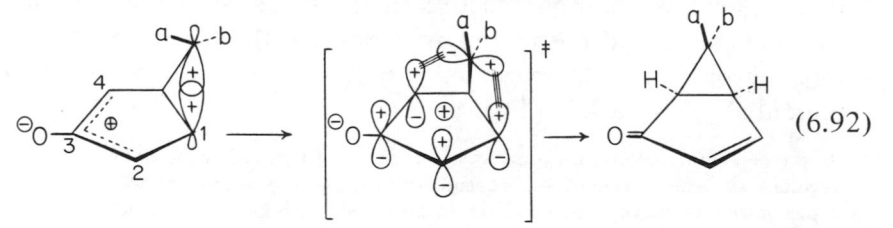

(6.92)

6.3.1.3   *6-electron processes*   The six electrons can be delocalized among five, six, or seven atomic centres which respectively delineates [1,4] [1,5], and [1,6] shifts. The [1,5] case provides nearly all of the examples in this category. In the known anionic [1,4] and cationic [1,6] migrations there is a lack of stereochemical and mechanistic information.

The [1,5] migration of hydrogen atoms is particularly well documented in thermal processes, which is not surprising since the favoured $[_\sigma2_s + _\pi4_s]$ pathway is available. It has been noted previously that an inversion at a hydrogen atom is not physically possible, and if the [1,5] hydrogen shift is studied in a cyclic molecule, then an inversion at the migration terminus can also be ruled out. Reaction (6.93) is just one of many such processes that are known at the present time, and adequately verifies the *supra-supra* pathway. The analogous shifts in acyclic systems, where the stereochemistry of the migrations are not so obvious, must also involve a similar interaction topology. Extensions of these reactions include homodienyl hydrogen shifts,† for example, reaction (6.94), in which the strained σ-bond of the cyclopropane ring plays the part of one of the usual π-bonds (see, for example, Frey and Walsh (1969)).

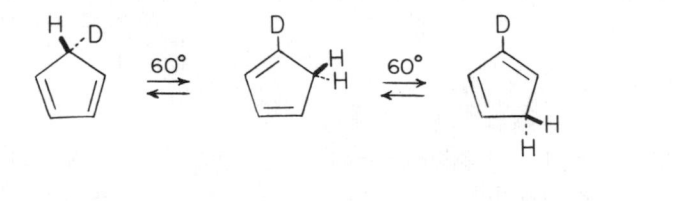

$$(6.93)$$

$$(6.94)$$

The thermochemical [1,5] shifts of atoms other than hydrogen are known, but are much less common; reaction (6.95) is an example. When there is a choice between a hydrogen atom migration and the shift of another group, the sigmatropic [1,5] hydrogen migration is always observed to occur preferentially, (Equation 6.96).

† The prefix 'homo' indicates the presence of an additional atom. In this sense hexa-2,5-diene is the 'homodiene' analogue of penta-2,4-diene, and 1-methyl-2-vinylcyclopropane is the 'homo' analogue of cyclopentadiene. Vinylcyclopropanes have similarities with 1,3-dienes in pericyclic reactions.

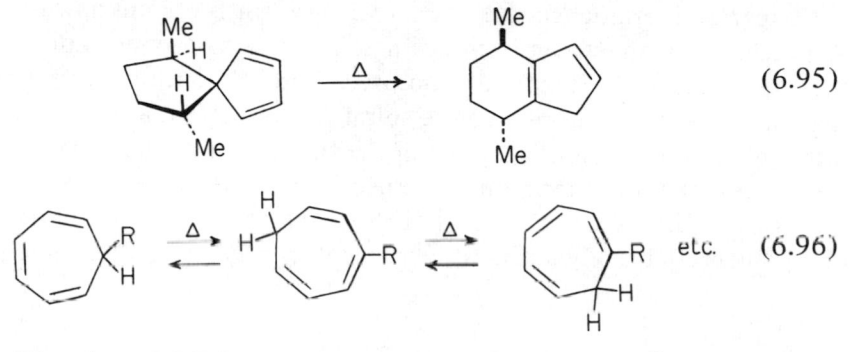

(6.95)

(6.96)

The equilibration of 3,7,7-trimethylcycloheptatriene at 300° (gas phase) with the 1,7,7- and 2,7,7-isomers occurs by way of an interesting sequence of electrocyclic changes and [1,5] carbon shifts, (Equation 6.97). This type of circulatory carbon atom shift in the three-membered ring also has been observed for other 7,7-disubstituted cycloheptatrienes.

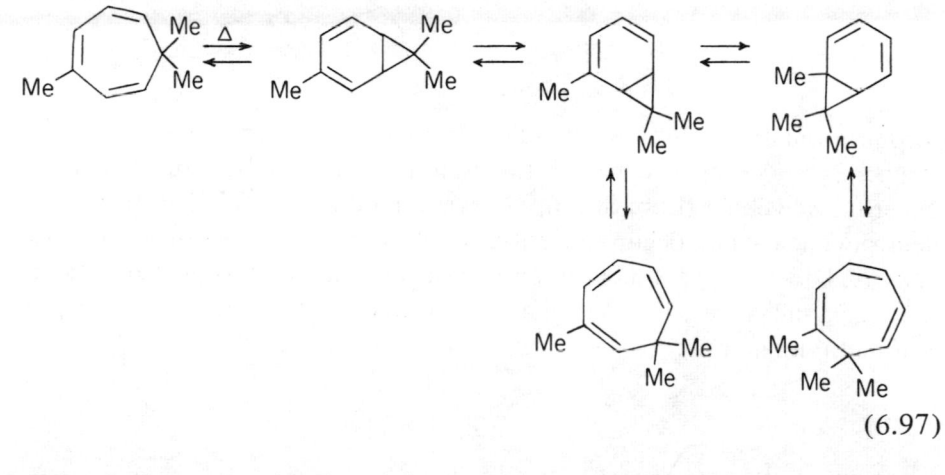

(6.97)

6.3.1.4 *8-electron and higher order processes*   The possible categories include [1,6], [1,7], and [1,8] shifts for the eight electron processes in anionic, neutral, and cationic systems. In each case the *supra-antara* or *antara-supra* interactions are the expected pathways, and therefore an inversion of configuration should occur either at the migrating centre or at the migration terminus. In many simple molecules this may not be geometrically possible. The [1,8] shifts are unknown.

Concerted thermochemical [1,7] hydrogen shifts are unknown in cyclo-heptatrienes or similar cyclic molecules. The best known example is given by the equilibration of vitamin D_2 and precaliferol (Equation 6.98). Presumably the reaction centres adopt a gentle spiral conformation, as indicated, to facili-tate the transfer of the H-atom from the top face at one terminus to the bot-tom face at the other terminus. The necessity for this type of conformation makes the rarity of thermal [1,7] H-shifts rather more understandable. The [1,5] shifts are usually available as competing processes. Thus O-deuteriated

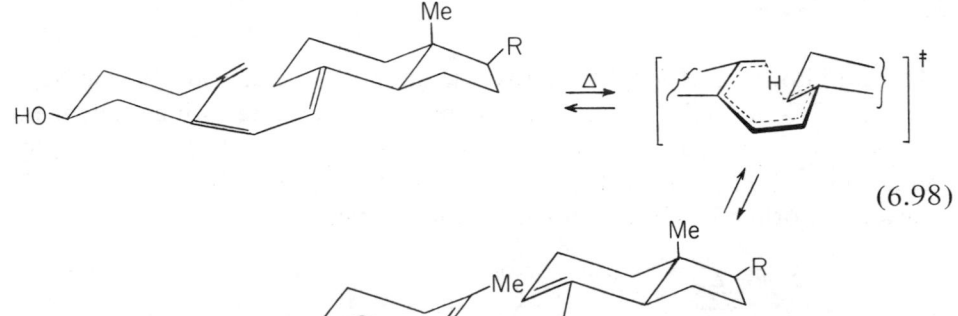

(6.98)

cis,trans- and cis,cis-2-(penta-1,3-dienyl) phenol on thermolysis at 121° furnish 2-ethyl-3-chromene with the deuterium label only in the 1-position of the ethyl side chain (Equation 6.99). An antarafacial [1,7] H-shift and an electrocyclic closure occur sequentially. With the trans,cis- and trans,trans-isomers, however, the 8-membered transition states are less readily attainable, and [1,5] shifts are observed. In addition, deuterium is found at the 3-position of the chromene ring.

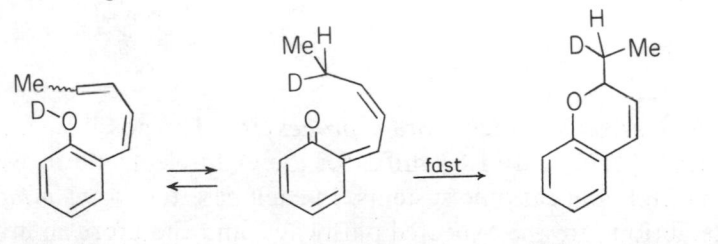

(6.99)

The thermal [1,7] sigmatropic migrations of atoms other than hydrogen appear not to be known. For alkyl shifts the antara-supra pathway is available (inversion at migrating carbon centre). The required $_\sigma 2_a$ interaction at a carbon

184

centre is rarely observed, however, in pericyclic changes, and the known cases relate to stereochemically rigid bicyclic systems (e.g. see Equation (6.90)). Even in molecules with a geometry favourable to a $[_\sigma 2_a + _\pi 6_s]$ alkyl shift, it is difficult to visualize circumstances in which the $[_\sigma 2_s + _\pi 4_s]$ interactions, a [1,5] shift, would not compete.

A number of examples of photochemical [1,7] hydrogen atom migrations are known, and reaction (6.100) summarizes several of these processes (R = D, Me, Et, OMe, C_6H_5 etc.). The same distribution of the isomeric products is not obtained in every case. For example, with R = C_6H_5 only 2-phenylcyclo-

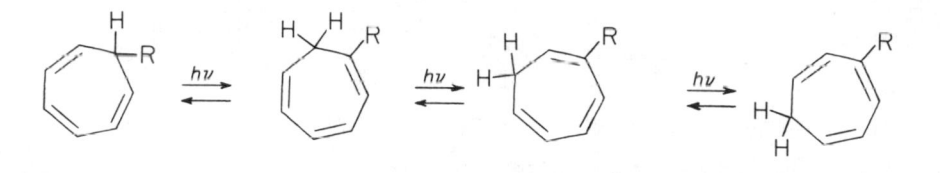

$$(6.100)$$

heptatriene is isolated. Methyl [1,7] migrations are observed in the photo-isomerization of 3,7,7-trimethylcycloheptatriene; a mixture of the 1,5,7- and 1,3,7-isomers is obtained.

The [1,6] shifts in pentadienyl anions have rarely been observed. Thermal [1,6] sigmatropic hydrogen shifts occur in the acyclic systems, but not in the analogous cyclic ions. This indicates that an antarafacial interaction on the π-system is necessary to the migration, as is predicted by the theory. Further confirmation for these results comes from the finding that the cyclic penta-dienyl anion is photochemically isomerized by a [1,6] hydrogen shift; the favourable $[_\sigma 2_s + _\pi 6_s]$ interaction is available to the excited state process.

Higher order [1,j] shifts are also comparatively rare. A thermal sigmatropic shift of order [1,17] has been described for a nickel tetradehydrocorrin, and an antarafacial light-induced [1,16] hydrogen migration, a $[_\sigma 2_s + _\pi 14_a]$ process, was the first of two key pericyclic changes in an elegent synthesis of (±)-palladium(II)-15-cyano-1,2,2,7,7,12,12-heptamethyl-*trans*-corrin perchlor-ate (Equation 6.101). A 'curly arrow' mechanism can not be written in any simple way; the positive charge may be regarded as being delocalized within the π-framework system.

185

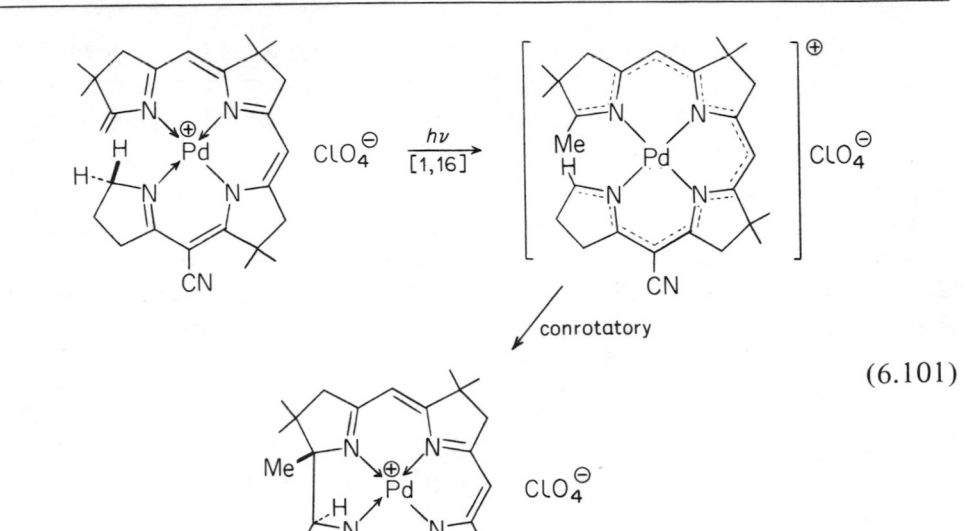

$$(6.101)$$

6.3.2. [i,j] shifts

6.3.2.1 *4-electron processes*   The formal possibility of $[i,j]$ shifts involving the delocalization of four electrons is limited to the five centre $[2,3]$ case, for example reaction (6.102), which appears not to have been observed.

$$(6.102)$$

6.3.2.2 *6-electron processes*   The six-electron category, yet again, is the one most abundant in examples, although all of these are for the six-centre $[3,3]$ rearrangement in neutral systems or for the five-centre $[2,3]$ migrations in 'anionic' molecules. The 'cationic' $[2,5]$ or $[3,4]$ migrations have yet to be discovered; these would require a 7-membered transition state.

The simple Cope† rearrangement (Equation 3.20) is the prototype for all migrations in the $[3,3]$ category. The predicted interaction modes are $[_\sigma 2_s + _\pi 2_s + _\pi 2_s]$, $[_\sigma 2_s + _\pi 2_a + _\pi 2_a]$, or $[_\sigma 2_a + _\pi 2_a + _\pi 2_s]$ which, in this particular

† Reviews: Rhoades (1963), and Doering and Roth (1963).

example, are mutually equivalent. In these thermochemical reactions the all-*supra* interaction is normally assumed to apply unless the molecular geometry dictates otherwise. There are two possible goemetrical arrangements of the atomic centres at the transition state of a Cope reaction (Fig. 6.3). The chair-like arrangement appears to be generally more favourable by about 6 kcal mol^{-1} (25 kJ mol^{-1}).

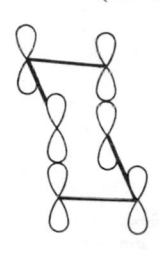

| (a) | (b) |

FIGURE 6.3
Possible geometric conformations in the prototype Cope reaction, (a) chair-like and (b) boat-like

The preference for the four-centre transition state (Fig. 6.3(a)) was deduced by Doering and Roth (1963) by their classical work on the dimethylhexa-1,5-dienes. The thermolysis (225°) of *meso*-3,4-dimethylhexa-1,5-diene yielded *cis,trans*-octa-2,4-diene, whereas with (±)-3,4-dimethylhexa-1,5-diene the rearrangement products obtained at 180° were the *trans,trans*- and *cis,cis*-octa-2,4-dienes (ratio (9 : 1). Both processes were highly stereospecific; for example, only about 0·3 per cent of the *trans,trans*-octa-2,4-diene was detected in the reaction of the *meso*-compound. The reaction pathways are illustrated in Equation (6.103).

Superimposed on the electronic effect, which distinguishes between the chair-like and boat-like arrangements, there is an additional steric preference for those conformations in which the bulky substituents are in equational positions. In the *meso*-hexadiene the two conformations are isoenergetic since one methyl group is axial, and the other equatorial. For the (±)-hexadiene, however, both methyl groups are either equatorial or both are axial at the transition state. The lower energy equatorial-equatorial conformer leads to the *trans,trans*-octadiene, which is therefore formed more rapidly. Since the *trans,trans*-compound also enjoys a greater thermodynamic stability, it is also the major product.

187

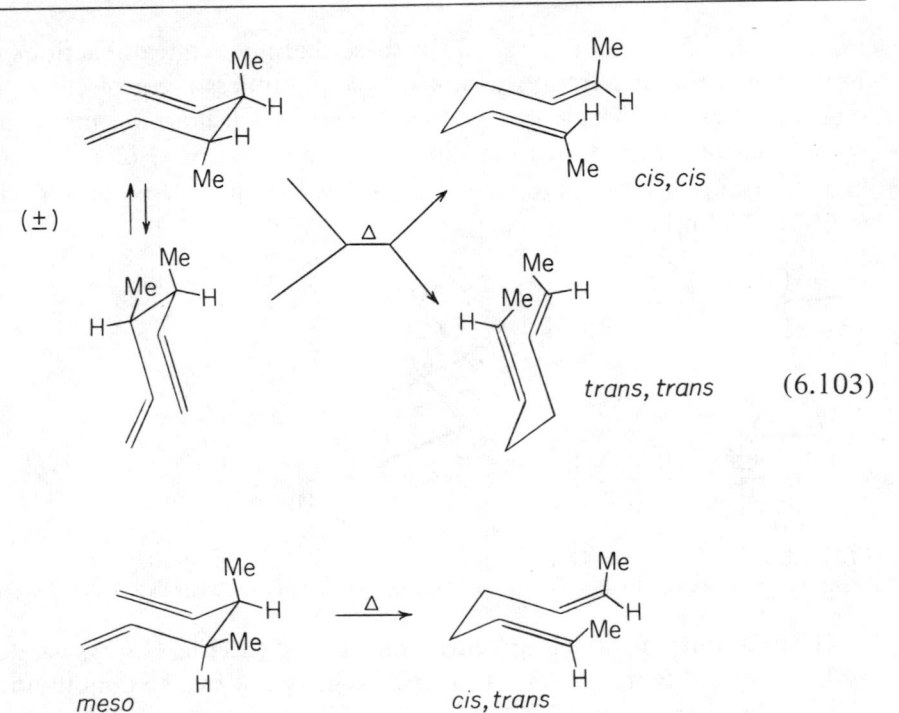

$(\pm)$

cis, cis

trans, trans   (6.103)

meso   *cis, trans*

The thermal rearrangements of optically active 1,5-dienes have also been studied, and the products found to have high optical purity. Where mixtures are formed, the major product is as predicted from the above steric considerations. It is thus not only possible to generate chirality at a remote centre, but also to be certain about the absolute stereochemistry at the new asymmetric carbon atom.

Temperatures in the region of 200–300° are frequently necessary in order to produce Cope rearrangements at a reasonable rate, and a mixture of the starting material and of the product(s) are often formed since these processes are reversible. However, conjugative stabilization by substituents at the transition state has the effect of increasing the reaction rate, and lower temperatures can then be employed. If this conjugation is transferred to the product molecule, the reaction may then be uni-directional. Likewise an energetic (i.e. strained) reactant molecule has the effect of making the rearrangement less freely reversible. The interplay of some of these factors is demonstrated in reactions (6.104) and (6.105). The low energy of the carbonyl group

188

apparently offsets the increase in molecular energy of the strained cyclopropane system, since in reaction (6.105) the equilibrium favours the left hand side. A similar stabilizing factor is also available in the formation of the non-aromatic product in the first stage of the Claisen rearrangement (see below). The boat transition state must be involved in the conversions (6.104) and (6.105). The reactions may be regarded as electrocyclic, but are normally classified as Cope (Equation 6.104) and Claisen-Cope (Equation 6.105) reactions.

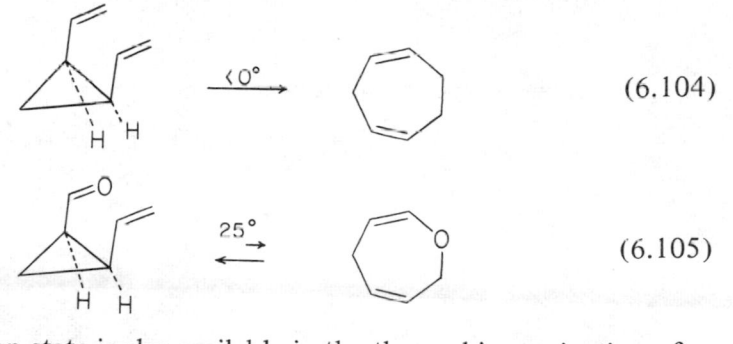

(6.104)

(6.105)

The boat transition state is also available in the thermal isomerization of *meso*-3,4-diphenylhexa-1,5-diene, as 37 per cent of *trans,trans*-1,6-diphenylhexa-1,5-diene is produced [cf. Equation (6.103)]. The main reaction product, *cis-trans*-1,6-diphenylhexa-1,5-diene (63 per cent), is formed *via* the four-centre interaction. This, and the previous results, show clearly that the six-centre interaction is energetically accessible if steric effects or molecular geometry so demand.

Apart from the Cope and Claisen-Cope rearrangements, a number of 'named' reactions are to be found within the category of [3,3] shifts;[†] reactions (6.106)–(6.111) are examples of some of these processes. The thio-Claisen rearrangement the sulphur analogue of reactions (6.106) and (6.107) is also well known. The all carbon atom counterpart of the Claisen rearrangement ((6.106); $O=CH_2$) was not discovered until it was realized that the final aromatization step required the presence of a strong base to promote the necessary tautomeric change. In reactions (6.107)–(6.111) the influence of steric factors on the stereoselectivity of the reactions is apparent. In reaction (6.109),

† Claisen rearrangements reviews: Rhoades (1963), Tarbell (1940), Jefferson and Scheinmann (1968), and Hansen and Schmidt (1969).

189

Claisen rearrangement

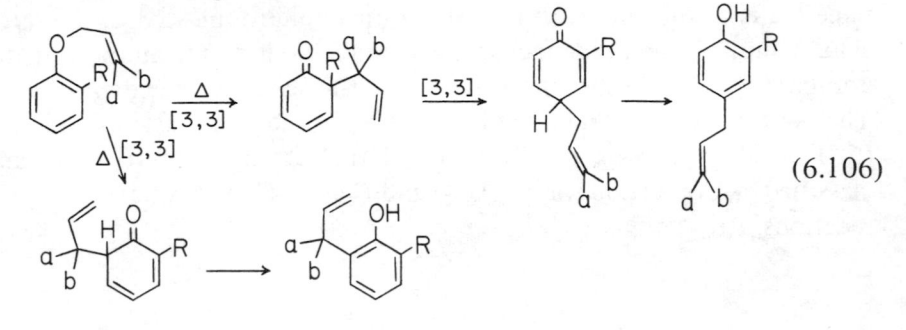

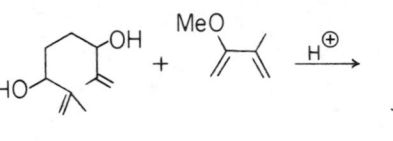

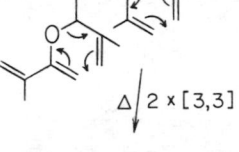

(6.106)

Claisen–Cope rearrangement

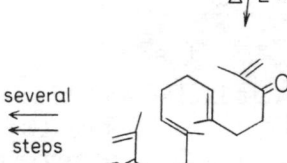

(6.107)

Squalene $\xrightleftharpoons[\text{steps}]{\text{several}}$

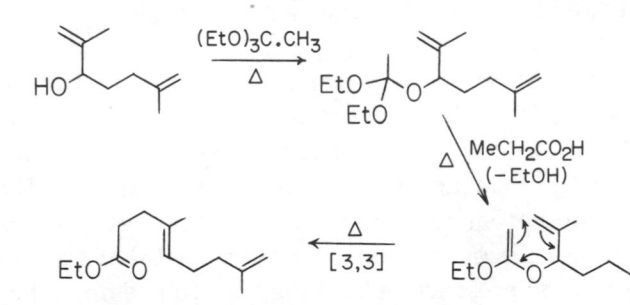

Claisen ortho–ester rearrangement

(6.108)

for example, there is a 9 : 1 preference for the formation of the *trans*-product. In one of the two possible four-centre transition state conformations, the methyl group adjacent to the σ-bond undergoing scission can be equatorial or

190

Amino–Claisen rearrangement

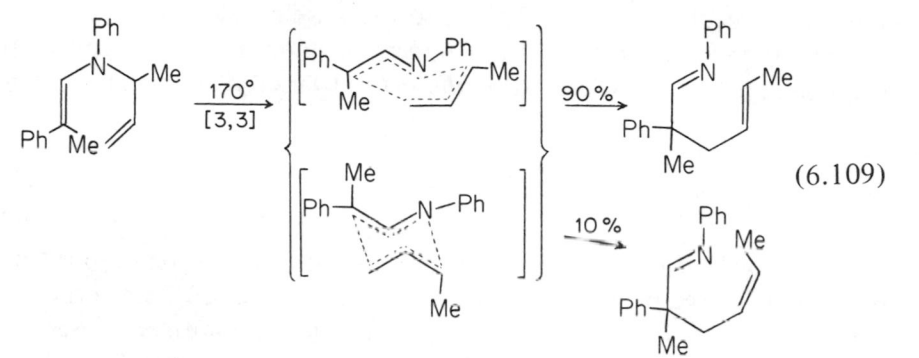

$$\frac{170°}{[3,3]}$$

90%

10%

(6.109)

Oxy–Cope rearrangement

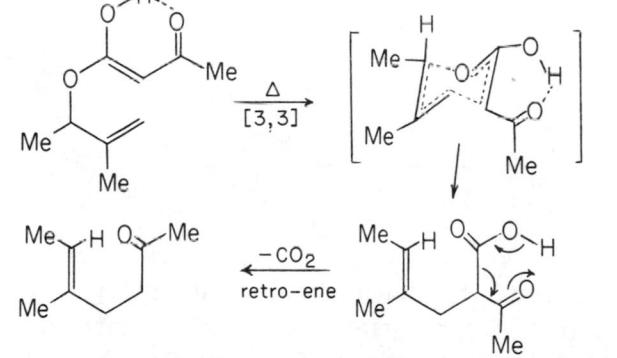

$$\frac{\Delta}{[3,3]}$$

(6.110)

Carroll reaction

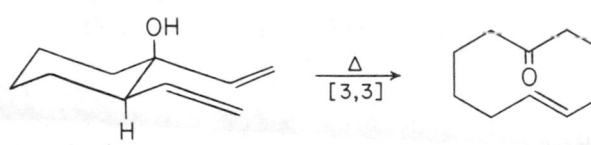

$$\frac{\Delta}{[3,3]}$$

(6.111)

$$\xleftarrow[\text{retro-ene}]{-CO_2}$$

axial. The axial conformer is more energetic because of the non-bonded 1,3-diaxial interactions, and it therefore only accounts for a small portion of the final product, the *cis*-isomer. Likewise the *trans*-alkene is formed in the other processes with fairly high stereoselectivity, and such reactions have been used extensively recently in the synthesis of natural products, particularly isoprenoids, in which this structural feature is present.

The oxy-Cope rearrangement generally is in competition with the retro-ene elimination reaction (6.112). These processes are considered in more detail in section **6.6**. On occasions the Claisen rearrangement is also susceptible to side reactions. The first of these, the *ortho-ortho* Claisen rearrangement, involves

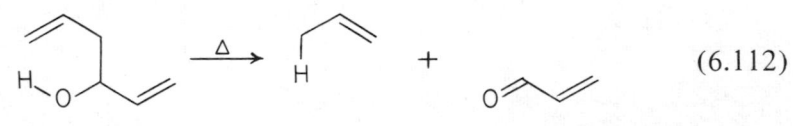

$$(6.112)$$

the migration, with inversion, of the allyl group from one *ortho*-position in the dienone to the other *ortho*-position, (Equation 6.113). Since the concerted [3,5] shift is geometrically improbable (a *supra-antara* interaction is predicted), a stepwise mechanism involving an intramolecular Diels-Alder reaction and a subsequent radical fragmentation is the most likely reaction pathway. The second side reaction is commonly known as the abnormal

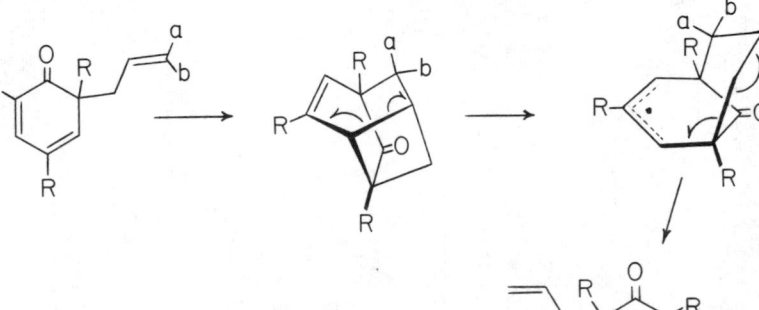

$$(6.113)$$

Claisen rearrangement. It arises when the allyl group has an alkyl substituent as indicated in Equation (6.114). The first-formed 'normal' rearrangement product is transformed by two consecutive [1,5] homodienyl hydrogen shifts into the abnormal product, (6.114).

The replacement of the allyl group by a propargyl group does not, remarkably, prevent the Claisen and the related rearrangements from occurring. The initial product inevitably possesses a cumulated double bond system (i.e. 1,2-diene), and additional reaction pathways may then become available, for example reaction (6.115).

192

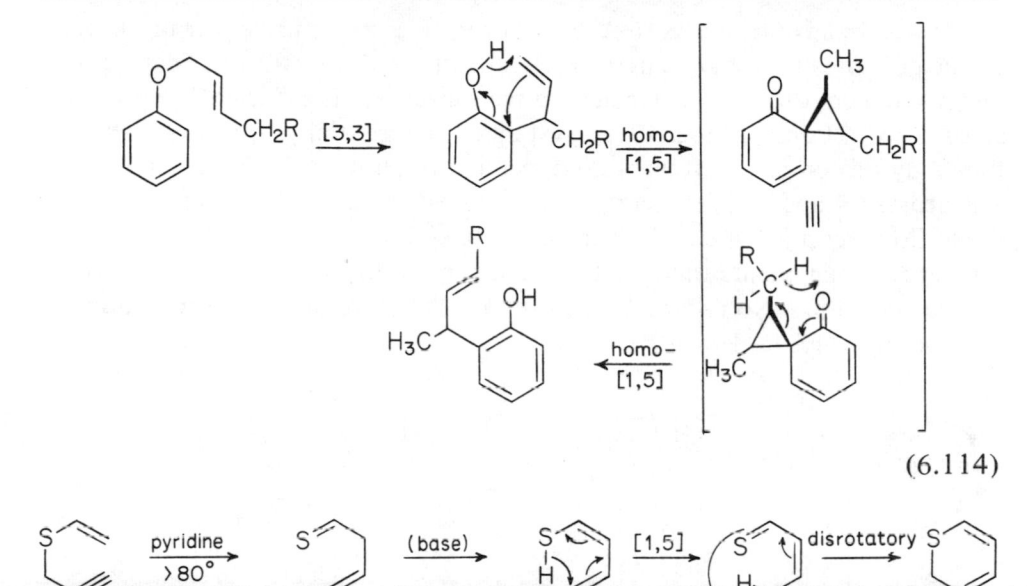

(6.114)

(6.115)

It was noted earlier that the Cope rearrangement is frequently reversible and, in a sense, is therefore degenerate. True degeneracy arises when the valence isomers are structurally identical. The prototype reaction of hexa-1,5-diene is a two-fold degenerate rearrangement; at sufficiently high temperatures the atoms C1 and C3 become equivalent, as do atoms C6 and C4. More extensive degeneracy has been detected in the thermal rearrangement of hypostrophene (Equation 6.116). Deuterium labelling studies have indicated that the five valence isomers are equilibrated at 35°.

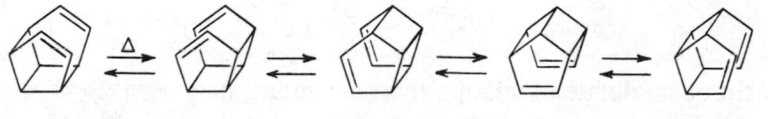

(6.116)

No other system, however, comes anywhere near the multiple degeneracy possible in the molecule bullvalene (59). This system was predicted to be capable of a 1 209 600-fold degenerate rearrangement (Doering and Roth,

1963) well in advance of its first preparation. The ^{1}H n.m.r. spectrum of bull-valene collapses to a sharp singlet at temperatures above $100°$, indicating that under these conditions the degenerate rearrangement is sufficiently rapid for all of the C—H units in the $(CH)_{10}$ system to be essentially equivalent, and they may be considered to move independently on the surface of a sphere. The atoms C4 and C6, for example, are bonded to each other in (59), but in a single Cope rearrangement they are separated by another atom, and after two further rearrangements they are two atoms removed from one another (Equation 6.117). No two carbon atoms are therefore permanently bonded to each other in this molecule.†

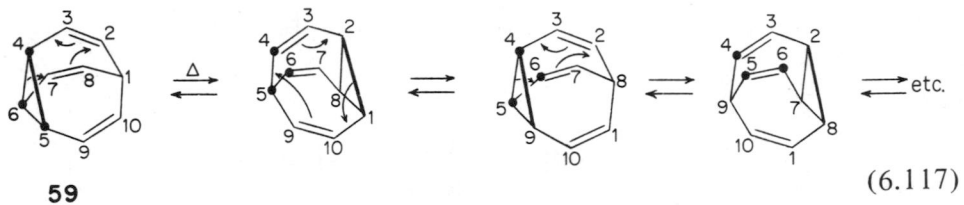

59

$$(6.117)$$

The majority of Cope rearrangements appear to take place by way of the all-*supra* interaction mode. The alternative allowed pathway involves a $[2_s + 2_a + 2_a]$ interaction which has been invoked occasionally to explain the topology of Cope rearrangements in certain geometrically rigid molecules. A possible interaction in this category has been mentioned previously (see Fig. 3.13(d)). Recent work on a related system (reaction 6.118) has cast doubt on this interpretation; the 'Cope' rearrangement could equally well be explained by two consecutive and allowed electrocyclic reactions.

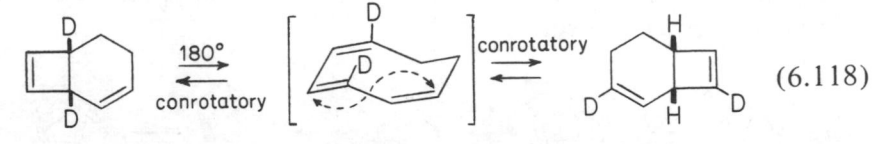

$$(6.118)$$

The cationic analogue of a Cope rearrangement, namely a [3,4] shift, has been observed (Equation 6.119). It occurs in competition with the alternative

---

† The total number of ways of arranging ten carbon atoms in 10! However, bullvalene has a three-fold symmetry axis, and only 1 in 3 of these arrangements is a truly independent structure; 2 in 3 structures differ from the third only by the rotation of the whole molecule in space, about this axis, through $120°$. The total number of valence isomers is therefore $(\frac{1}{3}) . 10! = 1\ 209\ 600$.

[1,2] and [3,3] migrations. In this example the [1,2]-shift could equally well be regarded as a [1,6] sigmatropic migration.

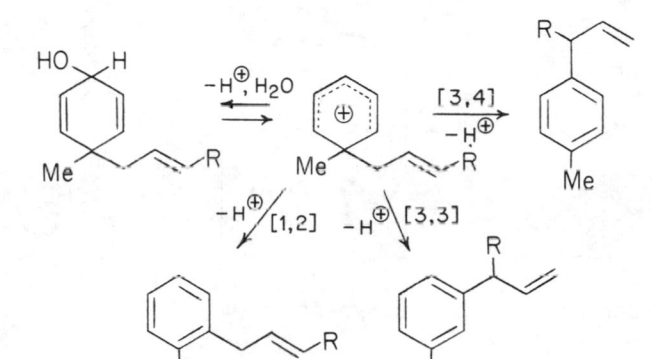

(6.119)

The anionic analogue of the Cope rearrangement, of which Equation (6.120) is the prototype, involves the delocalization of the six electrons over five atoms at the transition state.

(6.120)

Such reactions are the subject of fairly intensive study at the present time, and commonly one or more of the five atoms in the system is a hetero-atom (i.e. N, O, or S). Further modification of the type process includes the ability of a hetero-atom with a lone pair of electrons to take the place of the anionic centre. Additionally, allyl-substituted ylids undergo the rearrangement with equal facility, so that the total possible permutations is very large and the synthetic potential of these processes, as a consequence, is great. Among these processes are to be found the Wittig, the Sommelet-Hauser, the Meisenheimer, and sulphonium ylide rearrangements. A few typical examples are given in Equations (6.121)–(6.123). In Equation (6.121) the benzyl ether prepared from (S)-(+)-*trans*-3-penten-2-ol on treatment with butyl lithium at − 46° was found to rearrange to *cis*- and *trans*-1-phenyl-2-methyl-3-penten-1-ol (*cis: trans* = 17 : 83) which have opposite configurations at the chiral centre indicated. This elegant experiment proved that the migration involves a *supra-supra* interaction in Wittig rearrangements.

195

Wittig rearrangement

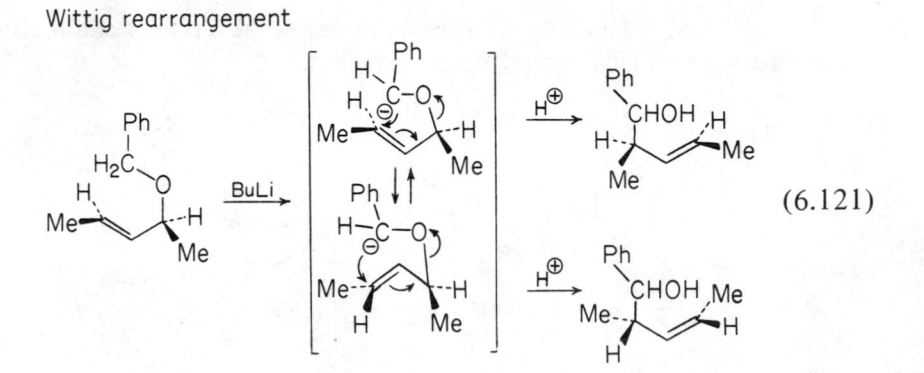

(6.121)

Sulphonium ylide rearrangement

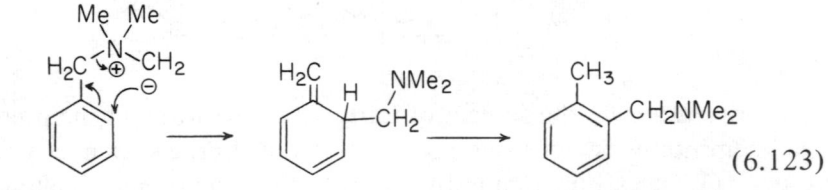

(6.122)

Sommelet – Hauser rearrangement

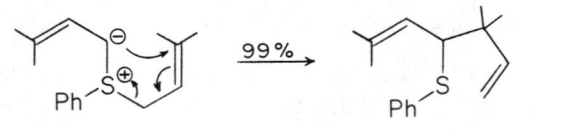

(6.123)

Radical cleavage recombination mechanisms are also known to occur in these reactions; for example the 1,2-shift of the allyl group without inversion is not uncommon. The radical pathway generally appears to have a higher activation energy so that the occurrence of the concerted [2,3] shift depends upon structural features and on the reaction temperature.

6.3.2.3   *8-electron and higher order processes*   In the case of [3,5] shifts the Woodward-Hoffmann theory predicts that for the thermochemical reactions there should be an odd number of antarafacial interactions. In the simplest context this means a *supra-antara* combination of the three-atom and five-atom components which, for flexible molecules, means that the antarafacial interaction is most likely on the larger component. Such migration is not

196

impossible, but no examples have come to light. The *supra-supra* combination requires photochemical activation and although a [3,5] shift in this category is known, the precise mechanism of the rearrangement is in some doubt.

The thermochemical [5,5] sigmatropic migration, on the other hand, has available the more favourable *supra-supra* interaction, but now a ten-membered transition state is required. A well documented example of this type is known, (Equation 6.124). Control experiments have ruled out the alternative pathways to the *p*-substituted phenol.

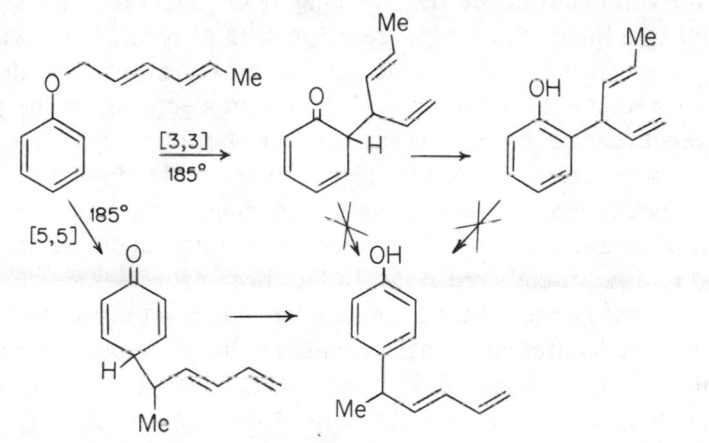

(6.124)

It is particularly interesting to note that the [5,5] migration proceeds about four times faster than the [3,3] rearrangement.†

6.4   Cheletropic reactions

The stereochemistry of cheletropic reactions has been discussed in Section **3.3.4.** The linear cheletropic reactions usually offer the best scope for orbital overlap and would normally be expected to be the preferred reaction pathways. Generally the extrusion reactions (i.e. the loss of the species :*Xyz*) are more numerous than cheletropic cyclo-additions because the :*Xyz* species is often a molecule of high thermodynamic stability, and in such cases the reactions are essentially uni-directional.‡

† For a concise review of aromatic sigmatropic rearrangements, see Hansen and Schmid (1969).
‡ Review: Stark and Duke (1967).

Consider Fig. 3.16; it is seen that $(k + 2)$ electrons are involved in the reaction, and further that two electrons are delivered from the hybrid (sp^n) orbital of $:Xyz$. This orbital, considered alone, can be acted upon in the supra-facial or antarafacial senses, and so can the k π-electron olefin. Therefore, there are the four usual combinations, namely *supra-supra, antara-antara, antara-supra,* and *supra-antara* (respectively Fig. 3.16(a) (i), (b) (ii), (a) (ii), and (b) (i)). When $(k + 2) = (4n + 2)$ electrons it will be expected, because of the general Woodward-Hoffmann rule, that the *supra-supra* or *antara-antara* interactions will occur in the thermal cheletropic reactions. These respectively correspond to a linear cheletropic reaction with disrotatory cleavage, and to a non-linear cheletropic reaction with conrotatory cleavage. The alternative pathways are reserved for the cases $(k + 2) = 4n$ electrons. In the photochemical reactions the usual cross-over relationship should apply.

Cheletropic reactions fill in the gaps in the possible sequence of ring sizes obtainable by cyclo-addition reactions. The cheletropic processes refer to the formation or cleavage of 3, 5, 7 . . . membered rings; cyclo-additions normally refer to 4, 6, 8 . . . membered rings. In fact both processes are closely related. The essential difference is that in the cheletropic reactions both terminal orbital lobes are located at a single atomic centre of one of the participants, and are necessarily orthogonal. In normal cyclo-additions the orbitals concerned are located at the termini of both of the components, and within each component these orbitals are considered to be parallel.

6.4.1   *4-electron processes*

This category corresponds with the formation or cleavage of three-membered rings. In thermochemical reactions the *antara-supra* and *supra-antara* modes are to be expected and of the two the linear process (Fig. 3.16(b) (i)), the *supra-antara* mode, may be ruled out for reasons based on geometry and orbital overlap. The low energy pathway is therefore the non-linear process (Fig. 3.16(a) (ii)).

The forward reaction (ring formation) is limited to the reactions of high energy species such as carbenes and nitrenes with the ethylenic molecule. Concerted cyclo-addition reactions are limited to a few singlet carbenes ($:CR_2$) and nitrenes ($:NR$) and these reactions are completely stereospecific. Equation (6.125) represents the general situation, and lack of stereospecificity is usually taken as evidence for the incursion of triplet reactions.

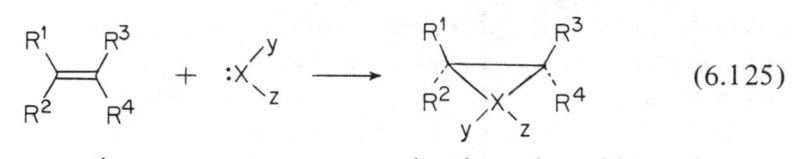

$$(6.125)$$

The extrusion reactions are more numerous, but here the evidence for concertedness if often very thin. Certain species, for example SO_2 (Equation 6.127) and N_2O (Equation 6.126) are extruded stereospecifically, while with others (e.g. N_2) the stereospecificity is dependent on the method of formation of the labile three-membered ring system (i.e. the diazine), and yet other species (e.g. SO) generally appear to be ejected non-stereospecifically. Further work is necessary in this area before the general trends in chemical behaviour

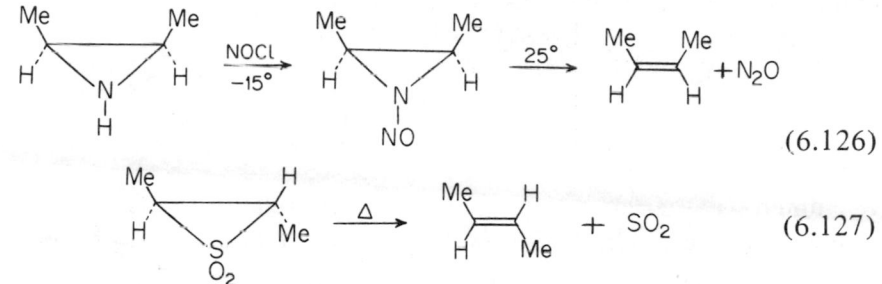

$$(6.126)$$

$$(6.127)$$

and reaction mechanism are known; similar comments apply to the photochemical processes in this category.

6.4.2   6-electron processes

The formation or fragmentation of five-membered rings characterizes this category. The cyclization process is mainly the province of SO_2, but even here the extrusion reaction occurs readily. The *supra-supra* mode is likely to be the preferred pathway, that is a linear cheletropic reaction with disrotation. The transformations summarized in Equation (6.128) amply verify these predictions,

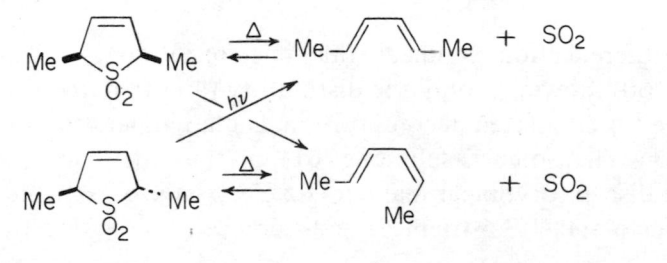

$$(6.128)$$

and the photochemical extrusions, although not completely stereospecific, very largely follow the predicted pathway (i.e. linear with conrotation). The loss of nitrogen from diazenes also follows the predicted pathway (Equation 6.129). In the case of carbon monoxide, although detailed stereochemical

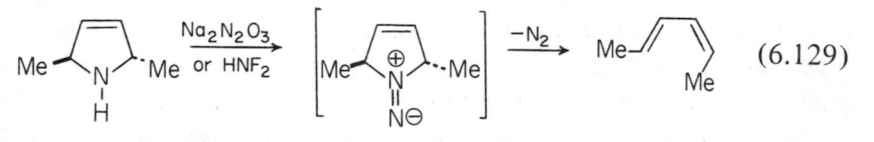

$$(6.129)$$

data is lacking, the extrusions likewise appear to be concerted. The cyclopentenones are particularly labile if an aromatic product can be formed, (Equation 6.130).

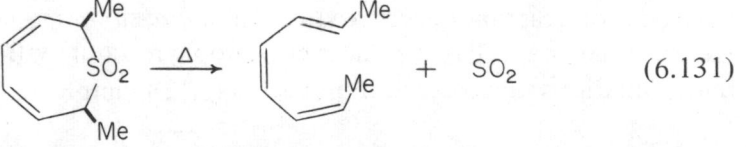

$$(6.130)$$

Numerous other cheletropic fragmentations related to the above are now known, and the experimental results are in good accord with expectation.

6.4.3   8-electron and higher order processes

Thermolysis of 2,7-dihydrothiepine dioxides gives trienes and sulphur dioxide. The *cis*-2,7-dimethyl compound is converted into *trans,cis,cis*-octatriene (Equation 6.131) while the *trans*-isomer gives the *trans,cis,trans*-octatriene. The stereospecificity is greater than 97 per cent and the results clearly indi-

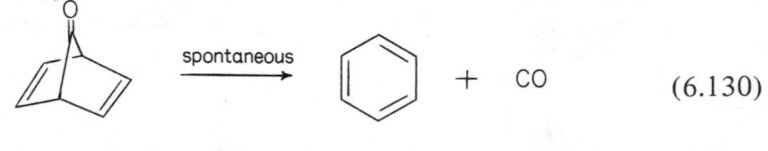

$$(6.131)$$

cate the preference for the linear (this time conrotatory) extrusion. With the sulphone (60), however, only the disrotatory (and therefore non-linear) mode is available for concerted decomposition, and a temperature of 250° is required for reaction. The isomeric sulphone (61), on the other hand, can fragment in a concerted disrotatory linear manner (six electron process), and decomposes at 100° to cyclo-octa-1,3,5-triene. The difference in activation free energies

200

between the linear and non-linear processes has been roughly estimated at 10 kcal mole^{-1} (42 kJ mole^{-1}), but (60) may react by a multistep pathway. This section is otherwise lacking in examples, and one or two apparently high order cheletropic reactions could equally well be regarded as processes involving the participation of fewer electrons.

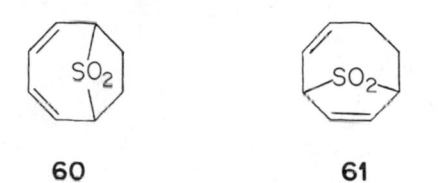

60   61

6.5   Group transfer reactions

The reactions in this category were defined in Section 3.2, but comparatively few examples have been disclosed in the literature. The known cases concern the transfer of hydrogen atoms and, in view of the definition, these processes must involve the delocalization of a minimum of six electrons. In fact *only* the six electron processes appear to be known which under thermal control should involve an orbital interaction of the type $[_\sigma 2_s + _\sigma 2_s + _\pi 2_s]$, or $[_\sigma 2_a + _\sigma 2_a + _\pi 2_s]$, or $[_\sigma 2_s + _\sigma 2_a + _\pi 2_a]$. The first two of these can be realized in the favourable *supra-supra* combination of the two reactants, and are therefore the normally observed pathways. The best known example of this type of reaction is the hydrogenation of olefins by diimide, Equations (6.132) and (6.133); Hünig *et al.* (1965). One or two carbon analogues of this reaction are

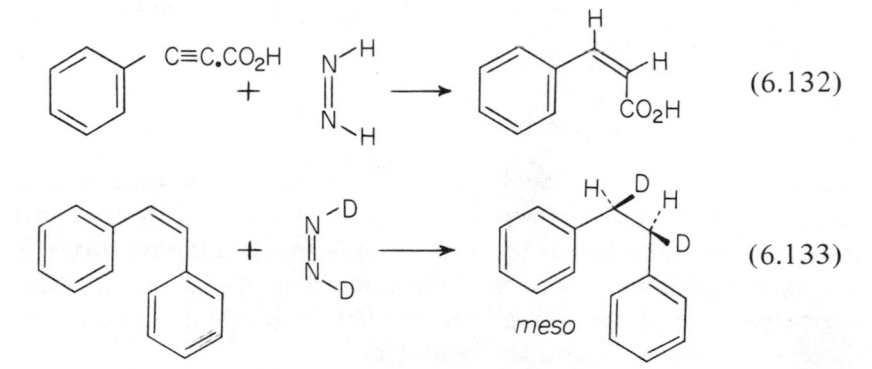

(6.132)

(6.133)

meso

also known. In reaction (6.134) the *supra-supra* interaction is clearly involved, but in other cases the stereochemistry of the transfer is not known. Stereo-chemical information is also lacking in the transfer reactions involving more than six electrons. The stereochemical information on its own, however, is at best rather tenuous evidence for concertedness. In reaction (6.134) the *cis*-1,2-

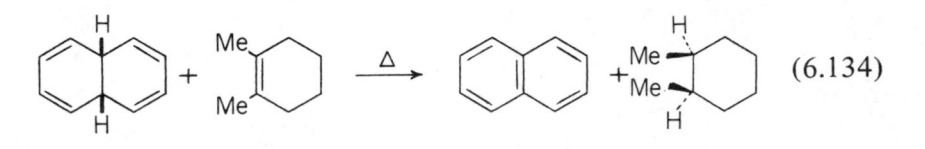

$$(6.134)$$

dimethylcyclohexane is formed in only 6·6 per cent yield and although none of the *trans*-compound was detected the reaction could nevertheless be non-concerted. The product of the defined stereochemistry might be expected from an intermolecular carbonium ion hydrogen transfer process, for example, as shown in Equation (6.135).

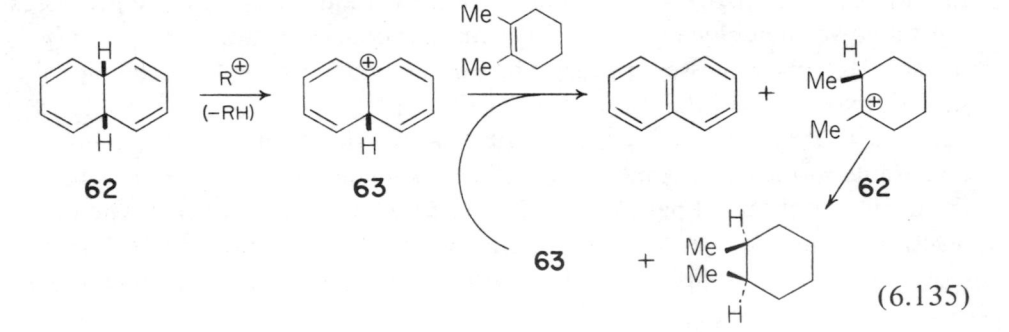

$$(6.135)$$

6.6   Elimination reaction

As outlined previously (Section **3.2**), reactions here considered as cyclo-eliminations are those in which n σ-bonds plus m π-bonds are transformed into $(n - 1)$ σ-bonds plus $(m + 1)$ π-bonds. Most of the reactions in this category have elsewhere in the literature been defined as cyclo-additions and sigmatropic rearrangements. It is felt that the particular classification adopted here is more rigorous and less confusing.

6.6.1   *4-electron processsses*

Reaction (6.136) is the prototype for cyclo-eliminations in this category; it is closely related to a [1,3] sigmatropic shift, and the reverse reaction is basically a $[_\sigma2 + _\pi2]$ cyclo-addition. In the thermochemical reactions the $[2_s + 2_a]$ interaction should be observed if concerted, and this topology has been shown

$$(6.136)$$

previously to be of rather low probability. Thus, 1,3-cyclohexadiene is decomposed at elevated temperatures mainly by a radical chain process, and the uncatalysed addition reactions of simple molecules to olefins likewise generally involve stepwise processes.

6.6.2   *6-electron processes*

Reaction (6.137) is the obvious extension of the simple 1,2-elimination discussed above. The favourable $[_\sigma2_s + _\sigma2_s + _\pi2_s]$ interaction is predicted by the general Woodward-Hoffmann rule for the thermal reactions, and one or two such examples have been described; Frey and Walsh (1969). Both 2,5-dihydrofuran and 1,4-cyclohexadiene are decomposed unimolecularly into hydrogen and respectively furan and benzene. The activation parameters and isotopic substitution experiments (i.e. D for H) strongly suggest that the eliminations are concerted. Likewise *cis*-3,6-dimethyl-1,4-cyclohexadiene is smoothly pyrolysed at 260° to give only *p*-xylene and hydrogen. On the other hand the *trans*-isomer is more stable and is decomposed at higher temperatures mainly into toluene and methane. It appears that pyrolytic eliminations leading to methane or ethane proceed by radical-chain mechanisms. An interesting reaction is that between bromine and cyclopentadiene which yields *cis*-3,5-dibromocyclopentene as the main product. There is, however, no evidence that the reaction is concerted and significantly butadiene and bromine react to form *trans*-1,4-dibromobut-2-ene which cannot be the product of a pericyclic reaction.

The most important process in this category is the so-called *ene*-reaction (Equation 6.138)†, to which must be added a number of closely related

† Review: Hoffmann (1969).

pyrolytic cyclo-eliminations and their retrogressions. The *ene*-reaction is commonly in competition with the Diels-Alder cyclo-additions, and explains why it is frequently classified as a cyclo-addition process itself. Also it is

$$\text{(structure)} \rightleftharpoons \text{(structure)} + \text{H—H} \qquad (6.137)$$

$$\text{(structure)} \rightleftharpoons \text{(structure)} + \text{(structure)} \qquad (6.138)$$

found that the reactivity of the two components in the reverse of reaction (6.138) parallels the structure reactivity relationships found for Diels-Alder components; reaction is facilitated by an electron rich *ene*-component and an electron deficient enophile. A strong preference for *cis-endo* addition also further correlates the two processes.

The *cis* stereochemistry is readily seen in reaction (6.139), whereas the *endo* stereospecificity is rather more subtle. This was originally demonstrated for the reactions of *cis*-but-2-ene, *trans*-but-2-ene, and of cyclopentene with enophiles. For example *cis*-but-2-ene reacts with maleic anhydride to furnish the *threo*-adduct as predicted in Equation (6.140), whereas the *trans*-olefin gives the expected *erythro*-adduct. The best evidence for concertedness comes from the analogous reaction of maleic anhydride with optically active 3-phenylbut-

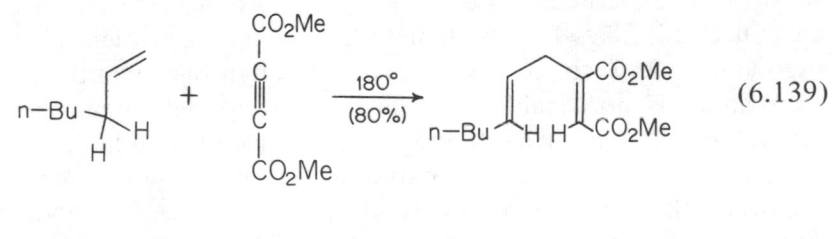

$$(6.139)$$

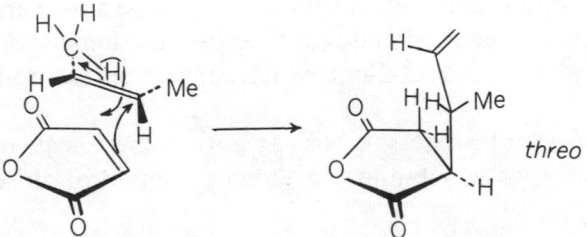

$$(6.140)$$

threo

1-ene; an optically active adduct is obtained. Nevertheless in a few systems stepwise mechanisms of lower activation energy are known to operate.

Retro-ene type reactions; that is the thermal eliminations related to Equation (6.138), are very much more common when one or more of the six atomic participants is a heteroatom, and notably oxygen. Such reactions are useful methods for olefin formation and for decarboxylations. A few typical examples are given in Equations (6.141)–(6.147).† The pyrolysis of *threo*-1-acetoxy-2-deuterio-1,2-diphenylethane (cf. Equation (6.141)) likewise yielded

Ester pyrolysis

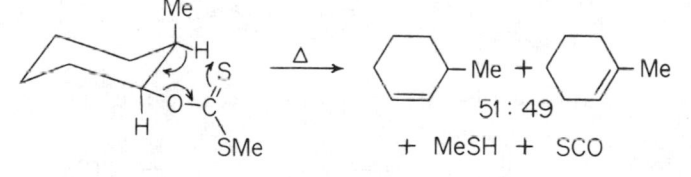

$$\qquad\qquad (6.141)$$

Xanthate pyrolysis (Chugaev reaction)

51 : 49

+ MeSH + SCO

$$\qquad\qquad (6.142)$$

β—Hydroxyketone pyrolysis (cf. retro—aldol)

$$\qquad\qquad (6.143)$$

trans-stilbene, but without the deuterium label. Reactions of the type (6.141), (6.142), and (6.145) have the disadvantage of generally producing mixtures of olefinic products if there is more than one type of removable hydrogen atom.

† Useful surveys of these and related pyrolytic *syn*-eliminations are to be found in the texts by Carruthers (1971) and Gilchrist and Storr (1972); reviews: DePuy and King (1960), Hoffmann (1969).

β-hydroxyolefin pyrolysis (cf. Prins reaction)

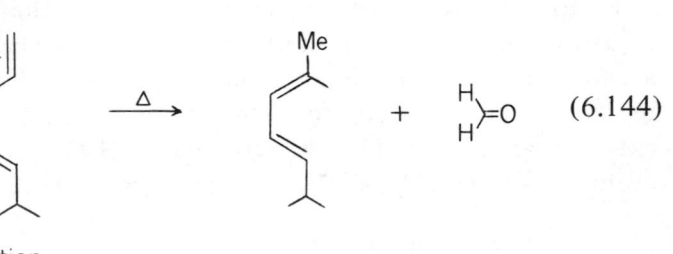

$$ \xrightarrow{\Delta} \qquad + \qquad \tag{6.144} $$

Cope elimination

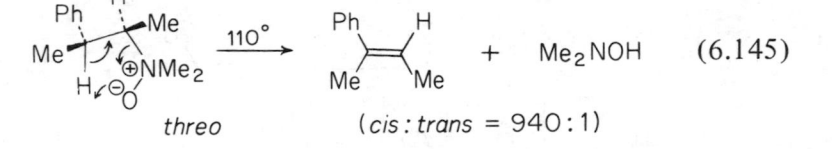

$$ \xrightarrow{110°} \qquad + \quad Me_2NOH \tag{6.145} $$

$threo$ $\qquad$ ($cis:trans = 940:1$)

Decarboxylation of β–ketoacids

$$ \xrightarrow[-CO_2]{\Delta} \qquad \rightleftharpoons \qquad \tag{6.146} $$

Decarboxylation of β,γ–unsaturated acids

$$ \xrightarrow{\Delta} \qquad + \quad CO_2 \tag{6.147} $$

In the open chain compounds the three methods produce closely similar results, and the main differences lie in the temperatures necessary to promote reaction.

Cyclo-elimination reactions involving more than six delocalized electrons appear not to have attracted detailed experimental study.

6.7   Miscellaneous topics

The purpose of this short section is solely to draw attention to the various extensions that have been made to the orbital symmetry concept. These include non-pericyclic concerted reactions,[1] orbital symmetry in inorganic chemistry,[2] and the oxidations of olefins, alcohols, and glycols by inorganic oxidants.[3] In addition a book of problems on pericyclic reactions has appeared.[4]

Among new concepts that have been put forward are the relationships between symmetry, topology, and aromaticity,[5] and bond stretch isomerism and polytopal rearrangements.[6]

A new class of pericyclic reaction has been defined,[7] namely dyotropic rearrangements (Greek *dyo* = two). This refers to reactions in which two σ-bonds simultaneously migrate intramolecularly. Two types of reaction fall into this category – type I in which the two σ-bonds interchange their positions (e.g. Equation 6.148), and type II in which no direct positional interchange occurs (e.g. Equation 6.149). Type I processes are of order [j,j], using an extension of the usual notion, for which there are a number of possible interaction topologies. In short, however, if the [2,2] dyotropic shift in reaction (6.148) is indeed concerted then it must involve a $[_\sigma 2_s + _\sigma 2_a]$ interaction.

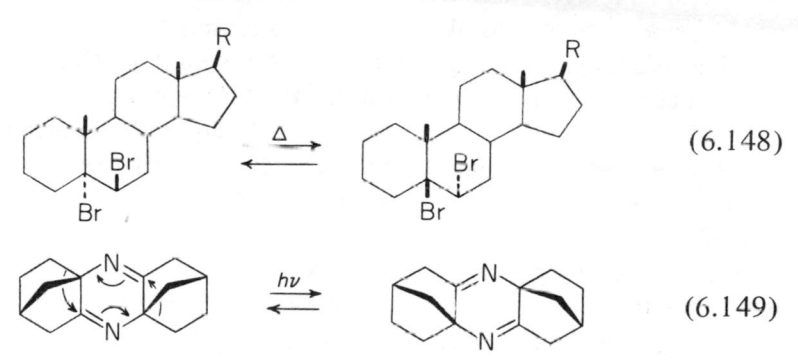

$$(6.148)$$

$$(6.149)$$

Purely geometrical considerations dictate that the bromine atoms must migrate along their initial sides of the π-system. The antarafacial interaction must therefore involve the utilization of a p-type orbital by one of the bromine atoms, but the inversion at this monovalent atom, of course, is not detectable in the rearranged product. The generality of dyotropic processes remains to be demonstrated.

A number of alternative theoretical treatments of pericyclic processes con-

For example see:[1] Gilchrist and Storr (1971), Miller (1968); [2]Pearson (1971); [3]Littler (1971). [4]Lehr and Marchand (1972). [5]Goldstein and Hoffmann (1971); [6]Stohrer and Hoffmann (1972); [7]Reetz (1972).

tinue to appear. These include the application of the principle of least motion,[8] orbital symmetry rules for unimolecular reactions,[9] extended valence bond theory, aromaticity and the Woodward–Hoffmann rules,[10] and the orbital phase continuity principle.[11] A 'curly' arrow symbolism[12] (utilizing three types of arrow to denote electron shifts and orbital interaction topology), which has a basis in resonance theory, has been put forward as a simple means for depicting and predicting pericyclic reactions.

A particularly stimulating series of papers[13] have dealt with the importance of donor-acceptor interactions and the degree of polarity of the transition state in determining stereospecificity in thermal and photochemical reactions. Among thermal [2 + 2] reactions, for example, it is suggested that there is a reactivity spectrum from the one extreme of non-polar cyclo-addition where both addends have similar electron donor or acceptor abilities to the other extreme, near ionic cyclo-addition, where the two addends have divergent electronic characteristics. Within these limits the majority of cyclo-additions are regarded as concerted and the lack of stereospecificity reflects the outcome of several concurrent well-defined and competing processes, rather than the general existence of a totally non-discriminating intermediate such as a biradical. This is a major divergence from the Woodward–Hoffmann classification into concerted and non-concerted reactions. The newer idea is that only at the non-polar end of the scale, and where the donor and acceptor electronic energy levels have widely disparate energies, are the [2 + 2] reactions likely to have unfavourable concerted pathways, and a two step mechanism should then operate.

The 'forbidden' processes that are known to occur comparatively readily have been discussed from a related viewpoint.[14] It was concluded that in the main the processes are concerted if only one C—C bond suffers cleavage, and that substituents which introduce low-lying excited singlet states can dramatically enhance the rates of such reactions by increasing the anharmonicities of the potential energy curves.

Several other important contributions by theoretical chemists have been made, from time to time, in discussions on the stereochemistry of pericyclic reactions.[15] Unfortunately space does not permit discussion of these ideas here.

[8] Tee and Yates (1972); [9] Pearson (1972); [10] van der Hart, Mulder and Oosterhoff (1972); [11] Goddard (1972); [12] Kaneko (1972); [13] Epiotis (1972). [14] Schmidt (1972). [15] For example see Salem (1968), (1969) and Trindle (1970).

Appendix I

Determinants

A determinant is an arrangement of quantities (elements) in rows and columns in which the number of rows equals the number of columns. The number of rows is called the *order* of the determinant. Thus

$$\begin{vmatrix} a & b \\ c & d \end{vmatrix}$$

is a determinant of order 2, whereas

$$\begin{vmatrix} 1 & 3 & 7 \\ 2 & 1 & 6 \\ 5 & 2 & 9 \end{vmatrix}$$

is a third order determinant.

The line which may be drawn from top left to bottom right (and in this case containing 1, 1 and 9) is referred to as the leading diagonal.

Evaluation of a determinant

(a) *Second order*

$$\begin{vmatrix} a & b \\ c & d \end{vmatrix} = ad - bc$$

i.e. the difference of the products of the elements on the diagonals, taken in the order shown. Thus, the determinant is merely a convenient representation of this result.

(b) *Third and higher order* These determinants must first be broken down into a number of second order determinants which can then be evaluated as in (a).

209

The value of a determinant of order 3 or greater
= (The first element of the first row x the determinant formed by striking out the row and column containing the first element)
− (The second element of the first row x the determinant formed by striking out the row and column containing the second element)
+ (The third element of the first row x the determinant formed by striking out the row and column containing the third element)
etc., continuing the sign alternation.

e.g. (1)

$$\begin{vmatrix} a & b & c \\ d & e & f \\ g & h & i \end{vmatrix} = a \begin{vmatrix} e & f \\ h & i \end{vmatrix} - b \begin{vmatrix} d & f \\ g & i \end{vmatrix} + c \begin{vmatrix} d & e \\ g & h \end{vmatrix}$$

$$= a(ei - hf) - b(di - gf) + c(dh - ge)$$

These three new determinants are called the *minors* of a, b and c. If the sign is included, they are called *cofactors*.

e.g. (2)

$$\begin{vmatrix} a & b & c & d \\ e & f & g & h \\ i & j & k & l \\ m & n & o & p \end{vmatrix} = a \begin{vmatrix} f & g & h \\ j & k & l \\ n & o & p \end{vmatrix} - b \begin{vmatrix} e & g & h \\ i & k & l \\ m & o & p \end{vmatrix}$$

$$+ c \begin{vmatrix} e & f & h \\ i & j & l \\ m & n & p \end{vmatrix} - d \begin{vmatrix} e & f & g \\ i & j & k \\ m & n & o \end{vmatrix}$$

These third order determinants can then be simplified further as in e.g. (1)
N.B. This method could, of course, be applied to second order determinants, in which case the cofactors are single terms rather than determinants.

210

Problem I.1   Solve the following determinants for the values of y.

(a)
$$y = \begin{vmatrix} 4 & 2 & 1 \\ 3 & 1 & 4 \\ 2 & 1 & 6 \end{vmatrix}$$

(b)
$$y = \begin{vmatrix} 1 & 2 & 5 & -3 \\ 4 & 2 & -1 & 7 \\ 5 & 3 & 8 & -2 \\ -2 & 1 & 4 & 5 \end{vmatrix}$$

(c) Solve the equation

$$\begin{vmatrix} 2x & 5 \\ 9 & x+3 \end{vmatrix} = \begin{vmatrix} 5 & 4 \\ 13 & 3x \end{vmatrix}$$

The use of determinants in the solution of simultaneous equations
For a set of homogeneous linear equations of the form

$$a_1 x + b_1 y + c_1 z = 0$$
$$a_2 x + b_2 y + c_2 z = 0$$
$$a_3 x + b_3 y + c_3 z = 0$$

it can be shown that

$$\begin{vmatrix} a_1 & b_1 & c_1 \\ a_2 & b_2 & c_2 \\ a_3 & b_3 & c_3 \end{vmatrix} = 0 \qquad (\text{I.1})$$

and also that

$$\frac{x}{\begin{vmatrix} b_2 & c_2 \\ b_3 & c_3 \end{vmatrix}} = \frac{-y}{\begin{vmatrix} a_2 & c_2 \\ a_3 & c_3 \end{vmatrix}} = \frac{z}{\begin{vmatrix} a_2 & b_2 \\ a_3 & b_3 \end{vmatrix}} \qquad (\text{I.2})$$

211

or
$$\frac{x}{\text{cofactor of } a_1} = \frac{y}{\text{cofactor of } a_2} =$$

$$\frac{z}{\text{cofactor of } a_3} \quad \text{etc.} \qquad (\text{I.3})$$

These are general results for all sets of n such equations containing n variables.

Problem I.2

Given

$$2x + 8y + 2z = 0$$
$$3x + y + 2z = 0$$
$$x + 4y + z = 0$$

find

$$\frac{x}{y} \quad \text{and} \quad \frac{x}{z}$$

Appendix II

The solution of the secular equations

In Hückel calculations, it is necessary to solve the secular equations for the energies and coefficients. Thus, we have to solve for E and $c_1, c_2, c_3 \ldots c_n$ a set of equations of the type:

$$c_1(H_{11} - ES_{11}) + c_2(H_{12} - ES_{12}) \ldots c_n(H_{1n} - ES_{1n}) = 0$$
$$c_1(H_{21} - ES_{21}) + c_2(H_{22} - ES_{22}) \ldots c_n(H_{2n} - ES_{2n}) = 0$$
$$\vdots$$
$$c_1(H_{n1} - ES_{n1}) + c_2(H_{n2} - ES_{n2}) \ldots c_n(H_{nn} - ES_{nn}) = 0$$

There are various methods available but perhaps the simplest is by determinants.

The equations have the same form as the set of equations in Appendix I (Equation I.1). We can, therefore, write

$$\begin{vmatrix} (H_{11} - ES_{11})(H_{12} - ES_{12}) \ldots (H_{1n} - ES_{1n}) \\ (H_{21} - ES_{21})(H_{22} - ES_{22}) \ldots (H_{2n} - ES_{2n}) \\ \vdots \qquad \vdots \qquad \qquad \vdots \\ (H_{n1} - ES_{n1})(H_{n2} - ES_{n2}) \ldots (H_{n2} - ES_{nn}) \end{vmatrix} = 0$$

Making the appropriate substitutions (i.e., $H_{11} = H_{22}$, etc., $= \alpha$; $S_{11} = S_{22}$, etc., $= 1$; $S_{12} = S_{23} = 0$ and $H_{rs} = \beta$ or 0, depending on whether r and s are adjacent),

213

this gives

$$
\begin{vmatrix}
\alpha - E & \beta \text{ or } 0 & \cdots & \beta \text{ or } 0 \\
\beta \text{ or } 0 & \alpha - E & \cdots & \beta \text{ or } 0 \\
\cdot & \cdot & & \cdot \\
\cdot & \cdot & & \cdot \\
\cdot & \cdot & & \cdot \\
\beta \text{ or } 0 & \beta \text{ or } 0 & \cdots & \alpha - E
\end{vmatrix} = 0
$$

At this stage, it is convenient to divide each term by β and putting

$$
\frac{\alpha - E}{\beta} = x.
$$

The determinant then reduces to

$$
\begin{vmatrix}
x & 1 \text{ or } 0 & \cdots & 1 \text{ or } 0 \\
1 \text{ or } 0 & x & \cdots & 1 \text{ or } 0 \\
\cdot & \cdot & & \cdot \\
\cdot & \cdot & & \cdot \\
\cdot & \cdot & & \cdot \\
1 \text{ or } 0 & 1 \text{ or } 0 & \cdots & x
\end{vmatrix} = 0
$$

Note that each term on the leading diagonal is x and all the other terms are unity (for adjacent atoms) and zero (for non-adjacent atoms).

(a) *To determine the energy levels*

In principle, it is only necessary to multipy out the determinant and solve the equation for x (and hence E). Now, if there are n atomic orbitals in the basis set, the determinant is of the order n, which on multiplying out yields an equation involving x^n. Solution of such equations (to obtain n values of E) is normally straightforward for small molecules, but becomes difficult for larger molecules. In some cases, it is possible to utilize the symmetry of the molecule to simplify the problem but, in general, it is more convenient to use one of the computer programs written for the purpose.

(b) *To determine the coefficients*

For small molecules, the *ratios* of coefficients are readily obtained from the secular equations using the method given in Appendix I for solving homogeneous linear equations (Equation (I.3)). The ratios of coefficients, together with the normalization condition, yield the wavefunction.

$$\psi = c_1\phi_1 + c_2\phi_2 + c_3\phi_3 \ldots c_n\phi_n$$

If ψ is not yet normalized†, we may divide through by c_1, inserting a normalization factor N.

$$\psi = N\left(\frac{c_1}{c_1}\phi_1 + \frac{c_2}{c_1}\phi_2 + \frac{c_3}{c_1}\phi_3 \ldots \frac{c_n}{c_1}\phi_n\right)$$

If ψ is normalized

$$\int \psi^2 \, d\tau = 1$$

Thus

$$N^2 \int \left(\frac{c_1}{c_1}\phi_1 + \frac{c_2}{c_1}\phi_2 + \frac{c_3}{c_1}\phi_3 \ldots \frac{c_n}{c_1}\phi_n\right)^2 d\tau = 1$$

which, since

$$\int \phi_i\phi_j \, d\tau = 1(i = j) \text{ or } = 0(i \neq j)$$

gives

$$N = \frac{1}{\sqrt{\left[\left(\frac{c_1}{c_1}\right)^2 + \left(\frac{c_2}{c_1}\right)^2 + \left(\frac{c_3}{c_1}\right)^2 \ldots \left(\frac{c_n}{c_1}\right)^2\right]}}$$

Thus, the wavefunction and its normalization factor may be expressed in terms of the ratios of the coefficients, which are obtained from the cofactors of the secular determinant. To illustrate the method of working, the cyclopropenyl system is worked out in detail in Appendix III. For larger molecules, it is again convenient to use a computer.

---

† For other purposes it is convenient to choose the coefficients such that the wave function is normalized. Thus

$$\int \psi^2 d\tau = \int (c_1\phi_1 + c_2\phi_2 + c_3\phi_3 \cdots c_n\phi_n)^2 d\tau = 1$$

Since

$$\int \phi_i\phi_j \, d\tau = 1(i = j) \qquad \text{or} \qquad = 0(i \neq j)$$

then

$$c_1^2 + c_2^2 + c_3^2 \cdots c_n^2 = 1$$

Appendix III

HMO treatment of the cyclopropenyl system

Specimen Calculation

1 CH——CH 2

ĊH 3

The wave functions have the general form

$$\psi = c_1 \phi_1 + c_2 \phi_2 + c_3 \phi_3$$

The secular equations

$$c_1(H_{11} - ES_{11}) + c_2(H_{12} - ES_{12}) + c_3(H_{13} - ES_{13}) = 0$$
$$c_1(H_{21} - ES_{21}) + c_2(H_{22} - ES_{22}) + c_3(H_{23} - ES_{23}) = 0$$
$$c_1(H_{31} - ES_{31}) + c_2(H_{32} - ES_{32}) + c_3(H_{33} - ES_{33}) = 0$$

Using the usual approximations and nomenclature,

$$H_{11} = H_{22} = H_{33} = \alpha$$
$$H_{12} = H_{21} = H_{31} = H_{13} = H_{32} = H_{23} = \beta$$
$$S_{11} = S_{22} = S_{33} = 1$$
$$S_{12} = S_{21} = S_{31} = S_{13} = S_{32} = S_{23} = 0$$

the secular equations become

$$c_1(\alpha - E) + c_2\beta + c_3\beta = 0$$
$$c_1\beta + c_2(\alpha - E) + c_3\beta = 0$$
$$c_1\beta + c_2\beta + c_3(\alpha - E) = 0$$

216

The secular determinant is:

$$\begin{vmatrix} \alpha - E & \beta & \beta \\ \beta & \alpha - E & \beta \\ \beta & \beta & \alpha - E \end{vmatrix} = 0$$

For simplicity, divide each term by β and put

$$\frac{\alpha - E}{\beta} = x$$

Thus, the secular equations are,

$$c_1 x + c_2 + c_3 = 0$$
$$c_1 + c_2 x + c_3 = 0$$
$$c_1 + c_2 + c_3 x = 0$$

and

$$\begin{vmatrix} x & 1 & 1 \\ 1 & x & 1 \\ 1 & 1 & x \end{vmatrix} = 0$$

Multiplying out gives

$$x \begin{vmatrix} x & 1 \\ 1 & x \end{vmatrix} - 1 \begin{vmatrix} 1 & 1 \\ 1 & x \end{vmatrix} + 1 \begin{vmatrix} 1 & x \\ 1 & 1 \end{vmatrix} = 0$$

$$x(x^2 - 1) - 1(x - 1) + 1(1 - x) = 0$$

$$x^3 - 3x + 2 = 0$$

This factorizes to

$$(x + 2)(x - 1)(x - 1) = 0$$

$$\therefore \quad x = -2, 1, 1$$

or $\quad E = \alpha + 2\beta, \alpha - \beta, \alpha - \beta$

The π-energy levels are as shown in Fig. 1.18.

To illustrate the method for the determination of the coefficients, consider the wave function (ψ_1) corresponding to E_1.

Writing the wave function in terms of the ratios of the coefficients (Appendix II)

$$\psi_1 = N\left(\frac{c_1}{c_1}\phi_1 + \frac{c_2}{c_1}\phi_2 + \frac{c_3}{c_1}\phi_3\right)$$

where

$$N = \frac{1}{\sqrt{\left[\left(\frac{c_1}{c_1}\right)^2 + \left(\frac{c_2}{c_1}\right)^2 + \left(\frac{c_3}{c_1}\right)^2\right]}}$$

The ratio of the coefficients is obtained from the ratios of the appropriate cofactors (Appendix I). Thus,

$$\frac{c_1}{\begin{vmatrix} x & 1 \\ 1 & x \end{vmatrix}} = \frac{-c_2}{\begin{vmatrix} 1 & 1 \\ 1 & x \end{vmatrix}}$$

or

$$\frac{c_2}{c_1} = -\frac{(x - 1)}{(x^2 - 1)}$$

Similarly

$$\frac{c_3}{c_1} = \frac{1 - x}{x^2 - 1}$$

For this wave function, $x = -2$

$$\therefore \quad \frac{c_2}{c_1} = 1 \quad \text{and} \quad \frac{c_3}{c_1} = 1$$

Also

$$N = \frac{1}{\sqrt{(1 + 1 + 1)}} = \frac{1}{\sqrt{3}}$$

$$\therefore \quad \psi_1 = \frac{1}{\sqrt{3}}(\phi_1 + \phi_2 + \phi_3)$$

In most examples, the other wave functions can be found merely by inserting the appropriate values of x in the cofactors. In the case of degenerate orbitals, this method is no longer satisfactory. Thus, if you substitute $x = 1$

into the cofactors, the ratio of the coefficients become

$$\frac{c_2}{c_1} = \frac{c_3}{c_1} = \frac{0}{0}$$

Clearly another method must be used.

In fact, there are an infinite number of pairs of orbitals corresponding to the two degenerate energy levels which satisfy the necessary conditions in that they have the right energy, are normalized (i.e., $\int \psi_2^2 \, d\tau = \int \psi_3^2 \, d\tau = 1$) and are orthogonal ($\int \psi_2 \psi_3 \, d\tau = 0$). However, having decided on one wave function, the other one may be determined. A convenient approach is to put one coefficient equal to zero. The secular equations are

$$c_1 x + c_2 + c_3 = 0$$

$$c_1 + c_2 x + c_3 = 0$$

$$c_1 + c_2 + c_3 x = 0$$

For orbitals ψ_2 and ψ_3, $x = 1$. Assume that in ψ_2, $c_2 = 0$

$$c_1 + c_3 = 0$$

$$\therefore \qquad c_1 = -c_3$$

or $\qquad \dfrac{c_3}{c_1} = -1$

Thus

$$\psi_2 = N(\phi_1 - \phi_3)$$

$$= \frac{1}{\sqrt{2}} (\phi_1 - \phi_3)$$

The coefficients of ψ_3 must now be chosen such that it is both normalized and orthogonal to ψ_2. Thus, for orthogonality

$$\int \frac{1}{\sqrt{2}} (\phi_1 - \phi_3) \psi_3 \, d\tau = 0$$

i.e.

$$\int \frac{1}{\sqrt{2}} (\phi_1 - \phi_3)(c_1 \phi_1 + c_2 \phi_2 + c_3 \phi_3) \, d\tau = 0$$

On multiplying out and putting $\int \phi_i \phi_j d\tau = 0 (i \neq j)$ or $= 1(i = j)$

$$\frac{1}{\sqrt{2}} (c_1 - c_3) = 0$$

$$\therefore \quad c_1 = c_3$$

But

$$c_1 + c_2 + c_3 = 0$$

$$\therefore \quad c_2 = -2c_1$$

Thus

$$\psi_3 = c_1 \phi_1 - 2c_1 \phi_2 + c_1 \phi_3$$

Normalising

$$\psi_3 = N \left(\frac{c_1}{c_1} \phi_1 - \frac{2c_1}{c_1} \phi_2 + \frac{c_1}{c_1} \phi_3 \right)$$

$$= \frac{1}{\sqrt{6}} (\phi_1 - 2\phi_2 + \phi_3)$$

The orbitals are sketched in Fig. 1.19.

Appendix IV

Answers to problems

Problem 1.1
See Section 1.13.

Problem 1.2

$$\psi_3 = \frac{1}{\sqrt{3}} (\phi_1 - \phi_3 + \phi_5)$$

Problem 2.1
Resonance energy of cyclobutadiene = 0.

Problem 2.2
The π-bond orders in butadiene are:
$$p_{12} = p_{34} = 0\cdot894$$
$$p_{23} = 0\cdot447$$

Problem 2.3
Fulvene is non-aromatic (has a zero resonance energy).

Problem 2.4
Resonance energy of (planar) cyclo-octatetraene = $-\beta$ (i.e. an anti-aromatic compound).

Problem 3.1
(a) (i) [2 + 4]
     (ii) [14 + 2]

(b) (i) *supra-supra*
   (ii) *antara-supra* (see Equation (6.76) and pertinent discussion).
(c) *endo*-addition (see Fig. 4.4 and Equations (6.48)–(6.52)).
(d) *endo*-addition.

Problem 3.2
(a) Reactions from Problem 3.1:
   (i) $[_\pi 4_s + _\pi 2_s]$
   (ii) $[_\pi 14_a + _\pi 2_s]$ – see Equation (6.76) and pertinent discussion.
(b) Reactions from Problem 3.2
   (i) $[_\pi 4_s + _\pi 4_s]$
   (ii) Easier to analyse the reverse reaction, which is a $[_\pi 2_s + _\pi 2_s]$ process; the stereochemistry about the *trans*-ethylenic double bond involved in the cyclo-addition is retained in the formation of the tricyclic molecule. The forward reaction is a $[_\sigma 2_s + _\sigma 2_s]$ process.

Problem 3.3
This is a $[_\pi 4_a + _\pi 2_a]$ process (if concerted), and a mechanism based on this assumption is given in Equation (IV.1). Note that the cyclo-octatetraene ring is non-planar.

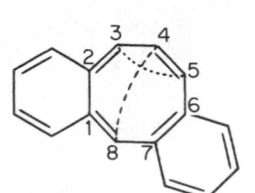 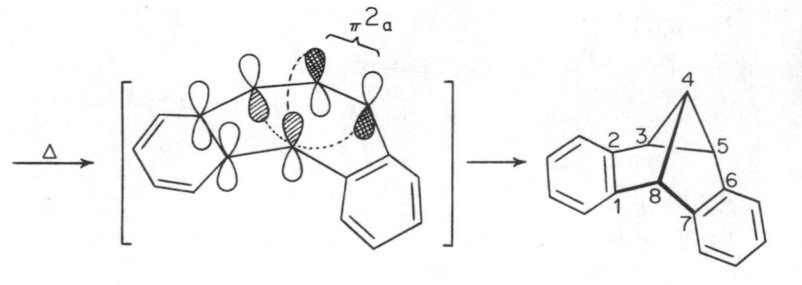

(IV.1)

Problem 3.4
(i)   disrotatory
(ii) disrotatory
(iii) The reaction clearly involves two consecutive electrocyclic reactions; the first yields the transient intermediate (2) which then suffers electrocyclic

closure to give the product indicated. This product can arise only if *both* steps involve disrotation (Equation (IV.2)) or *both* involve conrotation (Equation (IV.3)). The net observable change in either process is the same so

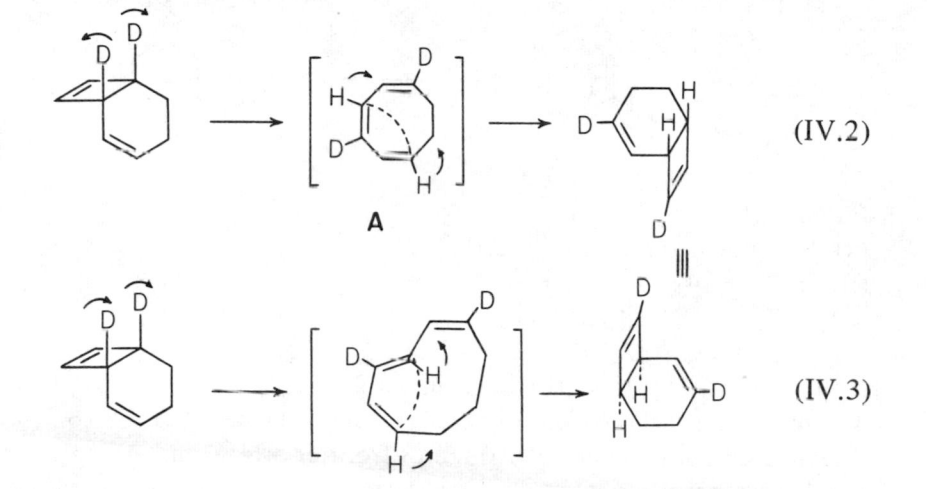

A

(IV.2)

B

(IV.3)

that a stereochemical distinction can only be made on the basis of the structure of the transient intermediate. If the intermediate had the structure (A), that is *cis,cis,cis*-cyclo-octatriene, it should be very much more stable than is suggested. An intermediate of structure (B), on the other hand, namely *cis,trans, cis*-cyclo-octatriene, is more reasonably expected to be labile on account of the *trans*-substituted double bond in a relatively small ring. Hence the evidence favours reaction (IV.3). This pathway accords with theory (Chapters 4 and 5).

Problem 3.5

(i) (ii) Reverse reaction is a $[_\sigma 2_s + {_\pi}4_s]$ process or a $[_\sigma 2_a + {_\pi}4_a]$ process; the forward reaction is $[_\pi 2_s + {_\pi}2_s + {_\pi}2_s]$ or $[_\pi 2_a + {_\pi}2_s + {_\pi}2_a]$.

(iii) Step 1, assuming the above mechanism for Problem 3.4 (iii) is $[_\sigma 2_s + {_\pi}2_a]$ or $[_\sigma 2_a + {_\pi}2_s]$; step 2 is $[_\pi 2_s + {_\pi}2_a]$.

Problem 3.6

(i) [1,5] shift (see Equations (6.93)–(6.96)).

223

(ii) [1,7] shift (see Equation (6.100) and discussion).
(iii) [3,3] shift, as indicated by Equation (IV.4).

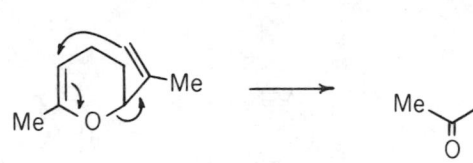

$$(IV.4)$$

Problem 3.7
(a) From Problem 3.6:
(i) $[_\sigma2_s + _\pi4_s]$ or $[_\sigma2_a + _\pi4_a]$
(ii) $[_\sigma2_s + _\pi6_s]$ or $[_\sigma2_a + _\pi6_a]$
(iii) $[_\pi2_s + _\sigma2_s + _\pi2_s]$ or $[_\pi2_a + _\sigma2_a + _\pi2_s]$ or $[_\pi2_a + _\sigma2_s + _\pi2_a]$
(b) (i) This is a [1,3] shift involving a $[_\sigma2_a + _\pi2_s]$ or a $[_\sigma2_s + _\pi2_a]$ interaction.
The migrating carbon atom undergoes inversion (see Equation (6.90) which
illustrates Woodward and Hoffmann's frontier orbital analysis of the problem).
(ii) Several steps are involved. The starting material is equilibrated with three
valence isomers by a series of [1,5] hydrogen atom shifts, Equation (IV.5).

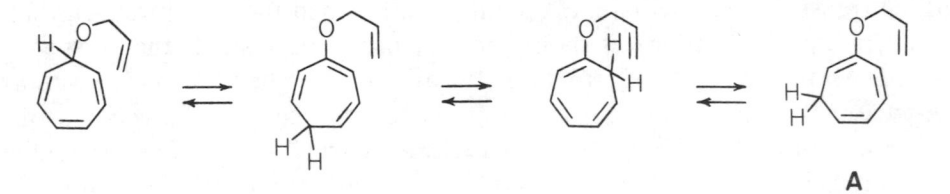

$$(IV.5)$$

Isomer (**A**) can undergo an energetically favourable [3,3] rearrangement
(Claisen rearrangement) to form the conjugated dienone (**B**), Equation (IV.6).

$$(IV.6)$$

A   B

224

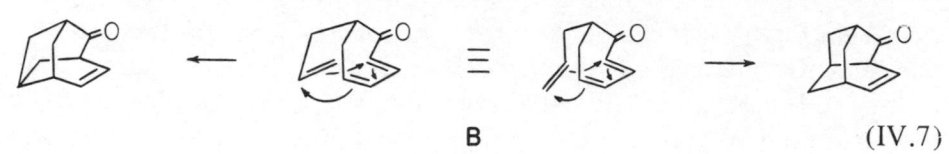

B (IV.7)

Among the various conformations that (B) can adopt, two are suitable for intramolecular Diels-Alder reaction by way of the $[_\pi 2_s + _\pi 4_s]$ pathway, Equation (IV.7).

Problem 3.8

Because of the bicyclic nature of the two sulphones, only scission with disrotation is geometrically feasible. The loss of SO_2 can additionally take place in a linear or non-linear manner. The bonding interactions are more reasonable in the disrotatory linear process which, other things being equal, should be the preferred pathway.

(i) The activation parameters are more or less as expected for a concerted six electron retro cyclo-addition type of process (cf. the data on p. 68). The linear disrotatory cleavage is therefore likely.

(ii) For what is essentially an eight electron retro cyclo-addition, the activation entropy is unusually low and suggests a decrease rather than an increase in the degrees of freedom at the transition state. This has been interpreted in terms of the less favourable disrotatory non-linear cheletropic fragmentation, but a complete change in mechanism seems more likely.

The conclusions for these reactions, if concerted, are in agreement with the theoretical interpretations (see Chapter 5 and Section 6.4).

Problem 4.1

For the various reactions in Fig. 4.3 only the 0_a, 2_s and 4_a interactions require summation. The total of such terms must be odd for a thermal pericyclic reaction and even for a photochemical process. Hence, all of the reactions shown are thermally allowed processes *except* the $[_\pi 2_s + _\pi 2_s]$ cyclo-addition which is an allowed photochemical reaction.

Problem 4.2

(i) $[_\pi 6_s + _\pi 4_s]$; only the $_\pi 6_s$ term is relevant, and hence the reaction is favourable under thermal activation.

225

(ii) From Fig. IV.1 it can be seen that for the *endo*-geometry the primary bonding interactions (≡) between HOMO-triene and LUMO-diene, or LUMO-triene and HOMO-diene, are stabilizing. However, the secondary interactions (---) are repulsive because of the phase dislocations. The *exo*-transition state geometry is therefore favoured because the destabilizing interactions are then absent.

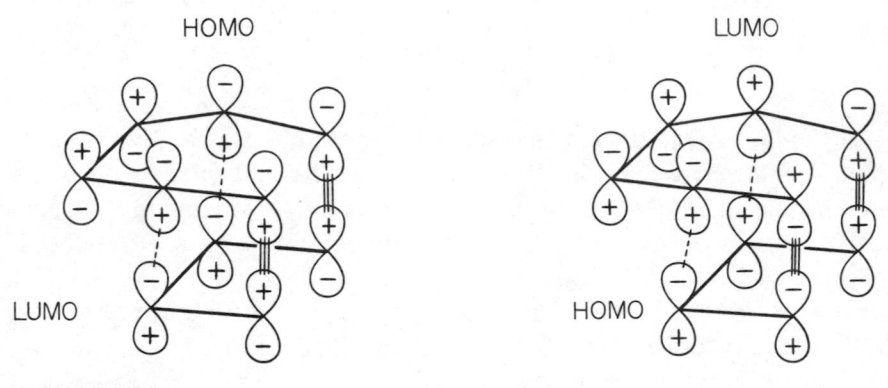

FIGURE IV.1
Frontier orbital analysis of the *endo*-geometry for the cyclo-addition of butadiene and hexatriene.

Problem 4.3
A series of $[_\sigma 2_s + {_\pi}4_s]$ electrocyclic and sigmatropic reactions are involved, as indicated in Equation (6.97) and the pertinent discussion.

Problem 4.4
The most obvious pathway, the $[_\sigma 2_s + {_\sigma}2_s]$ retro cyclo-addition, is symmetry-forbidden. The symmetry-allowed pathway involves first a $[_\sigma 2_s + {_\sigma}2_s + {_\sigma}2_s]$ retro cyclo-addition, which is followed by a $[_\pi 2_s + {_\sigma}2_s + {_\pi}2_s]$ Cope rearrangement, Equation (IV.8).

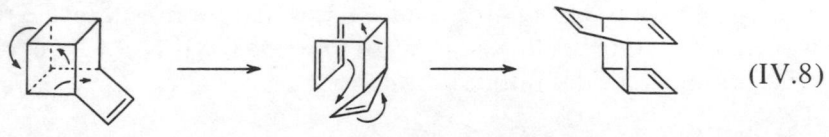

(IV.8)

Problem 5.1
Since six electrons are involved in the electrocyclic change (a $(4n + 2)$ system) the Hückel interaction (Equation (IV.9)) is the preferred pathway for the

thermal reaction which occurs with disrotation. The photochemical process therefore requires that Möbius transition state geometry which is available in the conrotatory mode.

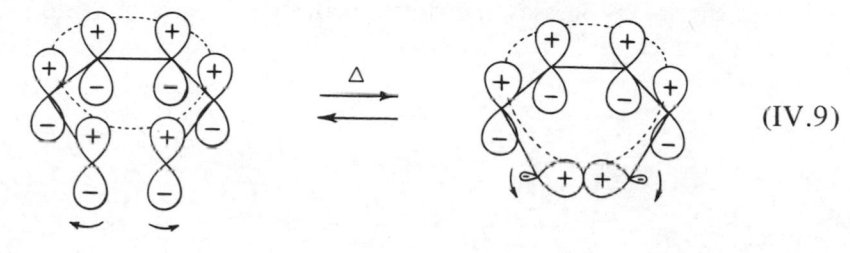

$$(IV.9)$$

Problem 5.2

The results are illustrated in Fig. IV.2; the phase dislocations are indicated by the zig-zag lines.

(a)

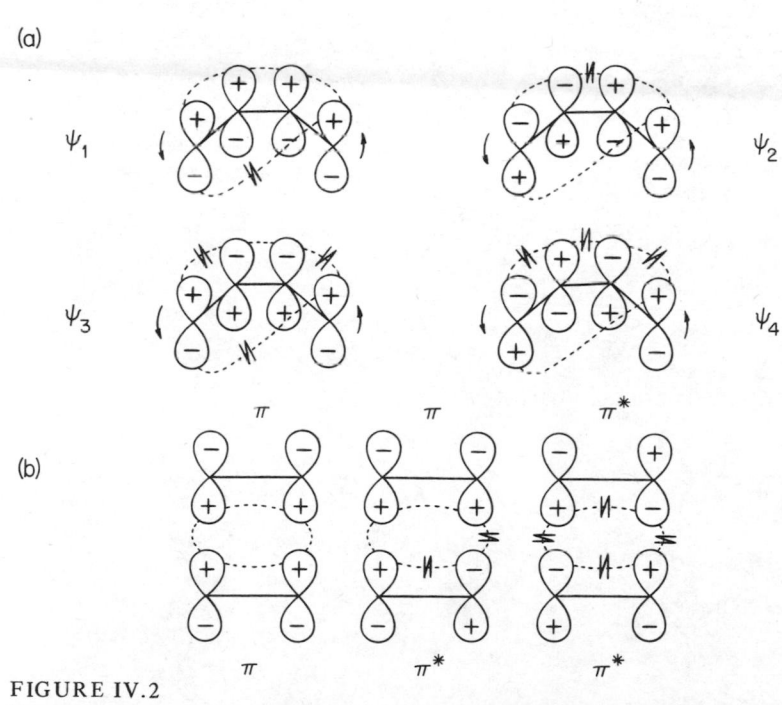

(b)

FIGURE IV.2

The Zimmerman analysis of (a) the cyclobutene-butadiene electrocyclic interconversion, and (b) the dimerization of ethylene, using all possible molecular orbitals as the basis set.

227

Problem 5.3

In each case there are $(4n + 2)$ participant electrons (i.e. 2 or 6) involved in the pericyclic changes. Hence the Hückel interactions are necessary for each of these thermal processes in order to provide aromatic transition states.

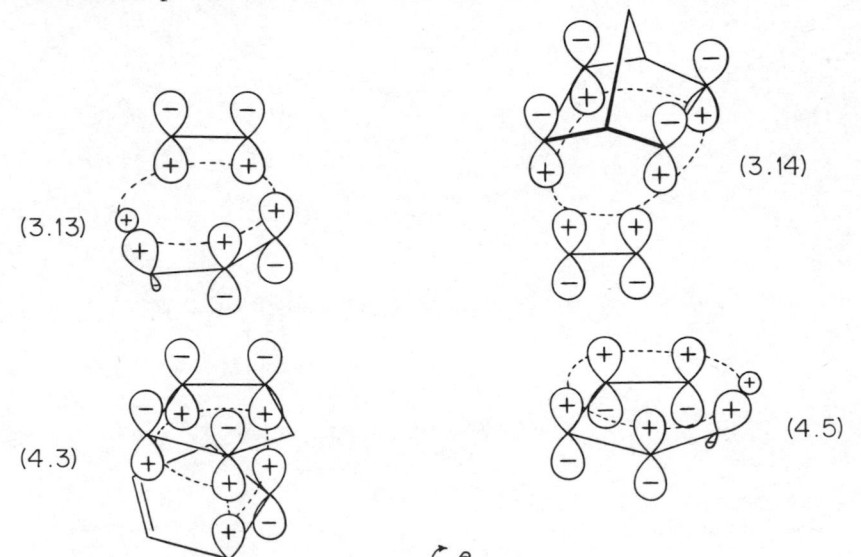

Problem 5.4

The orbital interactions are as illustrated.

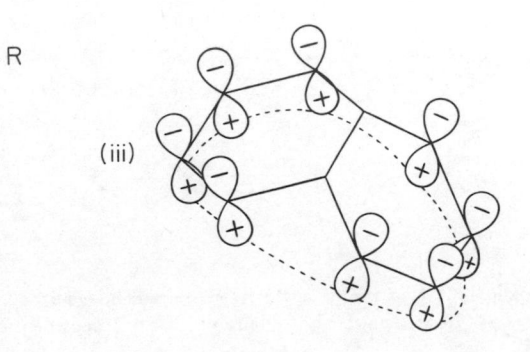

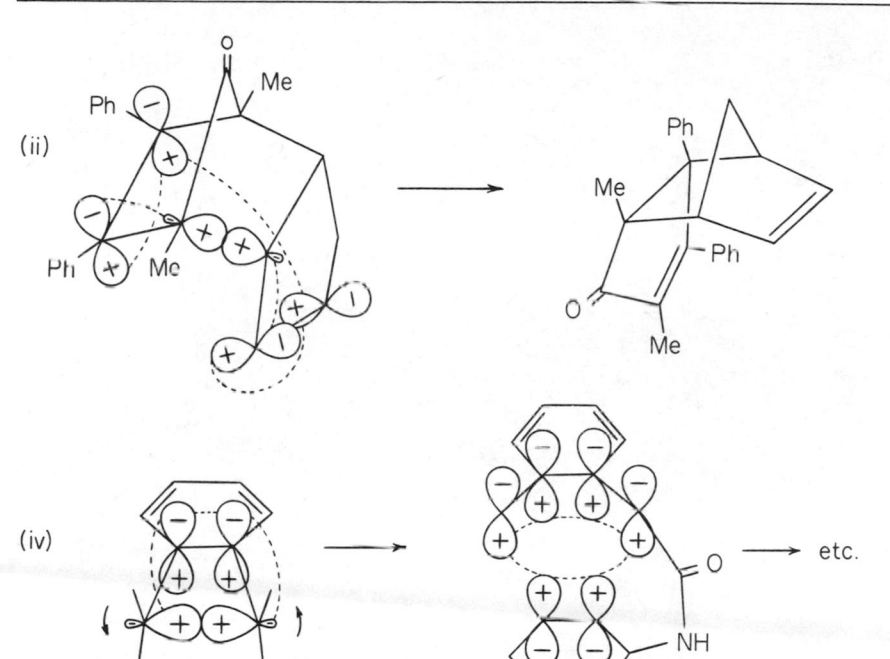

(i) A $(4n + 2)$ Hückel system, and the reaction is thermally favourable. The $[_\pi2_s + _\pi2_s + _\sigma2_s]$ pathway is involved in this example of the ene-reaction.

(ii) This is a [3,3] shift or Cope reaction. Molecular geometry dictates that the interaction should be of the $[_\pi2_a + _\sigma2_s + _\pi2_a]$ type. The transition state is of the $(4n + 2)$ Hückel type so that the thermochemical process is energetically favourable.

(iii) In this $[_\pi4_s + _\pi4_s]$ cyclo-addition process the eight electron Hückel transition state requires photochemical activation for aromaticity.

(iv) Two consecutive reactions are involved here. The first step, an electrocyclic $[_\sigma2_a + _\pi2_s]$ ring scission with conrotation, has a four electron anti-Hückel delocalized system. The second step, a $[_\pi2_s + _\pi4_s]$ Diels-Alder reaction, is characterized by a six electron Hückel transition state. Both steps are therefore thermally favourable.

Note the very elegant use of pericyclic reactions, for the purpose of organic synthesis, in reactions (iv).

Problem I.1
(a) $y = -11$; (b) $y = -475$; (c) $x = 1, 7/2$.

Problem I.2
$x/y = 7$, $x/z = -7/11$.

References

Baldwin, J. E. and Ford, P. W. (1969), *J. Amer. Chem. Soc.*, **91**, 7192.

Carruthers, W. (1971), *Some Modern Methods of Organic Synthesis*, Cambridge University Press.

Caserio, M. C. (1971), *J. Chem. Educ.*, **48**, 782.

Coulson, C. A. (1939), *Proc. Roy. Soc.*, **A169**, 413.

Coulson, C. A. (1951), *Valence*, Oxford University Press.

Coulson, C. A. and Longuet-Higgins, H. C. (1947), *Proc. Roy. Soc.*, **A191**, 39; **A192**, 16; (1948), *ibid.*, **A193**, 447, 456; **A195**, 188.

DePuy, C. H. and King, R. W. (1960), *Chem. Rev.*, **60**, 431.

Dewar, M. J. S. (1952), *J. Amer. Chem. Soc.*, **74**, 3341, 3345, 3350, 3353, 3355, 3357.

Dewar, M. J. S. (1966), *Tetrahedron*, Suppl. 8 Pt. 1, 75.

Dewar, M. J. S. (1967), *Aromaticity, Chem. Soc. Special Publ. No. 21*, 177.

Dewar, M. J. S. (1969), *The Molecular Orbital Theory of Organic Chemistry*, McGraw-Hill.

Dewar, M. J. S. (1971), *Angew. Chem. Internat. Edn.*, **10**, 761.

Dewar, M. J. S. and Gleicher, G. J. (1965), *J. Amer. Chem. Soc.*, **87**, 685.

Dewar, M. J. S. and Kirschner, S. (1971), *J. Amer. Chem. Soc.*, **93**, 4290.

Doering, W. von E. and Roth, W. R. (1963), *Angew. Chem. Internat. Edn.*, **2**, 115.

Dougherty, R. C. (1971), *J. Amer. Chem. Soc.*, **93**, 7187.

Epiotis, N. D. (1972), *J. Amer. Chem. Soc.*, **94**, 1924, 1935, 1941, 1946; (1973), *ibid.*, **95**, 1191, 1200, 1206, 1214.

Evans, M. G. (1939), *Trans. Farad. Soc.*, **35**, 824.

Fischer, A. (1964), in *The Chemistry of the Alkenes*, ed. S. Patai, Interscience, p. 1025.

Frey, H. M. and Walsh, R. (1969), *Chem. Rev.*, **69**, 103.

Frost, A. A. and Musulin, B. (1953), *J. Chem. Phys.*, **21**, 572.

Fukui, K. (1971), *Accounts of Chem. Research*, **4**, 57 and previous references cited therein.

Garratt, P. J. (1971), *Aromaticity*, McGraw-Hill.

Gilchrist, T. L. and Storr, R. C. (1972), *Organic Reactions and Orbital Symmetry*, Cambridge University Press.

Gill, G. B. (1968), *Quart. Rev.*, **22**, 338.

Goddard, W. A. (1972), *J. Amer. Chem. Soc.*, **94**, 793.

Goldstein, M. J. and Hoffmann, R. (1971), *J. Amer. Chem. Soc.*, **93**, 6193.

Hamer, J. (1967), *1,4-Cycloaddition Reactions*, Academic Press.

Hansen, J. J. and Schmid, H. (1969), *Chem. in Britain*, **5**, 111.

Hart, W. J. van der, Mulder, J. J. C. and Oosterhoff, L. J. (1972), *J. Amer. Chem. Soc.*, **94**, 5724.

Heilbronner, E. (1964), *Tetrahedron Letters*, 1923.

Hoffmann, H. M. R. (1969), *Angew. Chem. Internat. Edn.*, **8**, 556.

Hückel, E. (1931), Z. Phys., **70**, 204.

Huisgen, R. (1963), *Angew. Chem. Internat. Edn.*, **2**, 565.

Huisgen, R., Grashey, R. and Sauer, J. (1964), in *The Chemistry of the Alkenes,* ed. S. Patai, Interscience, p. 739.

Hünig, S., Müller, H. R. and Thier, W. (1965), *Angew. Chem. Internat. Edn.*, **4**, 271.

Jefferson, A. and Scheinmann, F. (1968), *Quart. Rev.*, **22**, 391.

Kaneko, C. (1972), *Tetrahedron*, **28**, 4915.

Kosower, E. M. (1968), *An Introduction to Physical Organic Chemistry,* Wiley.

Kraft, K. and Koltzenburg, G. (1967), *Tetrahedron Letters*, 4357, 4723.

Kwart, H. and King, K. (1968), *Chem. Rev.*, **68**, 415.

Lehr, R. E. and Marchand, A. P. (1972), *Orbital Symmetry (A Problem-Solving Approach),* Academic Press.

Littler, J. S. (1971), *Tetrahedron*, **27**, 81.

Longuet-Higgins, H. C. (1950), *J. Chem. Phys.*, **18**, 265, 275, 283.

Longuet-Higgins, H. C. and Abrahamson, E. W. (1965), *J. Amer. Chem. Soc.*, **87**, 2045.

Mango, F. D. (1969), *Adv. in Catalysis*, **20**, 291.

Miller, S. I. (1968), *Adv. Phys. Org. Chem.*, **6**, 185.

Onishchenko, A. S. (1964), *Diene Synthesis,* Davey.

Oosterhoff, L. J. and Lugt, W. Th. A. M. van der, (1969), *J. Amer. Chem. Soc.*, **91**, 6042.

Paquette, L. A. (1971), *Accounts of Chem. Research*, **4**, 280.

Pearson, R. G. (1971), *Accounts of Chem. Research*, **4**, 152; (1971), *Pure Appl. Chem.*, **27**, 145.

Pearson, R. G. (1972), *J. Amer. Chem. Soc.*, **94**, 8287.

Pettit, R., Sugahara, H., Wristers, J. and Merk, W. (1969), *Discuss. Farad. Soc.*, **47**, 71.

Phelan, N. N., Jaffé, H. H. and Orchin, M. (1967), *J. Chem. Educ.*, **44**, 626.

Platt, J. R. (1949), *J. Chem. Phys.*, **17**, 484.

Reetz, M. T. (1972), *Angew. Chem. Internat. Edn.*, **11**, 129, 130.

Rhoades, S. J. (1963), in *Molecular Rearrangements* Part 1, ed. P. de Mayo, Interscience, p. 655.

Roberts, J. D. (1962), *Notes on Molecular Orbital Calculations,* Benjamin.

Salem, L. (1968), *J. Amer. Chem. Soc.*, **90**, 543, 553; (1969), *Chem. in Britain*, **5**, 449 (see also ref. 3 for corrections).

Schmidt, W. (1972), *Tetrahedron Letters*, 581; *idem* (1971), *Helv. Chim. Acta*, **54**, 862.

Schrauzer, G. N. (1968), *Adv. in Catalysis*, **18**, 373.

Seltzer, S. (1968), *Adv. Alicyclic Chem.*, **2**, 1.

Stark, B. P. and Duke, A. J. (1967), *Extrusion Reactions,* Pergamon Press.

Stohrer, W-D. and Hoffmann, R. (1972), *J. Amer. Chem. Soc.*, **94**, 779, 1661.

Streitweiser, A. (1961), *Molecular Orbital Theory for Organic Chemists,* Wiley.

Tarbell, D. S. (1940), *Chem. Rev.*, **27**, 495.

Taylor, D. R. (1967), *Chem. Rev.*, **67**, 317.

Tee, O. S. and Yates, K. (1972), *J. Amer. Chem. Soc.*, **94**, 3074.

Trindle, C. (1970), *J. Amer. Chem. Soc.*, **92**, 3251, 3255.

Ulrich, H. (1967), *Cycloaddition Reactions of Heterocumulenes,* Academic Press.

Wassermann, A. (1965), *Diels-Alder Reactions,* Elsevier.

Woodward, R. B. and Hoffmann, R. (1965), *J. Amer. Chem. Soc.*, **87**, 395, 2046, 2511, 4385, 4389.

Woodward, R. B. and Hoffmann, R. (1968), *Accounts of Chem. Research*, **1**, 17.

Woodward, R. B. and Hoffmann, R. (1969), *Angew. Chem. Internat. Edn.*, **8**, 781; (1970), *The Conservation of Orbital Symmetry,* Verlag Chemie/Academic Press.

Zimmerman, H. E. (1966), *J. Amer. Chem. Soc.,* 88, 1564, 1566; see also (1969), *Angew. Chem. Internat. Edn.,* 8, 1.

Zimmerman, H. E. (1971), *Accounts of Chem. Research,* 4, 272.

Index

234